Family Planning in
Japanese Society

Family Planning in Japanese Society

Traditional Birth Control in a Modern Urban Culture

Samuel Coleman

PRINCETON UNIVERSITY PRESS
PRINCETON, NEW JERSEY

To My Parents
who have given me so much

Acknowledgments

I could not have conducted the research for this book had it not been for the assistance that Japanese and American colleagues and friends so willingly gave me. In Japan, medical specialists, paramedicals, and counselors in social work and family planning offered not only their time for interviews and discussions, but administered my questionnaires to their clients, provided me with introductions to other specialists as well as to prospective married couples for interviews, and—not least of all—encouraged me with their active interest in my research questions and the outcome of my efforts. Among the midwives, family counselors, and social workers, I wish to thank especially: Baba Tetsu, Chiga Yūko, Endō Kimiko, Fukazawa Michiko, Kanamatsu Sachiko, Katō Kayoko, Maruyama Misako, Mimori Toshiko, Nakayama Masu, Satō Shigeko, Satō Tae, and Tado Shizu. Among the physicians, who include specialists in private practice as well as educators, researchers, and administrators, I offer special thanks to: Kaneko Eiju, Maruyama Kazuo, Matsunaga Masaru, the late Muramatsu Hiroo, Muramatsu Minoru, Narabayashi Yasushi, Nitta Takeo, Nozue Genichi, Ōmura Kiyoshi, Ōtsuka Shōji, Satō Tsuneharu, Sugai Masatomo, Sugiyama Shirō, Tsuboi Hideo, Yamada Tetsuo, and Wagatsuma Takashi.

There were many social scientists who also gave freely of their time and energy. I feel particularly indebted to Shinozaki Nobuo, a fellow anthropologist who became Director-General of the Institute for Population Problems during my period of research in Japan. I also owe much to Aoi Kazuo, my advisor at the University of Tokyo, Hara Hiroko, and Yuzawa Yasuhiko. Students in the social sciences and health fields also gave me their help, and I also gained from their insights and expertise. Karasawa Yukiko generously extended numerous efforts. My special thanks also go to Hatō Mayumi, Kojima Hideo, Mutō Seiei, and Yamazaki Reiko.

Help came also from the ranks of various feminist groups.

I cannot overemphasize the extent to which the results of the intensive interviews with wives benefited from the skills and sensitivity of Sawanobori Nobuko, a self-employed marketing research specialist whom I first met through the Three Points Women's Project. Yamada Mitsuko, an activist in childbirth issues, provided indispensable aid and encouragement as well. My thanks also go to Iwatsuki Sumie, formerly of the Three Points organization, and the members of Himonji and the Shinjuku Lib Center. Friends gave me invaluable assistance at every stage of research. Tamura Shuji helped with a myriad of tasks and problems involved in relocating to Japan for an extended period, with assistance that began long before my research actually commenced. Despite her own demanding schedule, Eleanor Westney guided me through my initiation to computer data processing. Friends also provided important research contacts and information: my special thanks to Tom and Wenda Paton, Sunada Toshiko, and George and Willa Tanabe.

Various public and private institutions also provided valuable assistance, chief among them the Japanese government's Institute of Population Problems, with which I enjoyed an unofficial affiliation during the course of field research. I also thank the staffs of the Japanese Organization for International Cooperation in Family Planning, the Mainichi Newspapers' Population Research Council, the Japan Family Planning Federation, the Japan Association for Sex Education, and the Japan Association for Sex Research.

After field work, institutions and individuals in the United States gave me the assistance that enabled me to write this book. The task of turning data into a dissertation was helped along immeasurably by the cooperation I enjoyed from the staff at Columbia University's East Asian Institute, where I held a one-year affiliation as Junior Fellow until 1978. The resources, time, and assistance indispensable in producing a manuscript were made available to me by the Carolina Population Center in the course of a postdoctoral fellowship in population studies that began in 1979. Through courses and colloquia, as well as informal discussions, my colleagues at the Population Center gave me new insights and knowledge about important population-related issues as well as more sophisticated quantitative approaches to my data. My thanks go especially to Ronald Rindfuss and J. Richard Udry. Judy Kovenock and her staff made my use of the center's computer services simple and pain-free—no small feat—and Nancy Dole Runkle, through her programming skills, turned a semi-anarchic collection of text and tables into a very respectable looking manuscript. Lynn Igoe provided valuable editing help as well as welcome guidance in the mechanics of publishing a book. Kandi Stinson helped me through the maze of statistical testing techniques. Three colleagues at other institutions, Peggy Barlett (Emory University), John Money (Johns Hopkins University), and Patricia Steinhoff (University of Hawaii) gave me suggestions that greatly improved the rewritten manuscript.

My need for assistance from Japanese colleagues did not end with field work; a few Japanese associates have been burdened with my requests for clarifications, updates, and information to fill in gaps left standing when my field work ended. My deepest thanks for the kind and prompt replies to my inquiries go to Shinozaki Nobuo and his staff members at the Institute for Population Problems, as well as to Tomita Kōichi, Wagatsuma Hiroshi and Wagatsuma Takashi. Karasawa Yukiko and Yamada Mitsuko also gave me valuable supplementary information, and Kataoka Hiroko gave me useful suggestions regarding translations.

Books in the social sciences cannot be written without money—money for training, money for research, and money for writing. I feel obligated to make this undeniable, albeit crass, point in my acknowledgments because my country has entered an era of drastically reduced social science funding. I feel particularly grateful for the support that I have received, but I deeply regret the current trend that is making it more and more difficult for studies such as mine ever to materialize. My field research was supported by a dissertation research grant from the Social Science Research Council, and the writing of the dissertation by an award from the Japan Foundation. The postdoctoral fellowship that enabled the writing of this book was funded by the Public Health Service of the U.S. Department of Health and Human Services.

Other individuals in the United States and Japan deserve thanks. I can only hope that whatever insight and information that I have had to offer, and the bonds of good will formed in the course of the research, will in some small way reciprocate their assistance.

Samuel Coleman
Raleigh, North Carolina

NOTE

Japanese vocabulary, phrases, and proper names have been transliterated, using Hepburn romanization as it is used in *Kenkyusha's New Japanese-English Dictionary*, and names of individuals appear with the the family name preceding given name, in accordance with Japanese usage.

The results of statistical tests have been judged significant when they attain the .05 level of probability or less.

All monetary figures have been converted from yen into United States dollars at the rate of ¥ 280 to one dollar, the rate that prevailed during the time of field work.

Table of Contents

List of Tables

List of Figures

Family Planning in
Japanese Society

CHAPTER I

Introduction: How the Japanese Limit Fertility

This book is about how Japanese couples limit their fertility—why they use some birth control methods and do not use others. The Japanese pattern stands out among affluent industrialized countries because married couples rely heavily on induced abortion. Another remarkable feature of Japanese birth control is the small proportion of couples who make use of the post-World War II period innovations in contraceptive technology, particularly oral contraception and contraceptive sterilization; although many couples do attempt to prevent conceptions, they rely upon condoms and the calculation of female reproductive cycles. A country that is ultramodern in so many other respects has a family planning technology that was created in the 1930s.

THE WIDESPREAD USE OF INDUCED ABORTION

The Japanese Ministry of Health and Welfare annually publishes a statistical breakdown of induced abortions reported by obstetrician-gynecologists (Ob-Gyns). The rates (expressed as number of abortions in one year per one thousand women of reproductive age) based on these reported figures place Japan on the high end of the range of the Western European countries. In 1975, for example, Japan's rate of 25 abortions to every thousand women ranked below Denmark's 27, but registered somewhat above the figures for the United States and Sweden of 22 and 20, respectively, and well above France's 1976 rate of 12 as well as the rate of 11 in England and Wales in 1975.[1]

[1] Tietze 1979:26-28, 30, 35.

The estimates of Japanese demographers and public health specialists, however, place the actual number of abortions at anywhere from one and a half to four times the reported figures. Ob-Gyns in private practice underreport these operations because every unreported procedure brings in a fee that escapes taxation, and the great majority of abortions are performed in the private practitioners' own hospitals, where they can easily elude detection by monitoring agencies. This poses problems not only for income tax agents, who in the past have resorted to raiding obstetrical hospitals and counting empty anesthesia containers, but for students of population and public health as well, for it leaves us without firm statistics for studying the role of abortions in Japanese family planning.

Muramatsu Minoru, an Ob-Gyn who specializes in population and public health issues, has devised the most sophisticated approach to the problem of abortion estimates by calculating an expected number of abortions for a specific year based on married female population size, age composition, and extent of contraceptive use. His mean estimate (averaging assumptions of high and low contraceptive practice effectiveness) places the actual number of induced abortions to married women in Japan in 1975 at well over three times the reported number.[2] The resulting rate of 84 abortions for every thousand women of childbearing age puts Japan into the highest range worldwide, which is occupied by the Eastern European countries; it gives Japan twice Hungary's rate for the same year, slightly above Romania's 1973 rate of 81.[3] The estimate also means that pregnancies in Japan in that year were more likely to end in abortions than in live births. When Muramatsu's rates for each age group are spread over the average woman's reproductive years, we find that each woman experiences two abortions during her married life.

A 1969 nationwide survey of 29,880 women requesting abortions also provides an idea of the extent of repeat abortion

[2] Muramatsu 1978.
[3] Tietze 1979:33.

and its tempo: of the 63 percent who acknowledged at least one previous abortion, a fourth had received it less than 12 months before their request for another abortion.[4]

Married women account for the majority of legal induced abortion cases in Japan. A precise percentage cannot be derived from official records because marital status is not recorded, but the 1969 survey of women requesting abortions found that 66 percent of the applicants were currently married.[5] The result is close to the more recent informal estimates ranging around 70 percent given by Tokyo area Ob-Gyns.

The age distribution and rates by age for reported abortions also suggest that a sizeable majority of aborters among Japanese women are married. The distributions of reported abortions and their rates by age in Japan appear in Table 1-1, along with figures in the same categories for the United States. In Japan, the peak age group begins among women in their mid-20s; in 1976, the year for which the figures in Table 1-1 were prepared, average age at first marriage for women was 24.9 years. Moreover, the proportion of women who marry in their late 20s is very high: in 1975, 78 percent of Japan's women between the ages of 25 and 29 were currently married, in contrast to only 30 percent of women five years younger.[6]

The large proportion of married abortion recipients in Japan resembles the Eastern European pattern, in contrast to most of the Western nations, where unmarried women are more likely to be abortion recipients. During the mid-1970s, about three-fourths of the abortions performed in Czechoslovakia and Hungary were among currently married women; in the United States and Canada in the same period the yearly figures were in the range of 30 percent, and about 40 percent for England and Wales.[7] The United States age pattern reflects

[4] Calculated from figures in Kōsei-shō/Nihon Ishi-kai 1971:6.
[5] Kōsei-shō/Nihon Ishi-kai 1971:4.
[6] Calculated from figures in Japan, Office of the Prime Minister 1977:98.
[7] Tietze 1979:55.

Introduction

TABLE I-I
Distribution of Reported Abortions by Age,
Japan and United States, 1976

Age	JAPAN		UNITED STATES	
	Rate 1,000 Women	Percentage of Yearly Total	Rate 1,000 Women	Percentage of Yearly Total
<20	0.8	2.0	36.2	32.1
20-24	25.3	16.3	40.2	33.3
25-29	33.7	28.8	24.7	18.7
30-34	38.4	25.4	15.3	9.3
35-39	28.3	18.3	9.3	4.8
40-44	13.3	8.4		
45-49	1.4	0.8	3.7	1.8
TOTALS		100.0		100.0
		(664,106 cases)		(762,427 cases)

Sources: U.S.: Tietze 1979:49; U.S. Center for Disease Control 1978:21
Japan: Kōsei-shō 1981:23.

reliance on abortion chiefly among young unmarried women
and women who have completed their intended number of
children, whereas the Japanese pattern points to extensive use
among married women throughout their married lives and
relatively little use by women under 20 years of age. The
figures for Japan may underrepresent the actual number of
abortions among young women, for there is a strong suspicion
that doctors are less likely to report abortion cases in which
the recipient was unmarried.[8] On the other hand, there is an
important point that substantiates the low representation of
Japan's youngest women: Japanese youth have one of the
industrialized world's lowest rates of premarital sexual activity
for females as well as males.

[8] See Nakahara 1975:10; Taeuber 1958:276. Chapter 2 discusses
the reasons for underreporting of abortions to unmarried women.

A DEARTH OF MODERN METHODS
OF CONTRACEPTION

A high proportion of Japanese married couples do take steps to prevent conceptions; the extent of contraceptive practice in Japan is on a par with the West. In the mid-1970s, about 71 percent of Japanese wives capable of becoming pregnant were contracepting (an economical verb that means "applying a method of contraception"), a figure close to the 77 percent of American wives in the same category.[9] A current practice rate of 70 percent or more is typical of industrialized countries.

The Japanese contraceptive repertory, however, differs radically from that of many other countries: very few Japanese couples make use of the contraceptive technology that has developed since the early 1960s, in the form of oral contraceptives (pills), greatly improved intrauterine devices (IUDs), and simpler sterilization procedures. These three methods, collectively termed modern, accounted for well over half of contraceptive use in both developing countries and the English-speaking world as of the mid-1970s.[10] Figure 1 contrasts the percentages of methods used among currently contracepting wives in Japan and seven other industrialized countries, where the data are reliable and reasonably comparable. Belgium, with the second lowest distribution of modern methods, has roughly three times the proportion of Japan's modern method users.

The contrast among modern methods is greatest for pill use. Other statistics corroborate Japan's position at the lowest end of the scale of pill users; a calculation of the minimum percentage of women aged 15 to 44 supplied with oral contraceptives through commercial channels in the early 1970s finds Japan the lowest of 17 countries investigated.[11] Survey data

[9] These figures were calculated from information in Kōsei-shō 1976a:32 and Ford 1978:265; the percentages were standardized to the age composition of United States women.

[10] Nortman 1977:18; Stokes 1977:9; Nortman typifies Japan as a "lone holdout" in the trend of increased use of modern methods.

[11] Piotrow and Lee 1974:9.

Figure 1: Distribution of Contraceptive Methods Among Currently Contracepting Married Women in Japan and Seven Other Industrialized Countries, in Percentages, 1974-1978

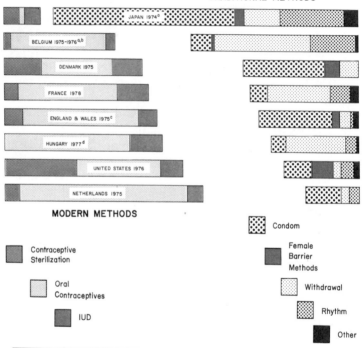

[a] Total exceeds 100.0 due to separate calculation of multiple methods.
[b] Dutch-speaking Belgians.
[c] Mothers of legitimate infants less than five months old.
[d] Wives under 40 years of age.
Sources: Japan, figures calculated from Kōsei-shō 1976a:33 and Nohara 1980:187; Belgium, Cliquet et al. 1978:76; France, figures calculated from Leridon 1979:26; Denmark, figures calculated from Leridon 1981:99; England and Wales, figures calculated from Cartwright 1978:4; Hungary, Wulf 1980:46; United States, figures calculated from Ford 1978:265; Netherlands, NIDI 1978:12.

from Ireland in 1973, when the importation and sale of contraceptives was illegal, show 15.6 percent of contracepting
married women relying on the pill,[12] easily six times the proportion of Japanese wives using oral contraception at that
time.

Japan also ranks low in extent of contraceptive sterilization,
although the international contrast is not as sharp as that for
the pill, and comparison becomes difficult because statistics
on contraceptive practice either omit sterilization or do not
specify what proportion of operations represent procedures
that were contraceptive as opposed to the medically necessary.
Against an 11.7 percent of sterilizations for all reasons among
couples with at least one live birth in Japan in 1974, a 1973
Vancouver study found about 17 percent of mothers of childbearing age or their husbands had had sterilizations specifically for contraceptive purposes.[13] Figures for contracepting
married mothers in England and Wales, however, are closer
to the Japanese level; 7 percent relied on sterilization for contraceptive purposes in 1975.[14]

The great majority of Japanese couples who contracept rely
on two traditional methods: condoms and rhythm (the calendar method, also known as the Ogino method). The degree
to which they have adopted condoms is particularly striking:
Japanese couples probably have the highest condom use rate
in the world. In 1974, three-fourths of currently contracepting
wives reported condom use. The highest use rate available for
any other developed country is for Finland—a 1967 figure of
42 percent.[15] The percentage of couples who use periodic
abstinence is also remarkably high, considering that Japan has
only a handful of Catholics; in 1974, a fourth of wives then
using contraception were relying on rhythm. The only other
country claiming a higher rate of use in the mid-1970s was

[12] Wilson-Davis 1975.
[13] United Community Services of the Greater Vancouver Area
1974:169.
[14] Cartwright 1978:4.
[15] The figure is derived from information in Leppo, Koskelainen,
and Sievers 1974:58.

Ireland, where over half the wives sampled claimed rhythm as their method.[16]

Despite the large role that traditional methods play in Japanese family planning, few couples employ female barrier methods (which include mechanical devices such as caps and diaphragms as well as spermicidal preparations). In contrast to fewer than 4 percent of contracepting Japanese wives claiming use of any female barrier methods, about the same percentage of women in West Germany are using spermicides,[17] and over twice that percentage of contracepting wives in the United States are using diaphragms or spermicidal foam. Foam is unavailable in Japan. Spermicides are sold in the form of jellies or foaming tablets. One other distinctive feature of Japanese contraceptive practice is the multiple use of methods. Independently calculated percentages for each method among current users presented in the 1974 World Fertility Survey total 137 percent. The single greatest multiple use category is condoms and rhythm.[18]

IMPLICATIONS OF THE JAPANESE PATTERN

What makes the Japanese pattern of birth control remarkable is what it implies about method acceptability. Heavy reliance on induced abortion has been the hallmark of Japanese fertility limitation since the end of World War II. In the West, the legalization of abortion has been opposed by religious groups, in particular the Roman Catholic Church, and—until very recently, at least—it was assumed that women have an intrinsic preference for contraception over abortion. The case of Japan has prompted some well-known population specialists to suggest that the absence of a Judaeo-Christian tradition opposing abortion has made the operation more of a realistic birth control alternative in Japan, or that there may not be anything more intrinsically desirable about preventing a preg-

[16] Wilson-Davis 1975:437, 440.
[17] Querido and Schnabel 1979:146.
[18] Kōsei-shō 1976a:33.

nancy than ending it in its early stages of development.[19] Could it be that Japanese culture creates an easy acceptance of abortion?

The extensive use of condoms and periodic abstinence in Japan also raises questions about the acceptability of these two methods of birth control. The widespread use of modern methods throughout most of the world reflects two benefits: these methods provide a high degree of physiological contraceptive effectiveness, and they free couples from having to apply a contraceptive method whenever they have sexual intercourse.

The former feature means fewer unwanted pregnancies due to *method* failure, in which the contraceptive did not protect against pregnancy even though it was used correctly and consistently; the latter feature greatly reduces unwanted pregnancies due to *user* (or psychological) failure, in which the contraceptive was used incorrectly or not at all. Condoms can be as effective as IUDs if they are used correctly and with complete consistency, but the price is an interruption of intimacy and a physical barrier to sexual contact—so much so that one family sociologist in the United States suggests that condoms symbolize "some denial of sexuality in its full marital context."[20] Rhythm is not only the least effective of contraceptive methods in use today; it also poses the greatest obstacle to marital sexuality, since it demands that the couple refrain from sex during a long portion of the female cycle. Among contracepting women in the United States, those who rely on rhythm report the lowest coital frequencies.[21] Perhaps our assumptions about the sexual frustration inherent in these methods is unwarranted in the Japanese context. Then again, Japanese husbands and wives could be placing a lower priority

---

[19] See Lader 1966:133; Lee 1973:349; Lorimer 1954:235; and Taeuber 1958:282. A widely read book on abortion by sociologist Kristin Luker (1975:7) suggests that the case of Japan challenges the assumption that women prefer contraception over abortion.

[20] Rainwater 1960:153.

[21] Westoff 1974:138.

on sexual expression than do couples in the West, with the problem of contraceptive effectiveness alleviated by access to induced abortion.

Method availability poses another critical factor.[22] The modern contraceptive methods and the diaphragm typically share an important disadvantage: medical specialists must actively participate in making these methods available, which could raise their cost and make them less obtainable than simpler methods. Hence the term *medical methods*, which connotes the need for a provider having specialized training. (The term will be used for the category of the diaphragm plus the modern methods.)

Do Japanese couples have the range of choices enjoyed by men and women in other affluent industrialized countries? The present pattern of birth control in Japan could be a result of the way in which family planning services are delivered by that country's medical industry, rather than of the preferences of Japanese couples. If Japanese men and women are indeed using a set of fertility limitation methods which they dislike, the next step would be to identify the obstacles which prevent them from enjoying more appropriate contraception. The investigation would demand both an examination of the medical care and family planning service delivery systems as well as an analysis of the characteristics of that small minority of Japanese couples who have broken away from the mainstream and are using modern contraception despite the extra difficulty of obtaining it.

The Japanese birth control pattern could also mean that couples are opting for the safest possible mix of birth control alternatives. Modern contraceptive methods, like induced abortion, pose the possibility of ill effects on health. The pill in particular has been linked to health dangers, among them fatal diseases of the circulatory system. In terms of the mortality risks associated with the various methods, women in

[22] For discussions of the importance of access to quality medical assistance for contraceptive adoption and use, see Coleman and Piotrow 1979:92-93, 96; Jaffee 1964:469-70; Scrimshaw 1976.

the West are safest when they use barrier methods and rely on induced abortion for their contraceptive failures.[23]

Any explanation of a country's birth control pattern must involve assumptions about the nature of marriage and sexuality, since every fertility limitation method demands trade-offs for one or both partners in health safety, sexual expression, and expense, as well as agreements about childbearing intentions. Indeed, the area of abortion and contraception offers a critical arena for reassessing assumptions about contemporary family dynamics in Japan. Some observers hold that Japanese wives enjoy ultimate authority in domestic matters. Does the widespread use of condoms substantiate that view, since condom use requires male cooperation? What does the widespread use of contraceptive methods that inhibit sexual gratification say about the role of sexuality in Japanese marriages? Is it a sign that the traditional family theme of subordinating the conjugal relationship to other family functions has persisted, despite the appearance of the modern nuclear family? Most observers agree that the Japanese woman has low status, and yet she has access to induced abortion, which Americans typically regard as the pinnacle of reproductive rights. Is this assessment of the Japanese woman's status mistaken, or is there more to learn about formal and informal restrictions on induced abortion that give Japanese husbands more control over reproduction?

THE STUDY

I went to Tokyo to explore these issues in mid-1974 and spent two years and four months gathering data. Much of my research took the form of anthropological observation. I gleaned observations concerning couples' marital roles, life-styles, and courtship patterns not only from day-to-day interactions with friends and acquaintances, but from the mass media as well. These sources also proved valuable for determining attitudes toward induced abortion. Discussions and interviews with

[23] Tietze and Lewit 1979.

Japanese specialists in the areas covered by this study were particularly helpful; in all, 93 specialists in family planning, obstetrics and gynecology, public health, the women's movement, the social sciences, family counseling, and the pharmaceutical industry gave me information and opinions.

More detailed information about my research methods appears in the Appendix, but the two highly structured investigations I conducted deserve some description here. I developed a self-administered questionnaire that investigated social background, marital life-style, pregnancy history, current contraceptive practice, frequency of sexual intercourse, and attitudes toward contraception and abortion. Ob-Gyns, family planning counselors, and paramedical personnel distributed the forms to patients at eight obstetrical hospitals and family planning facilities in the Tokyo-Yokohama conurbation. Of the 1,020 forms distributed, 635 were returned and found usable. Compared to all women of reproductive age living in the Tokyo-Yokohama area, the questionnaire respondents were somewhat younger, and a higher percentage had an education beyond high school. Nearly three-fourths of the respondents (73 percent) were living in nuclear households, and the group's average number of children was 1.5.

The distinctive features of Japanese contraception appear among the women in the clinic survey conducted for this study. A breakdown of methods used by contracepting wives appears in Table 1-2. Despite the fact that six of the eight questionnaire distribution points have family planning programs, the basic pattern of extensive reliance on condoms pertains, and only a fourth of the contracepting wives were using oral contraceptives or IUDs. Fewer than 2 percent were using a female barrier method, and about 30 percent claimed use of more than one traditional method. The respondents evidently underreported the extent to which they had experienced abortions; only 27 percent claimed ever to have had one or more abortions. Marital abortions accounted for over 80 percent of the total of 236 abortions reported, although respondents probably underreported premarital abortions more than marital abortions.

TABLE I-2

Percentage Distribution of Contraceptive Methods
in Use Among Currently Contracepting Japanese Wives,
Tokyo Area Clinic and Hospital Sample, 1975-1976

Condom Only	36.0
Periodic Method* and Condom	24.2
IUD	16.6
Oral Contraceptives	8.1
Condom and Other Traditional Method(s)	5.5
Female Sterilization	3.5
Periodic Method* Only	2.2
Diaphragm,** Spermicides	1.7
Miscellaneous Traditional	0.9
Male Sterilization	0.7
Interruptus Only	0.7
TOTAL	100.1
(N = 458)	

Total percentage exceeds 100.0 because of rounding.
* Includes both rhythm (Ogino) and basal body temperature.
** Includes condom and diaphragm combination.

I also conducted a series of intensive structured interviews
with 22 couples who were not involved in the questionnaire
study. Three sets of interviews were conducted in the Kansai
area (Kyoto, Osaka, and Kobe), one in Nagoya, and eighteen
in Tokyo and Yokohama. The interviews began in April 1976
and ended in November. (This phase had to await the development of networks for finding satisfactory interviewees as
well as development of my Japanese language skills to the
point where I could feel sufficiently confident in a structured
interview session.) Prospective interviewees were approached
informally by Japanese friends and colleagues who had as-
sisted in earlier phases of the research; personal relationships
between these people and the interviewees appeared to be a

major determinant of the interviewees' willingness to participate. The interviewee sample had a larger portion of wives with a four-year college degree than the questionnaire group, as well as a somewhat higher age.

I interviewed husbands, and a Japanese female colleague, Sawanobori Nobuko, interviewed each of their wives. We conducted our interviews separately, with one exception. Each interview began with demographic questions about family members (such as ages, the couple's regions of origin, and education). Spouses were then asked open-ended questions about domestic roles and their satisfaction with their spouses' performance in household activities. The interviews progressed to the topic area of marital affect, with questions such as the qualities that the marriage partners liked most and least about one another then and now. Desired number of children and the couple's actual reproductive history were then taken up, including history of contraceptive use. The final topic area was conjugal sexuality, including frequency of intercourse and relative strengths of both partners' sexual desire.

The results of surveys conducted by Japanese specialists also play an important part in this study. I offer them to the reader not only because they provide a valuable—if not indispensable—supplement to my own primary data, but also because many of these study results are published only in Japanese, which puts them out of reach of the non-Japanese specialist. The surveys are taken primarily from the mid-1970s to match the immediate time period of my own field observations as closely as possible. The most useful survey data come from a unique series of nationwide polls conducted by the Population Problems Research Council, a private organization created by the Mainichi newspapers in 1949. The Mainichi surveys have been conducted biennially since 1950, thus offering the world's longest consecutive series of family planning surveys. (Many of the results are published in English by the Population Problems Research Council with the assistance of the Japanese Organization for International Cooperation in Family Planning.) The Japan World Fertility Survey, conducted by the Ministry of Health and Welfare in 1974, has also provided a valuable source of supplementary data. Appendix C provides more information on major family planning surveys in Japan.

The fertility limitation system I encountered in Japan offers induced abortion, but in a social context of reproach. Modern contraceptive services are not readily available; the family planning movement is geared to providing condoms, and physicians are less committed to pregnancy prevention than to pregnancy termination. How couples respond to this situation reflects more than the range of available solutions; it also stands as a statement of their ability to deal effectively with an area of life that poses problems in every culture. The pursuit of effective contraception is particularly difficult for Japanese couples, however, because their marital sexuality is muted by female passivity and a deep gender role division in conjugal life. Their story deserves telling partly because so little is known of these aspects of Japanese life; Western readers have too often had to content themselves with fragmentary information or myths about subterranean female dominance and attitudes toward sexuality and induced abortion that are supposedly unencumbered with moral inhibition as they are in the Judaeo-Christian West. A related but more far-reaching reason for this study is to make Japanese family planning more understandable in human terms. The Japanese situation may be unique, but it results from processes and dynamics that are not. When we recognize certain universal human motives and dynamics that have played their part in shaping the Japanese pattern, we benefit not only in a more authentic view of Japanese society; we also move toward greater understanding of universal problems and issues that attach to the different fertility limitation techniques now being introduced in a great variety of cultural contexts.

CHAPTER 2

Resources for Terminating Pregnancies

There is probably no other industrialized country that can claim the degree of access to legal abortion over the last thirty years that Japan has had.[1] Such permissiveness has not always been the case, however; Japan entered the twentieth century with a law that strictly prohibited abortion,[2] but the extraordinary circumstances in the early post-World War II period brought about a heavy reliance on the practice. In the ensuing years, abortion became the preserve of a well-organized group of medical specialists who have made it widely available to Japanese married women on a fee-for-service basis.

THE LEGACY OF THE EARLY POSTWAR EXPERIENCE

Japan's economic and social structure was devastated by its defeat in World War II. As the country entered the second half of the 1940s, it experienced a severe shortage of basic necessities and a near-complete destruction of industrial capacity, problems that were only aggravated by the presence of 6.5 million demobilized troops and repatriated civilians who had poured back onto the country's four main islands by 1948.

The return of large numbers of men meant that their wives would be exposed to pregnancy. Although families were beginning—or resuming—to have children postponed by the war, there was a leap in the occurrence of unwanted fertility as well; as one indication of this rise, rates for infanticide and infant abandonment rose to their highest level in postwar Japan between 1945 and 1950, nearly trebling their 1940

[1] Daniel Callahan's 1970 book provides an excellent international review of abortion law; for an update, see Tietze 1979.

[2] Ōta 1967:26-27.

level.[3] There was little knowledge of contraception or access to various contraceptive methods, however, since the government had previously actively suppressed contraception and instruction in family planning. The first of the nationwide Mainichi family planning surveys in 1950 found that about two-thirds of couples in their childbearing years had never practiced contraception.[4] Supplies of contraceptives were grossly inadequate: the production and sale of condoms and spermicides in the late 1940s could meet the needs of only one out of seven married couples of reproductive age.[5]

It was under these circumstances that large numbers of Japanese women turned to induced abortion: pressed by stringent economic conditions and lacking the means to control conception, they sought ways to end their unwanted pregnancies. Perhaps because of the atmosphere of thriving black markets, physicians were no longer threatened by the law against abortion; not only were Ob-Gyns providing them, but other physicians and even veterinarians began performing abortions on a regular basis.[6]

The government responded by acting on the recommendations of the country's Ob-Gyns; the prewar law regulating abortion was replaced with a more liberal law that would confine the procedure to competent practitioners. The most recent prewar law providing grounds for legal abortion, the National Eugenic Law of 1940, was patterned after the law in Nazi Germany, and allowed induced abortion only to save the mother's life or to eliminate specific genetic defects. The new law of 1948, the Eugenic Protection Law, recognized rape and leprosy as legitimating reasons for performing induced abortions, as well as hereditary illness and cases where the mother's life would be endangered by pregnancy or birth. Spouse consent was also required. In the following year, the law was revised to extend legal availability greatly; Article

[3] Inamura 1975:41.
[4] Population Problems Research Council 1970:98.
[5] Taeuber and Balfour 1952:114-15.
[6] Ōta 1976:358-59.

14, Paragraph 4, allowed abortion "when there is risk that pregnancy or birth will cause substantial harm to the health of the mother due to physical or economic reasons." The logic was essentially maternal health protection, but the clause added a socioeconomic dimension as well.

The new Eugenic Protection Law also stipulated that abortions could be performed only by Ob-Gyns certified by their local medical association. These doctors were termed "designated physicians" (*shitei ishi*) when they had met the association's criteria for certification. The 1948 law required review of each application for abortion by a local committee, but this requirement was eliminated in 1952 in a revision which made each designated physician the sole arbiter of whether or not the patient's pregnancy qualified for legal abortion.

Japan's abortion law had created a unique category of specialists: unlike other medical specialists in Japan, who do not require certification, designated physicians must meet specific criteria formulated by their colleagues before they can perform abortions. Today, these qualifications include thirty months of training at an approved nonprivate hospital and a practice in a hospital or clinic having facilities for conducting major abdominal surgery. The certified doctor becomes a member of the organization of designated physicians, the "Maternal Protection Association" (*Bosei Hogo I Kyōkai*).

HOW THE LAW WORKS

Induced abortion is still prohibited under Japanese law by the Penal Code, but the Eugenic Protection Law defines specific exceptions to this prohibition. (There are actually two separate terms in Japanese for induced abortion: *chūzetsu* connotes legal abortion; *datai*, illegal abortion.)

The Eugenic Protection Law places the authority for deciding if a pregnancy is legally terminable on the individual examining physician. Although the "physical or economic reasons" clause has accounted for over 99 percent of all reported abortions since 1955,[7] there are no specific economic criteria that designated physicians are supposed to apply. The latest formulation of guidelines is the Permanent Vice-Minister's Circular of 1953, which defines those eligible as individuals receiving welfare, cases where the pregnant woman is the main breadwinner of the family, and cases where "birth or continuation of the pregnancy would qualify the family for welfare status."[8] The lattermost stipulation gives doctors their discretionary power. In practice, they do not ask for proof of economic status from their patients: the Maternal Protection Association asserts that the judgment of eligibility is a medical issue, not an economic one.[9] The irrelevance of the patient's economic status is revealed in the responses of women who had had abortions to a question about reasons for aborting in a 1969 nationwide survey: only 1 percent said that finances had become strained enough to qualify them for welfare.[10]

Other restrictions on abortion set forth in the Eugenic Protection Law also allow discretion to the individual physician. The law implies a limit on gestation period in its definition of abortion as "artificial expulsion of the fetus and appendant matter . . . in the period before the fetus is able to maintain life outside the mother's body" (Article 2, Paragraph 2). Although the government has defined this period as twenty-four weeks after the last day of the last menstrual period, the manual for designated physicians advises its members to make a comprehensive judgment for possibility of survival based not only on length of gestation but other considerations as well, such as the degree of fetal development.[11]

The requirement of spouse consent also leaves implementation to the doctor's discretion in actual practice. The patient's husband must provide his consent to the procedure unless he is "unascertainable, unable to declare his intentions,

---

[7] Kōsei-shō 1981:25.
[8] Nihon Bosei Hogo I Kyōkai 1966:10.
[9] *Ibid.*:11, Kashima 1975:92-93.
[10] Naikaku Sōridaijin 1970:19.
[11] Nihon Bosei Hogo I Kyōkai 1966:4-5.

or has passed away since the pregnancy began" (Article 14, Paragraph 3). The law, however, does not designate the form of consent. Local chapters of the medical association provide each practitioner with form sheets which require the names, address(es), and telephone number(s) of abortion recipient and spouse, as well as the paragraph number in Article 14 of the Eugenic Protection Law that is deemed applicable. Individuals validate written transactions and other documents with seals in Japan rather than with signatures, and the only seal required for a consent form is an inexpensive, unregistered seal. Since the more elaborate, registered seals are not required, it is quite simple for a woman to forge a consent by using a cheap ready-made seal (*sanmonkan*), which can be purchased at any stationery store for less than the equivalent of one U.S. dollar.

If it can be proved that a doctor performed an abortion on a married woman without the husband's consent, the abortion becomes an illegal abortion punishable under the Penal Code. Gynecologists vary in their assessment of the danger; one prominent member of the Tokyo Maternal Protection Association (a local chapter of the designated physicians' organization) stated bluntly: "If some angry husband were to come in here I'd tell him it's *his* problem, not mine. I'm a doctor, not a policeman." Other private practitioners are not as sanguine. Stories circulate among doctors of harassment by irate husbands and cases of blackmail. One story of an incident twenty years ago has it that a doctor was so harassed by one husband demanding a payment equivalent to about $8,000 that he secretly decamped and set up his practice elsewhere. Nevertheless, doctors are in agreement that cases of husband complaint are rare among stably married couples; common-law marriages, unmarried women, and divorces with immediate remarriage and pregnancy are more likely to become problem cases.

The Ob-Gyn's position in the potential legal dispute is weakened far more by negative attitudes toward abortion itself and an image of the doctor enjoying a lucrative abortion practice than the issue of male control over reproduction.

Hence this warning that appeared in an article on spouse consent in a major Japanese journal of obstetrics and gynecology:

> In the present state of affairs where some lawyers abhor the unwelcome stigma of "Japan the abortion heaven," you should bear in mind that there are young lawyers brimming with a feeling of righteousness that calls for making the doctor specializing in abortion an object of attack.[12]

I have found no instances of court cases based on the husband's accusation; such complaints are settled out of court, sometimes by cash payment. Even so, the husband who finds that his wife has secretly aborted against his wishes is likely to be too-embarrassed to publicize the fact in an open protest against a doctor. The Japanese husband who complains about his wife's abortion against his wishes risks an extremely unsavory reputation: he is supposed to be able to control his marriage, keep discord to a minimum, and not rely on outside sources to maintain his authority. As one legal specialist pointed out to an irate twenty-eight-year-old husband who wanted to take action against the Ob-Gyn who accepted his wife's forged consent form: "Your story sounds like you're slandering a doctor who's a complete stranger, using your own marital quarrel that a dog wouldn't touch, and he probably won't put up with it."[13] (The expression *fūfugenka wa inu mo kuwanai*, literally "not even a dog would eat a husband-and-wife spat," means that such quarrels should not be imposed on outsiders.)

The Eugenic Protection Law does not expressly forbid abortions to unmarried women: it simply makes no reference to them, so such abortions are not legally recognized. Although Ob-Gyns will provide abortions for unmarried women, they typically require the woman's parents to validate the consent form; less often, the doctor demands a consent form from the

[12] Okuyama 1975:37.
[13] Kashima 1975:93.

man who impregnated the patient. A few especially cautious Ob-Gyns said that they require the parents or sex partner to consent to the procedure personally.

There are instances of doctors who do not demand written consent forms, as indicated by legal disputes which later arise as well as repeated admonitions from the Maternal Protection Association.[14] The abortion without a consent form may reflect more than a physician's bureaucratic oversight; the procedure is easier to conceal from taxation. In the case of an unmarried woman, or a woman who otherwise does not meet the requirements of the Eugenic Protection Law, the disincentive to report is stronger still.[15] In addition, a few activists in the Tokyo women's movement and one practicing Ob-Gyn stated that unmarried women are also sometimes required to pay more for their abortions. In such cases, the Eugenic Protection Law works on behalf of the doctor, who has a stake in keeping abortion activity as covert as possible.

Although the formal pronouncements of the Maternal Protection Association and the statements of a few Ob-Gyns interviewed assert that abortion is not a procedure performed at the patient's request, actual practice amounts to availability on demand. The designated physicians' handbook states in bold black characters that "abortion is not a procedure performed at the patients' request," and a subsequent publication of the association reiterates the assertion.[16] Nevertheless, since doctors vary in their choice of conditions under which they will grant an abortion, all Ob-Gyns are aware that any prospective abortion patient they may turn down will eventually find a qualified and willing practitioner to abort her. Discussing the problem of working wives who want to abort their first pregnancy in order to keep their jobs, one doctor practicing in a residential area said that he tells such patients to give birth instead. Asked if it was a problem since the patient

[14] Okuyama 1975; Nihon Bosei Hogo I Kyōkai 1966:11-12; *Bosei Hogo I Hō* 1971.

[15] Taeuber 1958:276 makes this point, as does Nakahara 1975:10.

[16] Nihon Bosei Hogo I Kyōkai 1966:6; Sakamoto 1975:8.

could go elsewhere, he replied: "Yes, indeed! But I encourage them to keep the pregnancy anyway. Almost all of them just go away on me. However, I'm not that kind of doctor—I guess I'm a good boy." And, as one specialist observed in the professional journal *Sanka to Fujinka (Obstetrics and Gynecology)*: ". . . for the woman who wants an abortion, even if she is turned down by one or a number of doctors, in the end in practically every case she will receive an abortion from a doctor somewhere."[17]

Designated physicians are rarely prosecuted under the Eugenic Protection Law. The primary application of the law since its inception has been to weed out the uncertified abortionist and punish conspicuous cases of malpractice. In 1948 there were 427 infractions reported. The number of such cases declined rapidly to 76 in 1955, with only 5 cases ten years later. There is now no separate category for illegal abortion in the criminal statistics of Japan.[18]

FINDING AN ABORTIONIST

Tokyo has about 1,300 mini-hospitals with fewer than 20 beds operated by Ob-Gyns. Of about 270 private gynecological and obstetrical hospitals with over 20 beds, fewer than a third are as large as hospitals familiar to residents of the United States.[19] The great majority of abortions take place at the small hospitals. Abortions within the first three months of pregnancy are typically performed on an outpatient basis (without overnight admission), and such outpatient abortions are the speciality of the small hospitals, as opposed to the large public and voluntary hospitals, which require overnight admission. This is a source of the small hospital's attraction, for it offers greater convenience and ease in concealment for the patient. The abortion is performed in the morning and the patient is allowed to leave the hospital in the evening or

[17] Akasu 1973:1.
[18] Nakahara 1975:11.
[19] Tsuboi 1974:37, 47.

night of the same day. Public hospitals, on the other hand, prefer allocating their facilities to maternity and major gynecological surgery cases.

Doctors are allowed to advertise their services publicly in Japan, and Ob-Gyns are among the most well advertised of medical specialties. Signs announcing obstetrical and gynecological services are ubiquitous. Billboards are placed at train stations and street intersections, and neighborhood doctors also have signs placed on telephone posts. Some doctors also place large, easy-to-find advertisements in the telephone directory. The content of this advertising is limited to the name, location, and telephone number of the hospital; any specialities offered in addition to obstetrics and gynecology; and some statement about facilities, such as "complete surgical services available" or "inpatient facilities provided." Such signs are as likely to stress the convenience of the hospital's location as its services. The word "abortion" does not appear in such advertisements, but almost all of these advertisements have one feature that marks them as advertising for abortion services: the phrase "Eugenic Protection Law Designated Physician" (*Yūseihogohō Shitei Ishi*).

Advertisements attract abortion patients because it is assumed that Ob-Gyns are abortionists. It is doubtful that any more than a handful of Japanese women are aware of the implications of the words "Eugenic Protection Law Designated Physician" for abortion availability; a 1969 nationwide survey found that 48 percent of the respondents did not know that such a law existed. Of those who were familiar with the name of the law, fewer than a third (15 percent of the total questioned) knew that the law dictated the terms under which abortion could be performed, and fewer than 10 percent of these women knew that the law designates the qualifications for doctors who perform abortions, which is the main reason for including the designation in advertising.[20] The 1969 survey of women requesting abortions found a much higher level of sophistication, but even then only 68 percent of the respond-

[20] Naikaku Soridaijin 1970:31.

ents gave the correct (multiple-choice) answer that "the doctor who can do an abortion must be one who is designated under the Eugenic Protection Law."[21]

The dominant feature of the way Japanese women go about selecting an abortionist is their desire to preserve privacy. This means that impersonal sources of information often substitute for word-of-mouth communication with other women. In addition to the Ob-Gyns' advertisements, women's magazines occasionally offer an impersonal basis for selecting an abortionist, with articles that coach their readers in the selection of a facility by advising the woman to look for the designated physician signboard and appraise certain features of the facility, such as its cleanliness. As part of their strategy for concealment, many women do not go to the Ob-Gyn from whom they receive their other health care services, but instead travel to an unfamiliar community in order to maintain anonymity. As a result, a particular urban facility's abortion patient population has no well-defined geographical boundaries, in contrast to the clear delineation of other patient populations.[22] If complications develop, the patient is not likely to return to the doctor who originally performed the abortion.

SAFETY AND COST

The risk to the patient's life from induced abortion in Japan is on a par with rates in other industrialized societies. Japan's death rate for legal abortions per unit of population of women of reproductive age was identical to the rate for England and Wales and Denmark in the mid-1970s,[23] despite the greater frequency of the procedure in Japan. Comparison of the extent of complications and ill after-effects of abortion in Japan and other countries is complicated by varying criteria for complications. Available observations suggest, however, that elective

[21] Kōsei-shō/Nihon Ishikai 1971:3.
[22] See, for example, Soda et al. 1960.
[23] Tietze 1979:96.

abortion in Japan is not more hazardous to health than it is in other industrialized countries.[24]

Japanese Ob-Gyns prefer dilatation and curettage over the more recently developed vacuum aspiration methods, and about 90 percent of their patients get general anesthesia for the procedure.[25] Like any other surgical procedure, induced abortion is not entirely risk-free, but a major consideration is the point in gestation at which termination takes place: the earlier it is, the safer. Japanese women receive their abortions earlier in gestation than do women in the West, and somewhat later than in Eastern Europe.[26] This probably results in part from the greater proportion of teenage women receiving abortions in the West, since the very young are less likely to seek an abortion at an early point in gestation.[27] In addition, Japan and Eastern Europe are cultural areas where there is greater familiarity with induced abortion. In Japan, articles on abortion in women's magazines exhort their readers to have their abortions early, not only for safety's sake but to avoid greater expense as well.

As a rule, recipients of abortions in Japan pay for them out of their own pockets and without subsidy. Abortion is subsidized by the Livelihood Protection Act for the indigent, and is also available for as little as $30 for those eligible to use mutual aid association hospitals (e.g., families of public employees). There is no way to state with certainty what portion of abortions performed yearly are subsidized in these ways, but it is safe to assume that their numbers are few. The country has a national health insurance program that does pay doctors for abortions under certain circumstances. Abortions performed for "economic reasons" under Article 14, Paragraph 4, are not covered, but the same clause mentions "physical" reasons, and these are recognized as applicable for insurance

[24] Majima et al. 1973; Muramatsu 1967; Neubardt 1972.
[25] Majima et al. 1973:1335.
[26] Based on a comparison of figures in Kōsei-shō 1981:24 and Tietze 1979:64-65.
[27] Tietze 1979:61.

claims if the physician reports a somatic disorder. "Severe morning sickness" is a typical diagnosis used for such purposes. Although one occasionally hears of doctors who do a volume business in abortion by extending health insurance coverage to patients, the typical Ob-Gyn declines to do so. Remuneration to the doctor from insured procedures is much lower than that for procedures that are not covered; whereas patients in 1975 were charged at least $110 for an abortion within the first three months of pregnancy, the doctor would receive only about $16 for the same procedure under insurance. The difference results from government regulation of insurance remuneration, whereas the Maternal Protection Association sets fees for the operation when it is paid for by the patient. In addition, the paperwork involved in insurance procedures would create extra work for the hospital staff and also become a potential source of evidence of actual income from abortions that could prove incriminating to the doctor who is concealing procedures in order to evade income tax. Some doctors flatly deny that insurance could cover abortion except in rare cases where the woman is gravely ill, and one doctor complained of having to argue with patients who demand insurance coverage.

The cost of an abortion in Japan falls within the price range for abortions in the United States, but it represents a bigger expense to Japanese couples. In the mid-1970s, per capita income in Japan was only slightly over half the U.S. figure.[28] In terms of the average hourly wage, the expense represented nearly a week's wages.

[28] Keizaikikaku-chō 1976:93.

CHAPTER 3

Resources for Contraception

Although induced abortion is widely available in Japan, most contraceptive methods are not; organizational features of the health care and family planning delivery systems, together with Japanese law, severely limit the availability of medical methods. The commercial sector, by contrast, has developed the largest and most innovative condom distribution program in the world, while making family planning information a staple of magazine reading.

EARLY EXPERIENCES IN FAMILY PLANNING

Contraception and family planning are not a novelty of postwar Japanese society. Pre-World War II Japanese society was not lacking in its own pioneers of contraception, either. Two of its innovators in contraceptive technology became particularly prominent: Ogino Kyūsaku, who devised a formula for calculating infertile and fertile periods in the human female, and Ōta Tenrei, who designed the intrauterine ring. Both men were active in the 1920s and early 1930s, but Ogino's work became particularly well known internationally; his calendrical method of periodic abstinence, or calendar rhythm method, was almost identical to a formula independently devised by an Austrian researcher named Knaus, and the term Ogino-Knaus Method or Ogino Method has become a synonym for the rhythm method.

The makings of a viable family planning movement became evident in Japan in the late 1920s, and by the early 1930s privately run clinic activity—albeit modest—was on a scale comparable to England's in the same time period. By the mid-1930s, however, contraceptive research and organized family

planning efforts came into conflict with the country's en
pronatalism as Japan's leaders became more militarist
their foreign policy more aggressive. The government's po
of benign neglect turned to one of repression in 1936, a
within two years the birth control movement was gutted.[1] The
movement to provide contraception to the public did not reap-
pear until some twelve years later, after the old government
had been dismantled by the Allied Occupation.

Postwar family planning activity differed from prewar efforts in a fundamentally important respect: whereas the earliest promoters of family planning were guided by goals of
feminism, maternal health, betterment of the proletariat, and/
or eugenics, efforts since the end of World War II were—and
continue to be—directed at the reduction of induced abortions. The problem was not one of helping Japanese women
to control their births, but to substitute one form of birth
control for another.

One year after the creation of the Eugenic Protection Law
of 1948, a law was passed which permitted the manufacture
and sale of contraceptives. The first of the government's explicit attempts to substitute contraception for abortion, however, did not appear until 1952. In that year the Ministry of
Health and Welfare initiated a set of programs at government
health centers to provide family planning education, and established a course of training for counselors in contraception.
The health center programs were to be conducted at newly
established Eugenic Protection Consultation Centers. The
training course would entitle its graduates to fit diaphragms
and sell contraceptive materials.[2]

The government initiatives were marked by two important
shortcomings: inadequacy of funding and staffing, and the
failure to include physicians. Instead of creating new positions,
the government programs attempted to place the responsibility for teaching family planning on health center personnel,

[1] Haas 1975.
[2] Muramatsu 1966:11.

who were already occupied with other responsibilities. The new family planning counselor program made no provision for remunerating its field workers, either.[3]

For its contraception promoters, the government chose midwives, and made no attempt to include Ob-Gyns in any of its educational or service programs. Doctors were not incorporated into these early contraceptive campaigns, in all probability, because of their indifference or outright hostility. The government's contraceptive programs, unlike abortion, held no promise of added income. Indeed, widespread use of contraception would decrease the demand for abortion. A midwife who was active in promoting contraceptive instruction in Tokyo during the early postwar years found that doctors resented her activities. At one point one confronted her, saying, "If you keep this up it's going to ruin me!" An Ob-Gyn who had devoted considerable time and energy to teaching diaphragm use in the early years after the end of World War II also met with negative reactions from fellow Ob-Gyns, who branded his classes "repulsive" (*etchi*). His colleagues, by contrast, "were doing deliveries by night and abortions by day—some did so many abortions their fingers were calloused."

At the same time that the first efforts to provide contraception were made, the designated physicians were consolidating their organization and eliminating unsafe practitioners. In 1952, the same year that the government announced its efforts to replace abortion with contraception, Ob-Gyns received the authority individually to decide the eligibility of women seeking abortions.

Although midwives did not have a conflicting interest in induced abortion, neither did they find promoting contraception to be a very remunerative activity. The result was little activity in home visits or consultation clinics at the health centers.[4] Contraception also meant discouraging pregnancies that could result in delivery cases. Another Tokyo area mid-

---

[3] *Ibid.*
[4] *Ibid.*

wife who had been very active in providing contraception remembered being criticized by her midwife colleagues, who told her she was "cutting her own throat."

When the government saw that its family planning campaign at the health centers was failing, it responded by proposing that a private organization be established for the task. In late 1953, the Ministry of Health and Welfare approached Kunii Chōjirō (then Director of the Japan Association for Parasite Control) with its request for assistance. He drew up a proposal for an organization, the Japan Family Planning Association (JFPA). The government approved the proposal without criticism, but informed Kunii that it had no budget for JFPA activities.[5]

Faced with the refusal of government funding, Japan's family planning movement quickly devised its own strategy for self-support: condom marketing. In late 1954, the JFPA negotiated a very favorable deal with a major condom manufacturing company, which agreed to provide its product for a fourth of the retail price. The association created a new image for condoms by designing tasteful packaging and writing up packaging inserts promoting contraception for the sake of maternal and child health. Outlets such as women's clubs presented themselves in response to newsletter advertisements. The income went to hire staff and produce educational materials.[6]

During this same period, magazines were spreading information on contraception. In 1952, well over two-thirds of married men and women who claimed some familiarity with contraception had named magazines as one of their sources of information.[7] This was not a new role for the magazines; in the late 1920s and early 1930s the popular press had eagerly taken up the issue of birth control, with advice that was as explicit as censorship would allow. In 1926, for example,

[5] Kunii 1979:1.
[6] *Ibid.*:2.
[7] Okazaki 1977:140.

Fujin Sekai (Woman's World) introduced Ogino's work on periodic abstinence.[8]

By the mid-1950s, the most important features of Japan's contraceptive services delivery system had been cast: government participation was nominal; nonprofit efforts sustained themselves on condom sales and did not coordinate their actions with the medical profession; and the most salient promoters of family planning knowledge were the popular magazines. In 1955 the government added subsidies for distributing contraceptives to the indigent and provided token payments for counseling to family planning workers. This was the government's last contribution to the cause of promoting contraception, and in 1965 it dismantled the family planning budget category as a response to pronatalist political influences.[9]

The country's trend in fertility limitation since the early postwar years took a dramatic course, but the effects of the family planning promotion campaigns of the early 1950s were minimal. When the 1950s ended, Japan's people had accomplished an all-time first among twentieth-century nations: in ten years they had cut their crude birth rate in half, from 34 births per thousand population in 1947 to 17 in 1957, a level that they have maintained ever since. Their success in suppressing fertility was due in large part to the use of abortion. The absolute number of reported abortions reached its zenith in 1955, with 1,170,143 cases, and did not fall below the one million level until 1962.[10] In terms of an estimated actual rate based on the Muramatsu formulation, the peak occurred somewhat later; the frequency of abortion rose from 131.9 per 1,000 women in 1955 to over 138 in 1960.[11]

MODERN CONTRACEPTION AND THE LAW

Despite the dramatic technological advances in contraception that have come about since Japan's early postwar experience

[8] Haas 1975:25-29.
[9] Muramatsu 1966:15.
[10] Moriyama 1973b:21.
[11] Tietze 1979:30.

in family planning, Japanese law places unusually strict restrictions on the provision of all the modern methods. The restrictions are particularly severe in the case of oral ovulation suppressors: they cannot be dispensed for contraceptive purposes. Although the current legal status of oral contraceptives does not prevent physicians from prescribing them to patients, steroids cannot be labeled or advertised for contraceptive purposes, and family planning workers are not allowed to provide information on their use. Perhaps the most telling effect on availability of all, however, is the doubt about the pill's health safety that the government ban nurtures.

Japanese law also confines eligibility for sterilization to specific legally defined conditions. The legal requirements for sterilization, like those for abortion, are set forth in the Eugenic Protection Law. The law refers to sterilization as "eugenic surgery," and legal eligibility is limited to married couples for cases of hereditary illnesses, mental illness, leprosy, or danger to the mother's life or health. The latter category is stated in Article Two, Paragraph Four, "when there is fear of danger to the mother's life from pregnancy or birth," and Paragraph Five, "when the mother has several children and there is fear of deterioration in health from each occasion of delivery." Almost all sterilizations in Japan are performed with the recipient's consent and for maternal health reasons. In contrast with induced abortion, no special qualification is required for the physician performing sterilizations.

The legal status of contraceptive sterilization is quite ambiguous: one officer of the Japan Family Planning Association stated that it was "illegal." A prominent urologist stated that he limits his vasectomy patients to couples with two or more children "because it's required by law," although nearly half (43 percent) of reported sterilizations in 1975 fell under Paragraph Four of the Eugenic Protection Law, which makes no mention of number of children. Family planning counselors who oppose sterilization for contraceptive purposes cite the law, asserting that the procedure is not legally elective.

Of all modern methods, the IUD receives the most liberal treatment under Japanese law; any physician may insert one.

Nevertheless, clearance has been provided only for two ring-shaped IUDs made of inert materials, which excludes medicated devices and IUDs with copper. Before 1974, IUDs could not be manufactured or imported, and physicians could insert them only as part of clinical research studies. This stricture still applies to the nonapproved varieties of intrauterine devices.[12]

OBSTETRICIAN-GYNECOLOGISTS AND THE PILL BAN

In its actual application, the law does not prevent individual Japanese doctors from dispensing any modern form of contraception, including the pill. Currently, prescription of orals that are actually used for contraceptive purposes is an openly acknowledged fact. The stipulations for legal sterilization also allow liberal interpretation similar to the way designated physicians handle the law regarding induced abortion. But most of Japan's gynecologists do not promote modern contraceptive methods, and are content with the legal status quo if not actively supportive of it.

The government's hesitation to approve of the pill as a contraceptive has persisted because of concerns at several interlocking levels which in turn make the stance of the country's Ob-Gyns a linchpin in supporting the ban. Since the Thalidomide scandal of the early 1960s, activist groups have severely criticized the government's Drug Authorization Law for being too lax. Other drug-related incidents have also arisen, in particular neurological illness caused by Quinoform, a medication for diarrhea. Meanwhile, experiences of dramatic disease outbreaks caused by industrial wastes have intensified fear of "internal pollution" from drugs of dubious safety.[13]

The government has been beset by demands for compensation by victims of the side effects of government-approved drugs, and these demands have been accompanied by mass demonstrations at the Ministry of Health and Welfare head-

[12] Wagatsuma 1976:144.
[13] See, for example, Takahashi 1973.

quarters that have received nationwide publicity. A high official of the Ministry expressed the fear of what would happen if the pill were to be permitted for contraceptive use and if subsequent side effects emerged: "There would be demonstrators all over this place [the Ministry of Health and Welfare building]. It would be unwise to take chances like that." He added that "Abortion affects only the lower half of the body, but the pill has effects all over the whole body."

The issue is complicated by the present system of pharmaceutical laws and their loose enforcement, which allows a number of drugs that would require a doctor's supervision in the West to be sold without prescription at Japanese drugstores. Many Japanese assume that since oral contraceptives are legal in the United States they can be obtained without prescription at drugstores; in fact, Japanese women typically interpret the question of whether or not they would take the pill if legalized to mean its open availability at pharmacies. Doctors express concern over misuse of pills if the government were to approve them for contraception and women were to take them without medical supervision. There is also the fear that government approval will somehow increase availability of the pill to unmarried youths, thus encouraging premarital sexual activity. This fear is implicit in a popular image of a sexual rampage among adolescents in the United States, fueled by easy access to the pill.

Given these concerns, the Ministry of Health and Welfare is not about to authorize steroidal preparations for contraception without the approval of the medical community. The doctors' position, however, as articulated by the Maternal Protection Association, is that there are too many side effects and too many unknown hazards to warrant approval of oral contraceptives. The Maternal Protection Association poses an impressive political voice; its members are affluent, well organized, and politically self-conscious. Their interests are represented in the Diet, and members are kept informed of all political developments of consequence to them in the association's monthly newsletter, the *Nichi Bo I Hō*.

At its heart, the doctors' stance reflects a lack of interest in providing contraception. Although there are specialists with genuine apprehensions about the health effects of widespread pill use, such concerns are not sufficient to explain the medical community's support of a categorical governmental ban on one of the world's most widely used contraceptives. An inconsistency casts doubt on the assertion that the ban is a health protection measure; the governmental authorization in question is not whether steroidal preparations can be manufactured and sold, but whether they can be sold as contraceptives. Over-the-counter sale of preparations containing female hormones is not included in the prohibitions; one patent medication that is sold for inducing menstruation contains diethylstilbestrol,[14] a synthetic estrogen that has been strongly linked to cancer among the children of women who ingest it during pregnancy.

CONTRACEPTION VERSUS ABORTION IN THE OBSTETRICIAN-GYNECOLOGIST'S PRACTICE

In the present-day Japanese Ob-Gyn's practice, as in the past, promotion of inexpensive, effective contraception poses a conflict with income from induced abortion. The observation was made in the early 1960s by Koya Yoshio, an eminent Ob-Gyn and public health specialist, who stated that "Currently, those doctors who have been authorized by national law to perform abortions tend to oppose family planning as contrary to their professional interest in induced abortion."[15] The effect of this interest on the doctors' position regarding government approval of the pill was later unequivocally identified by Wagatsuma Takashi, one of Japan's foremost authorities on oral contraception; the association of Ob-Gyns has withheld support of authorization "to protect a primary source of its members' incomes, i.e., abortion."[16]

It is difficult to define precisely the typical private practice

[14] Matsuyama 1981:36.
[15] Balfour 1962:319.
[16] Quoted in Huddle, Reich, and Stiskin 1975:318.

Ob-Gyn's economic stake in induced abortion; individual doctors would not want to reveal the actual number of abortions they perform, not only because of a desire to conceal evidence of tax evasion, but to avoid the stigma that attaches to a large abortion clientele. Nevertheless, available data corroborate the widespread assumption that abortion represents a substantial part of Ob-Gyns' incomes. The total market value of reported abortions for 1975 represents about one hundred million dollars, exclusive of related fees (such as drugs and various miscellaneous charges). Doctors have been able to increase their fees for induced abortions well beyond the rate of inflation; baseline fees for first trimester abortions rose 545 percent between 1965 and 1975, in contrast with an overall increase of 225 percent in the consumer price index. During the same period, the cost of medical procedures rose only 54 percent.[17] As some indication of the extent of income gained from unreported procedures, an investigation of 723 obstetrical and gynecological facilities conducted by the Japanese government's tax bureau in 1973 unearthed over $8,900,000 in untaxed income, "practically all" of which was from unreported abortions.[18]

Other considerations also point to an important place for abortion in the economy of the Japanese Ob-Gyn in private practice. A seasoned practitioner can perform a first trimester abortion in five to seven minutes; the rapidity of the procedure allows some private practitioners to fit twenty or so operations into their daily schedule. A recent tendency has prompted the small hospital practitioner to rely even more on abortion for income; more women have come to prefer big hospitals for their deliveries, resulting in the loss of inpatients.

The fees that Japanese doctors place on the modern methods suggest a rule-of-thumb charge that amounts to the profit from one induced abortion per year from the same patient. Contraception, like abortion under the "economic reasons" clause,

[17] Calculated from figures in Mori 1975:112 and Japan, Office of the Prime Minister 1976:362-63.

[18] Nakahara 1975:9.

is a fee-for-service procedure; there are no health insurance programs that provide benefits for contraceptive materials or instructions. (The cost of oral contraceptives can be reimbursed by national health insurance, but the doctor must submit the expense as a course of therapy for an insured ailment, and insurance inspection teams composed of Ob-Gyns prevent their colleagues from dispensing pills under insurance on a large scale.)

As of the mid-1970s, a year's supply of pills could cost anywhere between $63.00 to $84.00, and additional fees accrue from physical examinations and laboratory tests required by the doctor who dispenses them. (The minimum fee for an initial examination is a little over $10.00.) An IUD insertion costs about $70.00, but doctors vary in their policies regarding removal and reinsertion, many insisting upon inserting a new device once every year, charging an additional $18.00 or so for the removal; for their patients, the yearly expense of an IUD comes to about $90. Since Japanese IUDs are made from inert materials, their effectiveness does not decrease with length of use; aside from the mistaken belief that prolonged use could result in difficult removal, there is no medical basis for the practice of frequent replacement.[19] The expense of sterilization cannot be calculated on a yearly basis, of course, since the number of fecund years that it covers varies depending upon the couple's ages. At the time of this research, tubal ligations in the Tokyo area cost between $180 and $535, depending on the individual doctor, type of facility, and length of hospitalization. Vasectomies cost somewhere between $100 and $215.

Few private practice Ob-Gyns provide contraceptive counseling and methods for their patients. The most striking omission of this service appears among abortion cases, where contraceptive counseling should be a matter of routine. Wives in the questionnaire sample who were currently using contraception were asked about their sources of contraceptive in-

[19] See Wagatsuma 1976:143.

formation; the correlation between the number of abortions they had received and whether or not a professional or para-professional had served as one of their information sources was not significant.[20] The Designated Physicians' Handbook does advocate post-abortion family planning guidance, but under specific circumstances only: cases of chronic disease, a debilitated physical state, or patients having the after-effects of toxemia of pregnancy.[21]

It is unlikely that Japanese Ob-Gyns fail to take a more active role in promoting contraception because their patients prefer that they do not. Wives in the interview sample were asked how they felt about receiving recommendations of contraceptive methods from an Ob-Gyn, and respondents were favorable to the idea with few exceptions. A few interviewees expressed a disappointment in the doctor's failure to provide contraceptive guidance. The strongest and most explicit criticism came from a 33-year-old wife with a high-school education:

> I'm very dissatisfied with gynecologists. Unless the patient brings up the discussion they won't tell you about contraception. Especially at private hospitals their reason is that they're short of manpower, so after birth there's no guidance whatsoever. Doctors are just too bent on profits only.

DOCTORS' ATTITUDES TOWARD CONTRACEPTION

The personal family planning performance of Ob-Gyns and their biases about specific contraceptive methods reflect their inability to act as providers of a range of effective contraceptive methods. The results of a survey on contraceptive guidance and personal contraceptive practice among Ob-Gyns in the Kantō area (Tokyo and surrounding prefectures) suggest

[20] Results were obtained using a Pearson correlation of the two variables.
[21] Nihon Bosei Hogo I Kyōkai 1966:17.

that Ob-Gyns are no less vulnerable to abortion than is the general public. The study was conducted in early 1975 by Satō Tsuneharu, a professor of gynecology at Gumma University. (He distributed a questionnaire to 500 Ob-Gyns, 221 of whom responded.)[22] Satō found 55 percent of the sample reporting that they had relied on abortion at least once. This rate is somewhat higher than the range of 40 percent to 50 percent for self-reported ever-experienced rates found in surveys of Japanese women in general.[23] One compensating factor is the higher age of doctors than is usual in a random survey sample (and, hence, a longer period of exposure to unwanted pregnancies). Of those who reported experiencing abortion, however, 56 percent indicated that they were not contracepting at the time of conception.[24] Satō was surprised at the relatively high rate of abortion among Ob-Gyns; this prompted him informally to ask professional acquaintances their attitudes regarding abortion, which elicited the response that abortion is "a good method of contraception" ([sic]— they used the word *hininhō*).

The doctors in Satō's survey also displayed a disinterest in diaphragms. The diaphragm ranks a lowly seventh in frequency among methods recommended by the doctors who responded to Satō's survey, below the rhythm method. (The IUD and pill were the methods most often recommended by Ob-Gyns, but the survey did not attempt to ascertain the extent or circumstances of contraceptive guidance among respondents.) The diaphragm also ranked lowest among methods used by the respondents and their spouses. Although only one percentage point greater in frequency, there were more physician couples relying on douching, an extremely ineffective method.[25] The fitting of diaphragms is confined by law to doctors and midwives, but in actual practice very few doc-

[22] Satō and Shigeshiro 1976.

[23] Naikaku Sōridaijin 1970; Roht and Aoyoma 1973; Mainichi Shinbunsha 1975.

[24] Satō and Shigeshiro 1976:83.

[25] *Ibid.*:82, 83.

tors ever offer them; if anything, they tend to identify the diaphragm derogatorily as a province of the midwife. The contraceptive methods relied on by the most physician couples were—as among laypeople—condoms and rhythm.[26]

Doctors are also typically biased against contraceptive sterilization, as evidenced in a publication written by a prominent Ob-Gyn which includes advice on family planning in question and answer form. The text is noteworthy not only for its casual attitude toward the possibility of an unwanted pregnancy after desired family size is reached, but its exaggeration of the legal restrictions on sterilization and the difficulty of reversal, and its suggestion that the procedure could rob marital sexuality of enjoyment as well.

Q.: I already have three children and I'm 35 years old, so I was wondering if I should just have my Fallopian tubes tied off. What is your advice?

A.: Tubal ligation (surgery in which the Fallopian tubes are tied and ova no longer pass through) is, properly speaking, not something that can be done freely. Under the Eugenic Protection Law, a Eugenic Protection Designated Physician can perform the operation with the consent of the patient and her spouse for illnesses due to bad genes and cases "when there is fear of danger to the mother's life from pregnancy or birth" and "when the mother has several children and there is fear of deterioration in health from each occasion of delivery." In addition, once ligated, reversal is completely impossible. Without a doubt, using contraceptives each time is troublesome. In addition, if you're absentminded you have a failure. However, sex when there is absolutely no possibility of pregnancy must surely run the risk of becoming a hollow thing. You're now 35 years old, so given just ten years or so your menses will end. Until that time, I recommend that the two of you continue cooperating, contracepting as you've done up until now.[27]

[26] *Ibid.*:82.
[27] Yamashita 1974:244.

Describing the urologists' attitude toward vasectomy, a urologist who himself has been very active in promoting male sterilization observed that urologists may not go so far as to deny the procedure to the patient who asks for one, but "they don't take a positive attitude; they feel their basic mission is to cure infertility." Performing the procedure in any numbers is not considered "an honest career (*seidō*)": urologists consider vasectomy in the same vein as cosmetic surgery, as opposed to "surgery which helps the disabled."

THE ACTIVITIES OF FAMILY PLANNING WORKERS

Japan's family planning organizations are also marked by several important limitations on both the extent and quality of contraceptive guidance that they offer. Since neither the government nor the family planning organizations put together statistics on the number of individuals who receive instruction or accept contraceptive methods, there are few indicators of the scale of nonphysician family planning assistance in Japan. The Ministry of Health and Welfare does not compile statistics on family planning activities at health centers. The national Mainichi surveys do suggest that a sizeable proportion of women have been exposed to information about contraception through the efforts of family planning field workers; in 1975, paramedicals accounted for about a fourth of the sources of information used by married women to acquaint themselves with contraception.[28] The usual form of instruction, however, is the group lecture; individual counseling is rare. The kind of information that can be imparted in the lecture format is important for providing an introduction to available options, but it does not impart the kind of practical advice and information that couples need for day-to-day application of a specific contraceptive method, especially if their method is not a modern one.

The content of family planning instruction in Japan focuses

[28] Mainichi Shinbunsha 1975:32.

on the traditional methods, and certain biases accompany the presentations. Both instruction and literature devote considerable attention to explaining two periodic methods, calendar rhythm and the basal body temperature technique (BBT), in which the user determines the point at which she ovulates through a minute shift in temperature. The Japan Family Planning Association also encourages those methods by selling calendrical record forms and specially graduated thermometers. There is little if any exploration of the problem of the inferior effectiveness rates of these methods relative to the barrier methods of contraception. The emphasis instead goes to applying the method correctly, which implicitly places the reason for any failures on the user's inability to calculate accurately. Instruction and literature do include attention to the female barrier methods, but the presentations thoroughly review the possibilities of failure when using spermicides without mentioning the fact that diligent spermicide use is considerably more effective than reliance on periodic abstinence.

The great majority of contraceptives provided by family planning workers are condoms. The Japan Family Planning Association supplies their contraceptives at wholesale prices to family planning workers, who then sell them to their clients at or below the retail market price. Condoms account for over 90 cents of every $1.00 of the Association's sales.

The strategies that family planning workers use to attract clients limit their audience to married women with children. Japan's family planning movement is very strongly oriented toward maternal health in rationale and outreach, and instructors typically incorporate classes in contraception into larger maternal health programs. The slogan of the Japan Family Planning Association is "Give birth to strong children, protect the mother's health, and build happy homes," and their advertisements and outreach posters feature mothers cuddling infants. Figure 2, an advertisement for condoms, is a typical depiction. The client who would feel most drawn to this orientation is the woman who has had at least one child

Figure 2: An Advertisement for Condoms in the
Japan Family Planning Association's Monthly Publication,
The Family Planning (Kazoku Keikaku)

丈夫な子をうもう
お母さんの健康をまもろう
明るい家庭をつくろう

●受胎調節に **F.P.スキン**

●F.P.のマークは
Family Planning　　　　　F.P.ゼリア　スキン
（家族計画）の頭文字です　　F.P.リンクル　ゼリー
〈発売元〉　　　　　　　　　F.P.フェザー　スキン

社団法人　日本家族計画協会事業部
東京都新宿区市ヶ谷砂土原町1-2保健会館内・電話269-2101㈹〒162

Source: *Kazoku Keikaku* 1976c.

and wants more: since these promotions emphasize the reproductive aspect of family planning, the woman who is unmarried or only recently married and postponing pregnancy
feels out of place—to say nothing of her partner. Young Japanese women who have gone to volunteer family planning
clinics in the United States express the wish that there were
similar facilities in Japan with a younger clientele, more privacy, and no display of childbearing and infant care themes.
   Family planning workers do attempt to reach newlywed
and engaged couples through classes organized at public health
centers. These activities do not appear to be reaching a significant proportion of young couples, however; although there
are no figures on the numbers involved, one informal estimate
suggests that fewer than one in ten of all newly married couples participate.[29] These programs are plagued by inadequate
funds and organizational problems in trying to schedule classes
in the evening for working people, as well as low participation
rates among men. Premarital classes are also limited by content restrictions: instructors do not teach specific contraceptive techniques to the unmarried.

   [29] *Josanpu Zasshi* 1976:21.

ORGANIZATIONAL LIMITATIONS

The limitations on Japan's contraceptive promotion effort result from specific organizational features of the country's family planning movement. Ever since the government instituted the criteria for bona fide contraception instructors, midwives have comprised the core of such personnel. Country-wide there are anywhere from 23,000 to 80,000 individuals who have had training as family planning counselors, but absolute figures are of little meaning since they do not reflect their present status and the extent of their activity. Well over one-half of these counselors are midwives. The recruitment of family planning workers from among midwives and public health nurses specializing in maternal and child health has acted to preserve the near-exclusive orientation toward mothers that originated some thirty years ago, when "protection of the mother's health" emerged as the rationale for promoting contraception.

The family planning movement's reliance on midwives in private practice as disseminators of contraception has also resulted in a steep decline in the number of active promoters of contraception. Midwives previously earned nearly all of their incomes from childbirth, but the situation has changed dramatically in the last thirty years or so, and the lion's share of delivery cases now go to Ob-Gyns. In 1947, 92 percent of births nationwide were attended by midwives, but by 1975 doctors had presided over 90 percent of births.[30] With this shift, far fewer women have been entering midwifery, and most of those who do are now employed by hospitals for their ability to oversee deliveries in the doctor's absence. Midwives in private practice are experiencing rapid attrition due to old age, and many who are still counted as family planning instructors have become completely inactive.

The competition between independent midwives and Ob-Gyns has inflicted another serious casualty on the promotion of contraception: these two important groups of specialists

[30] Japan, Ministry of Health and Welfare 1976:57. In Tokyo, approximately 95 percent of all births now take place in hospitals; Tsuboi 1975:323.

do not coordinate efforts to provide a full range of options
in contraceptive technology to Japanese couples. It would be
very difficult to generate the kind of cooperation between Ob-
Gyns and midwives that would allow an integrated program
of mutual referrals. The Director of the Japan Family Planning
Association once noted that public health personnel may not
be able to secure the cooperation of either group because of
their private practice interests.[31] This situation militates against
the promotion of contraceptive methods requiring a doctor's
services (IUD, pill, and sterilization) by midwives. Since the
Japan Family Planning Association does not educate the public
about oral contraception because of its legal status, the individual reached by the family planning instructor stands little
chance of learning about modern methods of contraception.

Instruction in contraception has yet to become a significant
part of a practicing midwife's income. If her client is indigent,
the government provides an instruction fee of only about
$1.50.[32] Some midwives say that they are reluctant to charge
fees for such instruction, since they feel that their efforts are
a public service. They do charge young mothers for assistance
and instruction in such infant care activities as bathing the
infant. A few midwives have recently begun to charge between
$10.00 and $17.00 for diaphragm fittings and instruction, but
the practice is far from widespread. The sale of contraceptive
materials offers far more material incentive to the family planning instructor than personal guidance and consultation. It is
difficult to state with any certainty the amount of midwives'
income represented by contraceptive sales, since the sources
of their income vary by the number of younger women in the
community who are currently having children; as a crude
estimate, however, between one-half and two-thirds of the
average midwife's income comes from selling contraceptives.
Under the family-planning-counselor-qua-contraceptive-
salesperson scheme, certain technical and economic considerations greatly favor condom promotion over the female in-

[31] Kon 1971:22.
[32] 1974 figure from Kon n.d.:2.

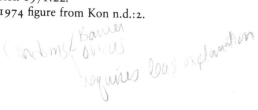

travaginal methods. Of all contraceptive devices, condoms require the least explanation: they are visible when applied, their use does not require chemicals, and they are sold in one standard size only. Since their mode of action rests solely on a mechanical barrier between male and female genitals, even individuals with an extremely low level of knowledge regarding reproduction can use them with a secure feeling of knowing how they work.

By contrast, no other contraceptive method places as many demands on the contraceptive counselor as the diaphragm; both counselor and client must have sufficient familiarity with the female genital tract for the counselor to fit the device properly and the client to accept it as a usable and effective method. The counselor needs a certain amount of manual dexterity as well as faith in the device itself to preserve and enhance the client's confidence, as well as the ability to explain the diaphragm's effectiveness despite the user's inability to see it in use. If the client has emotional resistance to manipulating her genitalia—which is highly prevalent among Japanese women—the instructor must help her overcome these feelings if the diaphragm is to be used effectively, if at all. The counselor also must keep a supply of all sizes (there are ten available in Japan) as well, and the possibility of contraceptive failure through improper sizing places yet another responsibility on the counselor. Spermicides pose some of the same problems, to a lesser extent; they are not visible when applied, and the user must handle her genitals in order to use them.

The wholesale and retail price structure of the methods distributed by the Japan Family Planning Association also encourages condom sales; the client who buys condoms provides more income for the independent midwife than does the diaphragm and spermicide user, even if condom use is decreased by nonuse during infertile periods.[33]

One other major feature of family planning activity in Japan appears to defy explanation in organizational terms: Why

[33] Calculated using figures in the Japan Family Planning Association's catalogue: Nihon Kazoku Keikaku Kyōkai 1976.

does so much effort go into promoting periodic methods, despite their lack of either effectiveness or profitability? One reason may lie in the problem of condom acceptability; since condoms pose an interference in sexual activity and male sexual sensation, their nonuse during infertile periods makes them more acceptable to couples who might otherwise reject condoms altogether. This way of relying on the infertile period is widespread among Japanese couples. (It receives more attention in Chapter 5.) The practice has been suggested to family planning counselors by Ogino Hiroshi, Chief of the Family Planning Department in the Japanese government's Institute of Public Health, and son of Ogino Kyūsaku.

> Which method is best? One can't say, in general. . . . Couples who become used to a variety of methods and apply them in combination use [contraception] longer and don't tire of it. The concept of the fertile period is fundamental here. For example, as one relatively widely suggested instance, after determining the interval in which pregnancy is possible, [the couple] uses mainly condoms during that time, and occasionally alternates with spermicide tablets, or alternates use of condom and diaphragm.[34]

CONDOM SALES IN THE COMMERCIAL SECTOR

Condoms represent by far the greatest volume of commercial contraceptive sales in Japan as well as the most innovations in marketing, advertising, and variety of nonessential features. Domestic market volume for condoms in Japan topped 4,800,000 gross a year in the mid-1970s.[35] This market is highly competitive, and although precise figures on sales volume are unavailable from condom manufacturers, an estimate of at least $156 million a year in total domestic sales would be conservative, given an average sale price of each piece at somewhere between $.20 and $.25.

[34] Ogino 1971:15.
[35] Kon n.d.:1.

The condom market in Japan is conspicuous in its proliferation of marketing strategies and techniques aimed at increasing availability through convenience of purchase, lessening of embarrassment during purchase, and enhancing familiarity with the product. A little over half of all condom sales are handled by pharmacy-cosmetic stores, which are relatively densely located; their density averages 14 per square mile nationwide, in contrast with a figure of .17 for health centers.[36] In the last ten years, however, commercial distribution through door-to-door sales has come to occupy a large share of the market, perhaps as much as 40 percent. More recently, sales through supermarkets and vending machines located on streets and sidewalks in front of pharmacies have also appeared. Vending machines have not added greatly to total sales, but the outlet through supermarkets appears to be a modest success.

Innovations aimed at lessening embarrassment at drugstores include locating condom displays next to the cash register, prewrapping boxes in nondescript paper, and pricing in denominations that do not require change in order to make the transaction as swift and inconspicuous as possible. Some condom packages include cards for reordering that the customer can pass directly to the salesperson without speaking, which also greatly minimizes interaction. The door-to-door commercial distribution of condoms is the greatest strategy of all for bypassing embarrassment. The first of the home sales companies (now the largest in Japan, with a yearly condom sales volume of over $17 million a year) was begun by a man whose brother operates a pharmacy; during visits to the brother's pharmacy he was struck by the discomfort and awkwardness of customers purchasing contraceptives, which inspired the idea of sales in the privacy of the customer's home.

Home sales companies now vie for ever-larger portions of the competitive door-to-door market, paying their saleswomen (known as "skin ladies") 30 percent to 50 percent commissions in addition to incentives such as vacation trips

---

[36] Katagiri 1974:5.

abroad. The saleswoman's income averages about $800 a month, and the most adept earn as much as three times that amount. Competition and high incentives encourage high-pressure sales tactics, including posing as midwives and discouraging the use of other contraceptive methods. In one approach which I experienced as a potential customer while at home, a middle-aged saleswoman promoted condoms by claiming that intravaginal chemicals cause frigidity, the pill causes severe eyesight problems after one year's use, and the IUD causes radical weight changes, can perforate the uterus, and is not very effective anyway. Waxing enthusiastic about the dangers of the IUD, she warned me that babies born as a result of IUD failures have a permanent ring-shaped deformity, emphasizing her point by making a circle on her forehead with thumb and index finger. Other saleswomen reported that they discourage pill use when asked, saying, "it makes you fat, affects your liver and eyes."

Condom advertising in Japan is highly visible in a variety of media. Advertising makes use of simple trademark symbols such as a hand making an "OK" sign (Figure 3) or the simplified silhouette of man, woman, and child, accompanied by the words "family planning," some reference to population problems, or the brand name of the product. Almost all drugstores have signs with these symbols, which appear constantly in a wide range of general audience and women's magazines as well as on billboards and late-night television commercials. During sales, supermarkets advertise discounted condoms by brand name together with feminine hygiene products and cosmetics (Figure 4).

The same technical features that give condoms a competitive advantage over spermicides in Japan's family planning movement pose yet a stronger advantage in over-the-counter sales, where interaction with the provider is minimal. Japanese law augments the condom's competitive edge; intravaginal chemicals can be dispensed only by pharmacists and certified family planning counselors, whereas the sale of condoms does not require such certification.

Figure 3: A Magazine Advertisement
for Condoms

Figure 4: A Supermarket Circular Advertising
Two Dozen Condoms
Sale Priced at ¥ 450 ($1.61).

BIRTH CONTROL EDUCATION IN
THE POPULAR MEDIA

The mass media, and magazines in particular, comprise the greatest source of contraceptive information for Japanese married women. The same Mainichi survey that found paraprofessionals providing a fourth of all information sources in 1975 also found that the media accounted for nearly a third of the multiple information sources claimed by respondents. Magazines constituted the single greatest source of information; 38 percent of the wives claiming knowledge of contraception named magazines as an information source.[37]

There are no sex education programs in Japan's public schools, nor is there an ongoing tradition of providing information on sex and reproduction through kin or community institutions. Until the early 1970s, sex education was referred to as "purity education" (*junketsu kyōiku*) among educators, its purpose to inculcate the importance of chastity. (Advocates of sexual morality instruction in public schools still use the term.)

It is doubtful that magazines serve as an adequate substitute for voluntary programs or folk institutions, either for information on sex in general or for the knowledge that can contribute to the best possible choice of contraceptive methods. Magazines carry distortions and misinformation, a result, as one Ob-Gyn concerned with family planning education put it, of "journalism's thoughtless commercialism."[38] Magazine articles are not written by health-care professionals; specialists may be consulted, but the product is neither their creation nor responsibility. The magazines' treatment of contraception generally exhibits the same biases in presentation that appear in family planning literature: articles highlight the possible hazards to health from modern methods, ignore female barrier methods, and uncritically promote condoms and rhythm and temperature methods for calculating cycles. If anything, the magazine articles devote even more attention to explaining

[37] Mainichi Shinbunsha 1975:52.
[38] Takemura 1973:55.

the periodic methods than do family planning publications. The subject lends itself well to treatment in print; as Muramatsu Minoru, Chief of the Public Health Demography Department at his government's Institute of Public Health observed, the method requires extensive explanation, which in turn makes lots of copy. The results, he once noted wryly, are "detailed enough to make a textbook on female reproductive physiology."

Even when they are factually correct, magazine articles are far from adequate as a source of contraceptive information and guidance. Although they serve a valuable function by introducing various methods to public attention, their information is neither precise enough nor extensive enough to answer questions and resolve problems posed by the individual conditions and needs of each user. Successful use of written materials also necessitates the various skills involved in translating written instructions and concepts into action, and these skills prevail only among the better educated. Indeed, those wives in the questionnaire survey who cited the media as an information source for their current method of contraception were slightly more educated. Women who rely on the media for information, however, are less likely to opt for modern contraception. The effects of media bias were evident in the significantly negative relationship between reliance on media information and the choice of a modern contraceptive method over a traditional one, despite the fact that more education among survey participants significantly increased the probability of choosing a modern contraceptive method.[39]

Negative media influence was probably behind the small percentages of women who indicated, when asked in a 1976 questionnaire survey, an interest in trying either the pill or IUD. The study involved over three thousand mothers-to-be

[39] Statistically significant results were obtained when using a multiple regression of a modern/traditional method dummy variable against the following seven independent variables: wife's educational level, husband's income, length of marriage, number of marital abortions, husband as source of information, professional as source of information, and media as source of information.

taking infant care classes conducted in 14 cities in Hokkaido and Kyushu, the northernmost and southernmost main islands of Japan, respectively. An impressive 72 percent of all those surveyed had heard about the pill through the media, but only 6 percent of those claiming to have familiarity with the pill expressed an interest in trying it after their anticipated birth. Similarly, 63 percent received their introduction to the IUD via the media, but only 11 percent of those knowing something about the method were willing to try it.[40] If a Japanese woman were to consider breaking out of the contraceptive status quo, she would not find a reliable escape route in popular magazines.

[40] Satō Fumi et al. 1977:37-38.

CHAPTER 4

Abortion, the "Necessary Evil"

Since so much of the appeal of modern contraceptive methods stems from their high level of effectiveness, the question arises of whether access to abortion in Japan has canceled out this source of preference for greater prevention capability. Could it be that Japanese couples' acceptance of abortion is great enough that they would have no preference between preventing a conception and ending a pregnancy? Because the Japanese rely so extensively on induced abortion for limiting their fertility, the question arises of whether they accept the operation emotionally more easily than do men and women in countries where abortion rates are lower. As Chapter 1 has noted, a number of population specialists have suggested that such is the case. A close examination of sentiment and behavior, however, does not bear out their hypotheses.

RELIGIOUS SENTIMENT AND SYMBOLISM

Since so much anti-abortion sentiment in the West comes from religious groups, a logical beginning would be to look for similar opposition among Japanese religious organizations. Indeed, both Japanese and foreign specialists have posed the suggestion that abortion is used frequently because religious opposition is alien to Japanese society.[1] A word about some unique features of Japanese religious expression is in order, because they could generate ambiguity about whether or not certain beliefs and behaviors are religious.

The nature of religious activity in Japan argues against defining religious expression solely in terms of the actions of an organized group. Edward Norbeck, a specialist on Japanese

---

[1] See Lader 1966:133; Lee 1973:349; Muramatsu 1967:78-79; Ōta 1967:2; 1976:329; Pohlman 1969:29, 403; Taeuber 1958:282.

religions, has estimated that only about a third of the population are members of organized religious sects.[2] This does not necessarily mean that the Japanese are an areligious people; rather, there is a more subtle division of labor than is seen among the religious organizations of the West, where each organization provides to a more or less stable membership its own complete set of rituals for life crises. In Japan, Shinto ceremonies are preferred for certain occasions such as weddings and new store openings, whereas matters relating to death and ancestral spirits call for Buddhist ritual. As a result, there is no inconsistency in claiming more than one religious affiliation, as the government's figures reflect: the total number of people claiming adherence to these two religious denominations exceeds the total population of Japan by over half.[3] In addition, the religions that have sprung up since World War II contrast sharply with the older religious bodies by offering explicit models for behavior and solutions for problems that emerge in everyday modern life. Buddhism and Shinto have been criticized for their lack of contact with the problems of daily life and for an other worldliness that does not respond to social change.[4] Some of the new religious groups, by contrast, focus on specific issues of day-to-day life, and their teachings influence popular thought far beyond the boundaries of their formal membership because their publications have a large-scale circulation.

The hallmarks of religious sanctions against abortion reside in statements or practices that base their authority on some supernatural or absolute, or reference to something sacred that must not be violated, as opposed to injunctions justified by pragmatic reasons. There should also be the threat of some supernatural form of retribution. Using these guideposts, religious themes opposed to abortion do emerge in Japanese culture.

[2] Norbeck 1970:4.
[3] Calculated from figures in Japan, Office of the Prime Minister 1976:11, 590-91.
[4] Norbeck 1970:68.

Buddhism claims more adherents than any other religion in Japan.[5] Japanese Buddhism is opposed to the practice of abortion, but its stance does not stand out in so many direct statements by the church leadership; the Buddhist clergy in Japan does not have a reputation for proclamations on matters of dogma, much less a well-developed casuistry, nor is there the exegesis that figures so prominently in Western theology. One relevant tenet which Japanese Buddhism emphasizes is the ideal of compassion, which demands entering into identity with all other beings by overcoming one's own sense of ego. To fail is to lose deliverance from the cycle of endless transmigration. Abortion is a case of the woman's egoism prevailing over her identity with her fetus. This position was set forth by a historian of Buddhist thought in the *Yomiuri Shinbun*, one of Japan's largest newspapers:

> . . . The problem from the Buddhist perspective relates to the abortion recipient's egoism . . . the issue is the humanistic murder of the fetus. There is no doubt that this "custom" is in complete opposition to the Buddhist value of life. . . . Buddhism, speaking with textbook strictness, regards the killing of animal and vegetable life as one and the same, and so it forbids killing any and all living things. However, in order to allow humanity to live with this textbook interpretation, it is necessary to consider the lamentable egoism of humanity, which cannot go on living without killing animal and vegetable. . . . Thus, Buddhism as an irony in this age pits the issue of the mother who would sacrifice herself out of compassion against the mother who would make a sacrifice of her fetus. . . . However, for following through on such principles, modern Buddhism's indecision can only be seen as disappointing.[6]

The article appeared when the government was introducing a proposal that would have restricted access to abortions. Its

[5] Japan, Office of the Prime Minister 1976:590.
[6] Yamaori 1975.

subhead is "Right or Wrong Undeterminable," but the stance attributed to Buddhism is decidedly anti-abortion.

Japanese Buddhism's stance on induced abortion also manifests itself in specific devotional practices. These practices appear to have their provenance in or before the Tokugawa Era (1630-1868), the latter half of which witnessed the extensive practice of infanticide and abortion. The aborted fetus (as well as the quickly dispached newborn infant) is referred to in Buddhist terminology as "water child" or *mizuko*, the Chinese characters for this term being simply "water" and "child." The word "mizuko" can also mean "unseeing child," with *mizu* representing the negative form of the verb "to see"; the child sees "neither the light of day nor its mother's face." The belief regarding the spirits of the unborn in the Edo Era held that they were "sent back" but not permanently; mothers prayed to them to be born to their families again in the future, a sentiment attested to by the practice of burying the remains under the house veranda or floors. In the meantime these spirits were in the Children's Limbo (*Sai-no-kawara*).[7] It was also during the Tokugawa Era that the practice began of erecting statues of Jizō, the guardian of children, for mizuko souls, and tumuli (*mizukozuka*) containing the bones of abortuses and neonates. As in Figure 5, the *mizukojizō* is usually a Bodhisattva clasping an extremely small infant to his bosom.

The erecting of such monuments did not end with the Tokugawa Era. A number of temples have constructed *mizukojizō* since World War II, among them three temples in the Tokyo area: Seiju Temple in Kita Ward, which erected its Baby's Requiem Monument in 1955; Teisen Temple in Bunkyo Ward, which constructed a stone monument named the "Spirit Tumulus for Mizuko Under Ten Months of Age" in 1960 (length of gestation is commonly calculated from the time of last menstrual period; hence a newborn is ten months old), and Hase Temple in Kamakura, which began offering miniature *mizukojizō* to worshippers since 1974. Within two years

[7] Higashi 1976.

Figure 5: Poster for a Mizuko Requiem
at Seigen Temple in Tokyo

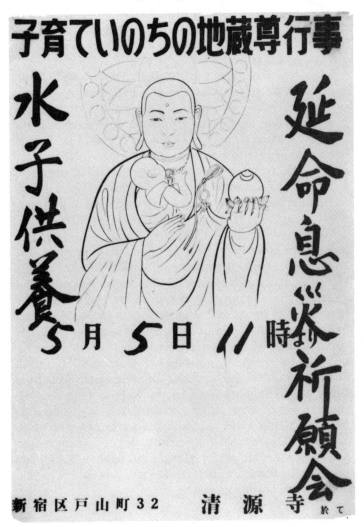

visitors placed over three thousand of the figures in rows on the temple grounds.[8]

Devotional practices are also attached to beliefs regarding *mizuko*, the most frequently observed being requiems or *mizukokuyō*. Such services are held regularly at the temples having Jizō monuments, and the Kaihisa Monastery in Tokyo has also conducted requiems for *mizuko*.[9]

Shinto has a relevant anti-abortion theme as well. As an immanently animatist collection of beliefs, Shinto attributes supernatural power to various objects as well as to the spirits of departed individuals, a power capable of intervening in the lives of the living. One of these powers is that of retribution through evil curse (*tatari*); an aborted fetus is able to place such a curse on the woman who aborts it. Hence, offering a *kuyō* acts as a means of placating the spirit.[10] Through syncretism the idea became fused with the concept of the transmigrating spirit in Japanese Buddhism.

There is one highly visible instance of an indigenous religious organization with an explicitly anti-abortion stance. The Seichō no Ie, whose English name is the "Home of Infinite Life, Wisdom, and Abundance," opposes contraception, but its anti-abortion stance is better known. The group is marginal in terms of its size as well as in its place in Japanese religious history; according to the group's own estimates, there are only approximately 30,000 active participants, and the organization began its activities only some fifty years ago. The content of its beliefs is extremely eclectic, drawing on elements from Christianity, Buddhism, and Shinto. Despite its modest position among religious movements, however, the organization produces a large variety of published works, some of which are not readily identifiable as Seichō no Ie publications. Seichō no Ie magazines are published at the rate of about 2.5 million per month, and the organization claims to have sold 14 million books in the last forty years.

[8] *Ibid.*
[9] Fuji 1974:147.
[10] *Kazoku Keikaku* 1976a:5.

Although anti-abortion statements appear frequently in tracts and magazines prepared for the White Dove Society (*Shiro-hatokai*), the women's arm of the Seichō no Ie, the single most comprehensive statement of the religion's position on induced abortion appears in its book on motherhood and abortion, *What's Important?* The author, Taniguchi Seichō, is the adopted son-in-law of the movement's founder, Taniguchi Masaharu.[11] The book's preface states that giving birth is a "great mission" given to women, and that

> when a woman obeys this "command of heaven" she is satisfied and can attain a feeling of "carrying out the mission." . . . When it is abandoned through abortion, she is tortured by a sense of guilt (*zaiakukan*) which says "I've killed our child." . . . (pp. 3-4)

On the nature of the fetus, Taniguchi states that

> We must respect human life. I don't think anyone would object to this point. . . . Some people seem to think "we must respect *big* lives, but we can kill *small* lives." But in these instances this is not a matter of a bug or a vegetable's life, but a fine human life. I said "a small life" but to state it more accurately it is the life called "the fetus." It is the same as "human life." The only difference is that it still resides in the mother's womb and is connected to her body through an umbilical cord. (p. 38)

The book frequently states that all human beings are endowed with eternal life, a belief that has strong implications for abortion as well, since it draws on the Shinto theme of retribution from an angered spirit:

> Medically speaking, the damage to the mother's body from abortion surgery is truly frightful. The feeling of destruction to the mother's body that it gives and the harmful influence on marital life are truly unfathomably

[11] Taniguchi 1975. Son-in-law adoption (*muko-yōshi*) is a practice for insuring continuity of the family name.

grave matters. This is the counteraction (*hansayō*) of the anger of a fetus' soul having been set adrift from darkness into darkness, as well as the "self-punishment" due to the human nature of husband and wife. (pp. 59-60)

Taniguchi's book comprises a pastiche of anti-abortion and pronatal arguments familiar to Western anti-abortion tracts, but the theme of reprisal brought on by the soul of an unplacated fetus is noteworthy because it is uniquely Japanese.

Unlike other religious organizations in Japan, the Seichō no Ie has matched its anti-abortion beliefs with political activities, including organizing mass petitions to the Diet to restrict the Eugenic Protection Law and media events that have boasted the participation of Diet members in the ruling Liberal Democratic Party. The organization has also conducted *mizuko* requiems regularly since 1961 at its shrine at Uji, near Osaka.

Japan's family planning movement has also made use of religious symbols as an attempt to reduce reliance on induced abortion. In 1962 a group of concerned family planning activists, led by Shinozaki Nobuo of the Ministry of Health and Welfare's Population Problems Research Institute, gathered funds for two *mizukojizō* statues that were placed in Osaka's Higashinari Health Center and in Seigen Temple in Tokyo's Shinjuku Ward as a conscious countermeasure to the country's high abortion rate.[12] Shinozaki explained that their purpose was to impress upon women "the gravity of the situation" and the "cruelty" of abortion by offering religious acts of contrition. Through requiems, he said, the woman offers up her apologies to the fetus. These services are held every year in May at Seigen Temple, if possible on Children's Day. Figure 5 reproduces an announcement of the service. Religious symbolism has also served as the medium for expressing gratitude to a midwife who taught a community contraception; the

---

[12] It is interesting to note that these public health activists organized their religious campaign in the same period that Muramatsu estimated as the actual high point in yearly total number of abortions, "around 1960"; Muramatsu 1970:104.

residents of Tokyo's Suginami Ward erected a Buddhist monument in honor of Hanyū Taki, a local midwife who pioneered in contraceptive instruction after the end of World War II. Inscribed are the words, "I clasp my hands in prayer for the souls of the unborn."

RELIGIOUS SYMBOLS IN SECULAR CONTEXTS

Just as religious activity in Japan does not conform to the Western pattern of participation, beliefs of a religious nature may not appear in easily recognizable packages. Certain religious themes have so thoroughly permeated society that no one religion or sect can lay exclusive claim to them; they have become symbols in the popular domain. In the process, some themes may have been reduced to a kind of shorthand whose implications are not immediately apparent to the outside observer. A popular women's magazine recently printed the story of a woman who had experienced 35 abortions in the span of 18 years.[13] The story, "Thirty-five Mizuko Sit on the Chopsticks in My Right Hand," details the aftereffects the woman experienced, including visitations from the spirits of the fetuses who were wronged. The woman, given the fictitious name of Takeda, is quoted as saying that sleep does not come easily, and when it does, "I invariably have nightmares. They're dreams of babies drenched in blood that come walking toward me" (p. 26). Awake, as well,

> When it's really bad I can't even hold chopsticks in my right hand. I get the feeling that the thirty-five *mizuko* that I've aborted are sitting heavily on my chopsticks, saying "this parent doesn't even have the ability to lift a chopstick." . . . Having repeated abortions thirty-five times up to now, both my mind and my body are in shreds. In the daytime, even when things are normal I feel like I've just been hit on the head with a bat. It's the

[13] *Shūkan Josei* 1976.

curse (*bachi*) of the *mizuko* that I aborted and my body will probably never return to its former state no matter what I do. . . . (p. 26)

Another popular woman's magazine, *Bishō*, included directions and a map to Seiju Temple in an article giving advice on how to conceal one's abortion. Headlining the insert about the temple is the admonition to "Read carefully, you who don't like contraception!"[14] Reference to religious symbols can be briefer still: in a young men's magazine article providing information on contraception, an Ob-Gyn who performs abortions is quoted as saying that he feels like "making an incense offering in the operating room after the surgery is over."[15] Certain phrases have passed beyond their original religious context as well. The most frequently used is "from darkness to darkness" (*yami kara yami e*), a staple of secular anti-abortion literature which uses the imagery of the fetus that never sees the light of day.

The ultimately secular expression of the theme of fetal spirits returning to wreak vengeance appeared in a men's comic burlesque, "I'm a Gynecologist."[16] The hero, an Ob-Gyn, dreams that he is sucked into his patient's uterus, where he is assailed by the fetuses that he had aborted. Two of the panels from the sequence are reproduced in Figure 6. The text for this comic includes an expression that appears in Seichō no Ie literature and other anti-abortion publications, the verb for burying, *hōmuru*, which also means casting aside or consigning to oblivion.

FETUS VERSUS INFANT

If Japanese culture were to make abortion more emotionally acceptable, there would be a clear-cut distinction between the fetal state and full-fledged human life; this mechanism would allow individuals to achieve a consistency of sentiment and

[14] Bishō 1976:150.
[15] Purēboi 1975:147.
[16] Kimura and Shichijō 1976.

Figure 6: Panels from "I'm a Gynecologist"

*"Yeah, we're the spirits of the miserable
fetuses that you threw away, chum!"*
*"And I'm the thousandth one that you
were about to do in!"*
Source: Kimura and Shichijō 1976:164-65.

action when seeking abortions so that they would not confront
the feeling that they were destroying a member of the human
community. This kind of emotional insulation is not evident
in present-day Japan: if anything, there is considerable symbolic confounding of fetuses, infants, and children. A 1968
survey conducted in Nagoya among 1,500 women over 15
years of age reflects the lack of one widely accepted definition
of human life that categorizes the fetus as nonperson; two-
thirds of the participants claimed the belief that the fetus is a
human life at the moment of conception, as opposed to "the
sixth or seventh month of the pregnancy" (4 percent) or being
"part of the mother until it is born" (22 percent).[17]

Typical colloquial expressions for abortion include "aborting a baby" (*akachan o orosu*) or "aborting a child" (*kodomo
o orosu*) rather than confining the expression to "aborting a
fetus" (*taiji o orosu*). Expressions like "taking life" or "killing
a child" also emerged frequently in informants' discussions
of induced abortion. Cartoon depictions of aborted fetuses
also liken them to infants, as in Figures 6 and 7.

[17] Hayasaka et al. 1973:20.

Figure 7: Cartoon Depictions of Fetuses

(left) An illustration accompanying text concerning an abortion performed without the husband's consent.
(above) "Family Planning Rambles: Abortion Heaven." The sign on the cloud says "Returned Goods."

Sources: Left, Kashima 1975:93; Right, *Kazoku Keikaku* 1976c:1.

POLLS AND SURVEYS OF ATTITUDES

In their responses to public opinion polls on abortion, fewer Japanese approve of the use of abortion than do Americans. The most refined indicator of public opinion among Japanese women is the Mainichi Survey's question, "What do you think about abortion?" with a fairly detailed set of alternative answers. The responses, along with the percentage of total response represented, have been translated and appear in Table 4-1 much as they did in the original questionnaire format.

The options provided for responses cast a certain degree of anti-abortion bias into the results. Those who gave unqualified

TABLE 4-1

Response to Mainichi Survey Question on Attitude
Regarding Induced Abortion, 1975

Question: What do you think of induced abortion (aborting after becoming pregnant)?	
(1) *I approve it*	9.2%
(please check up to 2 answers)	
1. It's only natural when times are hard	5.8
2. It's more convenient than contraception	0.6
3. I don't think it's a bad thing	1.5
4. I don't think it's a health hazard	0.6
5. Everybody's doing it	1.9
6. Other (state explicitly) + no answer	1.9
(2) *I approve it under certain conditions*	68.2%
(please check up to 2 answers)	
1. Only when birth presents a hazard to the life or health of the mother	58.0
2. When impregnated by force	23.9
3. To avoid inheriting harmful illnesses	26.1
4. When times are hard and contraception has failed	15.5
5. Other (state explicitly) + no answer	3.2
(3) *I don't approve it*	11.1%
(please check up to 2 answers)	
1. Because it's sin/immoral	3.1
2. It poses danger to the mother's health	8.1
3. Children are the gift of God	4.1
4. Religious reasons (name of religion: _____)	0.4
5. Other (state explicitly) + no answer	0.4
(4) *No answer/other*	11.5%

Source: Mainichi Shinbunsha 1975:34, 42; figures for subcategories have been recalculated to represent a percentage of all respondents.

approval—in essence, proponents of elective abortion—may not have been given enough alternatives to represent their reasoning adequately, which would explain why one out of five (1.9 percent among 9.2 percent) fell into the "Other/No Answer" category. There is no answer, for example, that reflects the sentiment that abortion is a matter of women's rights. Those who gave conditional approval were also limited; since respondents are limited to only two answers, those who agree with more than just two conditions have no way to express that opinion.

Taking these limitations into account, we find that a comparison with attitude surveys in the United States suggests that American women have a less restrictive attitude toward abortion. In a Gallup poll conducted in September of 1972, 38 percent of the female respondents approved of abortion with no legal restrictions. Regarding "mother's health" as a legitimate justification for abortion, the American white population registered an approval rate of about 87 percent. Even among Catholics, 82 percent approved in a March, 1972 survey.[18] By contrast, 67 percent of the 1975 Mainichi sample can be counted as approving of the same stipulation, 58 percent explicitly and 9 percent by recognizing abortion without limiting conditions.

Other tests of opinion on abortion in Japan also find a sizeable proportion of the female population expressing negative attitudes toward abortion or taking the opinion that its availability should be restricted. The 1969 nationwide survey of married women conducted by the Office of the Prime Minister included a question on attitude toward induced abortion. The question responses and their distribution in percentages follow.[19]

Question: what do you think about induced abortion? Please choose the answer that most closely resembles your feelings.

[18] Blake 1973:459; 449.
[19] Naikaku Sōridaijin 1970:27.

It is totally inexcusable	11%
I think it is a bad thing	29
I don't think it is good but it is unavoidable	48
I don't think it is bad	2
I cannot state absolutely	7
I don't know	3

A 1974 survey conducted in Tokyo for the city's Metropolitan Public Welfare Office sampled female respondents by occupation. Respondents were asked their attitude toward induced abortion, with answer choices on a five-point scale ranging from "I am opposed, it's improper" to "I am in agreement, it's correct," with "I can't say either way" midway in between. The opacity of both the question and the answers provided limit the significance of the results greatly, and probably accounts for the 33.3 percent neutral responses seen. Negative responses, however, accounted for a little less than half (47 percent) of the total responses, and, of these, most were answers indicating strong opposition (29 percent of the total responses). Even among women in the water-trades (*mizushōbai,* bar hostesses and demimondes), the group most lenient in its attitude regarding abortion, 41.7 percent expressed negative attitudes, half of them (21 percent of the group total) strongly negative.[20]

Restrictive attitudes were also expressed by a large number of respondents in my own questionnaire survey. The question was phrased as follows: At present there is a movement to revise present abortion law by recognizing abortion in cases of danger to the mother's life but not allow abortion in cases of economic hardship. What is your opinion? The question was designed to reflect as accurately and economically as possible the actual issue of government policy toward abortion, a familiar controversy. About a fourth of the respondents agreed that the law should be more restrictive:

[20] Tōkyō-tō Minsei-kyoku 1975:85-86.

I agree	24.4%
I disagree	43.1
I've never thought about it/ can't decide	28.5
No answer	3.9
Total	99.9
	(N = 635)

(Percentages total less than 100.0 because of rounding.)

Fewer than half of the respondents were able clearly to state opposition to making the law more restrictive. Confining the breakdown to those who committed themselves to an opinion, we see that nearly one out of three respondents favored making Japan's abortion law more restrictive.

THE DETERMINANTS OF A MORALLY ACCEPTABLE ABORTION

The Mainichi Surveys do show a majority of Japanese women approving abortion when the "life or health of the mother" are endangered. Other conditions that figure in popular morality are that the woman be married, have at least one child, and be financially overburdened. Under these conditions, abortion is a "necessary evil" (*hitsuyō aku*). The range of acceptable circumstances varies, of course, according to subculture: the most lenient set of acceptable conditions would probably be found among members of the water trades; the most restrictive view of justifiable circumstances probably belongs to Japan's Roman Catholics as well as to the pronatalist political sector, composed of economic expansionists who want a steady supply of young and inexpensive labor, and ultranationalists who fear that a stable or decreasing population would compromise Japan's international political power.

The rationales for abortion that have the most widespread acceptance are those that can negate the nearly universal but largely implicit fear in Japanese society that abortion, if broadly condoned, will have disruptive effects on family organization. It is probably this area of concern that generates anti-abortion sentiment among the greatest number of Japanese. (Individuals who harbor such feelings are not necessarily pronatalist in the strict sense, but pronatalist groups do appeal to their fears by stressing the argument that abortion has deleterious effects on the family.) The feared effects of abortion on the institution of the family can be summed in two related points: (1) the denial of maternity and maternal responsibilities by conferring the power to women to decide whether or not to give birth, and (2) the separation of sexuality from marriage and reproduction.

The central threat to the family from abortion is the rejection of motherhood posed by voluntarily terminating a pregnancy. The anti-abortion response to this threat assumes an ideology of childbirth and child-raising as woman's unique role, a role that is part of a natural order transcending individual predilections. The sentiment is epitomized by using the expression *sazukarimono* for children (a gift conferred on one by a superior), as opposed to *tsukuru mono* (something one has made oneself—literally, a product); the latter view regards children as a possession rather than as an independent entity. Commentators depict the product attitude toward children as a recent trend that is more "modern" and more rational, and hence fits nicely with the controlled fertility ideal of family planning.[21] The child as possession image also has a pejorative dimension, however; the mother who regards her child as a possession is able to do with it as she pleases. Editorialists and psychologists have blamed this attitude for a number of cruel and arbitrary ways of treating children, from arrogant manipulation and insensitivity to infanticide.[22] In a 1976 anti-abortion publication, Yoshida Tadao, Professor of Economics at Meiji University, brings the gift versus possession duality to his attack on abortion rights:

Do you suppose that it's a good thing for a man and woman to make this baby who has come to life into a personal possession? If I may use a mystical way of stating

[21] See, for example, Kunii 1974.
[22] Itō 1976; *New York Times* 1973.

it, I think that the baby is a *sazukarimono*. . . . [Pro-abortion feminists] consider the fetus their personal property. They think of it like a skirt or a blouse.[23]

Opposition to unsanctioned sexual behavior also contributes to anti-abortion sentiment, particularly regarding use of induced abortion among unmarried youth. Conservative lawmakers have blamed easy access to abortion as a cause of "free sex" (premarital sexual activity).[24] The objection to abortion for its purported effect on sexual morality also applies to the separation of sex and reproduction within marriage as well. In the words of one Diet member, "Sex as play is dangerous. No matter how love is glorified, doesn't a union of man and woman without the goal of bearing and raising children invite spiritual decadence?"[25] Prime Minister Satō Eisaku's vaguely worded denunciation of abortion in 1972 for its "corruption of sex and the social order"[26] could also refer to the separation of sexuality from reproduction within marriage. The recent campaign among family planning workers and a few Ob-Gyns to dissuade young wives from aborting their first pregnancies could also owe its atmosphere of urgency to a latent fear that couples are using abortion to put a priority on sexuality to the exclusion of childbearing.

These objections to the use of induced abortion require excuses for aborting that enhance the role of mother rather than conflict with it. Such reasons are summarized in the rationale of aborting "to protect the mother's health"—the legal stipulation under which virtually all reported abortions are performed. The use of motherhood as rationale reaches ironic heights in the name of the organization of physicians trained in abortion techniques, the "Maternal Protection Association" (*Bosei Hogo I Kyōkai*). The Eugenic Protection Law, as well as the literature both pro and con on abortion,

[23] Yoshida 1976:50-51.
[24] Kon 1973:182-83.
[25] *Ibid.*
[26] Moriyama 1973a:4.

uses the term "mother's body" (*botai*) to discuss the relationship between abortion and health, to the exclusion of the expression "woman's body" (*jotai* or *onna no karada*), a term used only by young women in radical feminist groups.

Economic hardship also serves as an acceptable rationale if the justification is posed in a way that reinforces the primacy of motherhood. The typical economic argument against restricting legal access to abortion comes from the assertion that inflation, inadequate housing, or the necessity that wives work make it difficult or impossible for wives to bear more children.[27] By posing the assumption that the pregnancies ending in abortion would otherwise be births that women actually *want* but cannot have, the argument supports motherhood.

The use of women's rights as an ideological justification for induced abortion is conspicuously absent in Japan, in contrast with Eastern European countries, where female emancipation is an official reason for laws that permit easy access to the operation.[28] The issue of women's control over their reproductive functions does receive some attention, but the stance takes on a form that has a decidedly Japanese flavor: the point is not so much freedom for women as it is the danger of government interference, like the oppressive pronatalist policy of the pre–World War II government. The argument's most serious proponents are few in number.

The lack of widespread support for abortion as a civil rights issue probably explains the curious rendering of the United States Supreme Court's landmark 1973 decision on abortion by the Japan Family Planning Federation in their "New Declaration" of March 1973, a statement in opposition to attempts to restrict abortion law. According to the Federation, the American court's decision affirmed "the *parental* right to give birth or not give birth to children," whereas the decision

[27] Moriyama 1973a:5; Nihon Fujin Dantai Rengōkai 1975:20; Hoshii 1974:104.

[28] For a contrast, see Callahan 1970:263 and Emily Moore's observations in Hall 1970:101.

had actually ruled that abortion is a *woman's* right under Constitutional guarantees of privacy.[29] The Federation's wording limits the issue to cases where the woman is married. It also implies her husband's agreement—the Japanese wording does not designate singular or plural for "parent."

WOMEN'S EMOTIONAL RESPONSES TO THE ABORTION EXPERIENCE

Since the dominant Japanese ideology only provides personal justification for abortion in the face of dire necessity, we should expect individual women to experience emotional difficulty in dealing with their abortions, or at least lack the means to interpret their decisions to abort in positive terms.

It is highly doubtful that severe psychological reactions occur among Japanese abortion patients. My own search found no instances of abortion patients requiring postoperative observation for emotional pathology, nor did I uncover any professional literature on psychological aftereffects. There are indications, however, that a sizeable minority of women experience unpleasant subjective physical aftereffects. In the 1969 nationwide survey conducted for the Office of Prime Minister, 30 percent of those who had reported receiving induced abortions identified "abnormalities" afterword, more than half described with such subjective symptoms as headache, pains in the loins, dizziness, and fatigue.[30]

Of the 11 women in the interview series who had experienced induced abortions, 2 reported adverse physical aftereffects. (Five others had complaints or reservations about their operations in one form or another.) One is a 26-year-old housewife who reported fatigue, menstrual irregularity, and swelling; the other woman, a 37-year-old housewife with three terminations, complained of pains in her loins. Both women specifically mentioned experiencing a sense of guilt. Ob-Gyns are familiar with the tendency among married patients with

[29] Quoted in Moriyama 1973a:5; emphasis added.
[30] Naikaku Sōridaijin 1970:24-25.

histories of abortion to complain of headaches, stiff shoulders (*katakori*), and abdominal pain, subjective symptoms that they say disappear when a subsequent pregnancy is carried to term. Doctors interpret this as alleviation of guilt, but no one has conducted any formal studies of the phenomenon. Two doctors identified such complaints as the result of Buddhist influence. In addition, Dr. Majima Suemaro, a Tokyo Ob-Gyn specializing in psychosomatic sterility, reported rare cases of psychosomatic sterility as a complication of induced abortion, which he identifies as the result of guilt feelings.

There are other signs that Japanese women have to cope with feelings of wrongdoing; family planning specialists and Ob-Gyns commonly use the expression "guilt feelings" (*zai-akukan*) to describe women's reactions to abortion, and a comprehensive medical text on induced abortion technique advises physicians to dispel the patients' emotional insecurity, "including shame and guilt feelings."[31]

Nationwide survey results in Japan suggest that guilt and remorse are widespread, but the survey forms fail to offer responses for women who may have felt feelings of relief, resolution of tensions, or the conviction that they had made the right decision.[32] Japanese anti-abortion and family planning literature often cites the results of this question posed by the Mainichi Survey to those women who reported at least one abortion:

How did you feel the first time you received an abortion?
(1) I thought I had done something bad. 32.9%
(2) I felt sorry for the fetus.
(3) I thought that I might not be able to have children.
(4) I had no feelings in particular.
(5) Other (state explicitly:).

In the 1975 survey, about a third of the respondents (32.9 percent) had answered that they felt they "had done something

[31] Ōmura 1972:35.
[32] All of these mental states have been investigated in the United States; see, for example, Osofsky et al. 1973.

bad," another third (33.5 percent) checked the second answer, and 14 percent either responded that they were without any specific feeling or marked "other."[33] Bias toward negative responses should be expected from this question, not only because there was no positive alternative offered, but also because the alternative answers that are negative are placed first and are most numerous. By contrast, when women in the previously mentioned 1968 Nagoya survey were given the alternative, "my mind was put at ease," 36 percent chose it as their response.[34]

Women who have had abortions have to contend with the accusation from anti-abortion adherents that they lack maternal compassion. The pejorative element of the "children as possession" image is one example, but the argument also crops up in ideological interpretations of history. Yoshida's anti-abortion tract takes up the familiar suggestion that the occurrence of infanticide and abortion in the Tokugawa Era makes the morality of abortion moot. Yoshida claims that women in the past felt great sorrow when they resorted to such practices, as evidenced by *mizuko* tumuli. In contrast, today there is an " 'OK, I've aborted my child, sayonara!' mood in postwar Japan, where women abort lightheartedly and don't even make a move to bury the fetus."[35] The attack on women's maternal sensitivity inspired one woman to investigate present-day religious practices surrounding abortion:

> I am slandered by those who say that present-day women abort with no more feeling than if they were removing a tumor; but as one woman living in these times I firmly believe that a mother's love for her child is the same in the present as it was in the past, and will probably remain so in the future: as long as there are *mizuko*, offerings (*kuyō*) will surely be continued.[36]

[33] Mainichi Shinbunsha 1975:34.
[34] Hayasaka et al. 1973:21.
[35] Yoshida 1976:52.
[36] Higashi 1976.

The argument poses a double bind for Japanese women's feelings about their abortions: to deny any emotional reaction is to negate one's sensitivity to childbearing as a woman; to express unhappiness is tantamount to admitting having done something wrong. One example from the interviews illustrates the general expectation that women should feel some sort of remorse; a 39-year-old artist who reported no problems from her two abortions mused that she had not pitied the "children" (i.e., fetuses, although she chose the word for child, *kodomo*) because "maybe I'm just a cut-and-dried (*dorai*) type."

One impression gained from the interviews is that if there is conflict in some aspect of the marital relationship it may find expression in the woman's feelings about her abortion experience. In one instance, a 44-year-old interviewee whose husband has a mistress believes that he was in the mistress' company when she had her abortion, and although she herself wanted to keep the pregnancy he persuaded her to terminate it. In addition to resentment toward her husband, she expressed mild regret: "There aren't any physical aftereffects, and emotionally it's not a very serious matter, but from time to time I find myself thinking, 'if it had lived. . . .' "

The expression of regret, "if it had lived," appears to be a feeling experienced by older couples. When younger, they may have been faced with economic pressures that ruled out keeping an unplanned conception. When they have passed into economic security, however, the memories of their reasons for not wanting a birth fade. Both partners can also nurture a feeling of loss if they had wanted a child of one sex but have children only of the other sex. In one example found among the interviewees, this unresolved feeling of loss was intensified by an ongoing family problem of the wife's resentment toward her mother-in-law. A couple residing with the husband's parents has three sons. Although the wife has wanted child-care assistance from her mother-in-law, she has not received it. When their second son was two years old the wife became pregnant but was in danger of losing the pregnancy to a spontaneous abortion. According to the wife, her doctor advised absolute rest, but she could not give up taking care of her two boys, and consequently was required to undergo an induced abortion. The incident dramatized the mother-in-law's lack of help. The wife stated that she had never complained to her husband about his mother's failure to help, but she did not want to live with her in-laws and resented his putting her in the present situation. She expressed the "hunch" that the aborted pregnancy was female, and she had related it to her husband, intensifying his sense of loss as well as hers. (The couple's third birth was an attempt to have a girl—a fact which the husband also related in his interview—but he denied that they had experienced any induced abortions.)

MEN'S ATTITUDES TOWARD ABORTION

Generalizations about Japanese men's feelings about abortion are harder to make, because opinion surveys on abortion in Japan sample women only, and men are much more reluctant to discuss the topic than are women. Popular assumption has it that the man is the impetus for an abortion: he is the person persuading his reluctant wife or girl friend in the television serials and bullying her in anti-abortion literature. Many health care specialists see the husband's reaction to his wife's abortion as relief at having been saved from the tight economic situation that would result from another birth. To the contrary, however, one piece of survey evidence suggests that husbands are more likely to promote childbirth than termination. In the 1975 Mainichi Survey, respondents who reported one or more abortions were asked whose opinion was mainly responsible for the decision to abort, and all respondents were asked the same question regarding the decision to have a baby. Respondents credited their husbands with decisive influence in about a third (32.2 percent) of abortion decisions and nearly half (48.1 percent) of birth decisions.[37]

Another appraisal of husbands' attitudes is that they are emotionally distant from the issue. Some family planning specialists share this view. Harasawa Isamu of the Japan Family

[37] Mainichi Shinbunsha 1975:34, 35.

Planning Federation has used a graphic ten-minute color film of an induced abortion to preface his family planning lectures to husbands, in order to overcome what he feels is their lack of closeness to the issue. In six interview cases, husbands either understated the number of abortions that their wives had reported or denied having had any, in conflict with their wives' reports. (There is no indication in any of these cases that the wives had concealed their abortions from their husbands.) A few family planning counselors suggested that these husbands had forgotten the events as a result of their separation from matters related to childbearing.

Behind husbands' difficulties in discussing the topic of abortion may lie embarrassment and consternation that stem, in turn, from either an unwillingness to cooperate in contraceptive use or a sense of defeated effort to prevent conceptions. Asked why Japanese men avoid discussion of abortion, male informants typically responded by saying that it was an "embarrassing" or "sleazy" (*darashiganai*) topic. Two interviewee husbands went beyond this answer, however, saying that underneath their exterior image Japanese men are quite selfish and, by separating themselves from the problem of unwanted conceptions, they fail to cooperate in preventing them. When confronted with the necessity of an abortion, they feel guilty (*ushirometai*).

The husbands' own formulas for successful contraception also make abortion a difficult problem for them to deal with openly. Husbands do not usually assess contraceptive methods in terms of their physiological effectiveness: rather, they view effectiveness as a function of the skill and intelligence of the user. Male informants used adverbs like "skillfully" (*umaku*) or "correctly" (*tadashiku*) to describe successful contraceptive use. This view is also symptomatic of unfamiliarity with modern methods. This stance invites a strong sense of personal failure and feelings of inadequacy for the husband who genuinely wants to avoid pregnancy but who is faced with a contraceptive failure. Whether because of their subrosa noncompliance or their sense of failure, the most difficult topic for interviewee husbands to discuss was the experience of contraceptive failures that ended in abortion.

ABORTION AVOIDANCE

100% effective

Despite the opprobrium that surrounds abortion in Japan, could it be that individual women there do not prefer conception prevention over pregnancy termination? Against the negative symbols and publicly expressed criticism of the practice, women know that reliance on abortion is widespread, which must prove a powerful factor in promoting emotional acceptability. Then, too, certain features of abortion are unmatched by contraception: abortion as an ex-post-facto method of pregnancy control is required only when the woman is pregnant. When used, it is 100 percent effective. Japanese family planning specialists believe that couples regard abortion as a means for "liquidating" errors in contraceptive use.[38]

Although the availability of induced abortion must surely encourage some risk-taking resulting in unwanted pregnancy, the available evidence points to a preference for preventing rather than terminating. The strongest disincentive among women to rely on abortion is that it is a form of surgery. Contrary to the popular idea that Japanese women are extremely stoic,[39] patients strongly prefer—if not insist on—general anesthesia instead of other forms of anesthesia. In the course of discussions and interviews, women expressed both the fear and dislike of abortion as a surgical procedure and the fear of subsequent sterility. For two of the interviewee wives, inadequate anesthesia made the procedure quite painful. Two Ob-Gyns reported patients with abortion experiences who developed a fear of pregnancy strong enough to reduce

[38] The knowledge that some method of eradicating unwanted conceptions is at hand should contraception fail is a factor in risk taking among American women according to Kristin Luker's 1975 study; see especially pp. 94-98.

[39] One example is Neubardt 1972:142, who suggests that Japanese women would make "ideal subjects" for local block anesthesia.

the frequency of marital intercourse to nil. Both doctors said that providing pills or IUDs effected a cure for the problem.

Japanese women who have experienced abortion are more likely to use contraception than those who have not had abortions. Such is certainly the case among women in the questionnaire sample: only 9 percent of the women who had experienced abortions were not contracepting at the time of the survey, in contrast to 31 percent of women with no reported abortions. Moreover, although the association was not strong, the consistency of contraceptive practice was significantly related to the number of marital abortions in a positive direction.[40] Conversely, an analysis of 1965 Mainichi Survey data by Muramatsu Minoru found that fewer than 10 percent of wives who had never used contraception reported having abortions.[41]

Women who have experienced induced abortions are also more likely to choose modern contraceptive methods. Among the currently contracepting wives in the questionnaire sample, the use of a modern method had a significant positive relationship with the total number of marital abortions when five other variables were controlled, among them length of marriage and husband's income.[42] (The choice of a modern method cannot be credited to the Ob-Gyns' intervention at the time of abortion: as Chapter 3 notes, there was no relationship between number of marital abortions and professional as a source of information for the currently used method.)

It also appears that a substantial proportion of pregnancies ending in abortions are the result of contraceptive failure as

[40] Similarly, a 1971 study conducted in Koshi prefecture found that women who relied on abortion also had more contraceptive experience than those with no abortions; Roht and Aoyoma 1973.

[41] Muramatsu n.d.:3.

[42] Statistically significant results were obtained using a multiple regression of a modern/traditional dummy variable against the following six variables: wife's educational level, husband's income, length of marriage, number of marital abortions, husband as source of information, and professional as source of information.

opposed to no use of contraception. Unfortunately, the questionnaire survey form did not require respondents to state which of their pregnancies resulted from contraceptive failures. (A question regarding number of contraceptive failures since marriage was posed separately.) Nevertheless, contraceptive failure accounted for 58 percent of all marital induced abortions among the study participants when the relationship was controlled for length of marriage and other pregnancy outcomes.[43] These results resemble the findings of a five-year clinical study of abortion patients in Tokyo in which 56 percent of the married patients had been using contraception.[44] The 1969 national survey of abortion patients conducted by the Japan Medical Association and the Ministry of Health and Welfare reported that 73 percent of abortion patients (both married and unmarried) were contracepting. Of these patients, however, nearly two-thirds reported that their use of contraception was not consistent.[45] In the 1969 nationwide Prime Minister's Survey, 46 percent of the wives who had experienced abortion attributed their unwanted conceptions to contraceptive failure.[46] These study results may have overstated the extent to which abortion resulted from contraceptive failure; Japanese clinicians believe that abortion recipients tend to overstate the occurrence of contraceptive failures for the sake of appearances. On the other hand, some Japanese women using the nonappliance methods of rhythm or interruptus do not regard them as contraceptive methods, so their failures would not be counted. Then, too, those women who did not use contraception reflect not only chance-taking or a prefer-

---

[43] The variable for number of contraceptive failures contributed an r square value of .578 when the dependent variable for total number of marital abortions was put in a multiple regression against number of contraceptive failures, length of marriage, and a variable summing all other pregnancy outcomes (live births, spontaneous abortions, etc.).

[44] Miyamoto 1973:9.

[45] Kōsei-shō/Nihon Ishikai 1971:15.

[46] Naikaku Sōridaijin 1970:19.

ence for post-conception birth control, but the unavailability of appropriate information and suitable methods as well. The Japanese married woman who would state a preference for abortion over contraception is a rarity: of wives in the 1975 Mainichi Survey who said they had never practiced contraception or had tried but stopped, fewer than 3 percent indicated that they preferred induced abortion.[47]

Other indications of a reluctance to rely on abortion lie in the issue of what women do with their unwanted pregnancies. The Mainichi Survey asks its currently contracepting wives if they would give birth or have abortions should their contraceptive method fail; in 1975, answers were in roughly equal proportions for both alternatives.[48] Nor does access to induced abortion absolutely guarantee that every woman will limit her fertility to her ideal level. There were 18 cases in the questionnaire survey of women who reported more children than they felt was the ideal for them. (In two additional cases, the excess was accounted for by the birth of twins.) Of these 18 wives, 10 had experienced one or more marital induced abortions, and these women as a group averaged twice the frequency of marital abortions among all women in the sample aged 35 to 44. Over half of their abortions (11 incidents) were between the time of their last desired birth and the subsequent undesired birth(s).

Occasionally individuals justify abortion-avoiding behavior in moral terms. One interviewee wife gave her opposition to "throwing away a life" (*inochi o suteru*) as her reason for not terminating an unwanted pregnancy, and a 33-year-old husband whose wife was taking oral contraceptives said that they preferred the pill because "abortion is killing a life." The consensus among Japanese married women, however, is not that the number of abortions can be reduced by raising peo-

[47] Mainichi Shinbunsha 1975:33.

[48] 38.4 percent and 37.5 percent, respectively, with the remaining 24.1 percent undecided or not answering; Mainichi Shinbunsha 1975:33.

ple's senses of morality or by making the law more strict; fewer than 20 percent of the respondents gave either of those answers in the 1969 birth limitation survey conducted for the Prime Minister's Office of Public Affairs. For 73 percent of those asked, the solution lay in the diffusion of accurate knowledge about contraception.[49]

[49] Naikaku Sōridaijin 1970:30.

CHAPTER 5

Making Do: Method Adoption and Performance

The case of induced abortion in Japan cautions us not to equate necessity with preference: just because women there rely on abortion extensively does not mean that they prefer it over other fertility-limitation alternatives. Similarly, the extensive use of condoms in Japan represents a response to the availability patterns described in Chapter 3 rather than an expression of preference over other contraceptive methods. The condom is not an appropriate family planning method for a large proportion of the Japanese couples who have adopted it; on the whole, Japanese condom users are not very satisfied with the method, and their dissatisfaction is reflected in practices that result in unwanted pregnancies. Nor do a substantial number of husbands provide the level of cooperation that condoms necessitate for optimal protection from pregnancy. Nevertheless, individual couples must chart their own lonely courses for controlling births, with condoms as the universal point of departure.

USERS' ATTITUDES TOWARD CONDOMS

Contrary to an image of positive acceptance that the widespread use of condoms suggests, few Japanese husbands are likely to make positive statements about them. Although every couple but one in the interview group of 22 couples had used or were currently using condoms as a family planning method, there were no enthusiastic endorsements from any of the husbands. Two male interviewees (both currently using condoms) provided at best neutral appraisals: one (29 years old) said, "You hear people complain that it's not the real thing, but that's not a disadvantage for me"; in the other instance of acceptance, a 36-year-old husband married for ten years said, "I've been using them so long I've grown used to them."[1] When asked to name positive features of the condom, five of the husbands interviewed (two of whom still relying on the method) could name no positive features at all.

To judge by statements from the couples in the interviews, condoms posed an obstacle to sexual gratification, particularly for men. The husband's major objections to condoms concerned the dulling of sensation from use, and both men and women often referred to condoms as "troublesome" (*mendōkusai, wazurawashii*, and *hanzatsu*), a reference to the break in foreplay or sexual intercourse necessitated by application. Wives' statements were, on the whole, not as negative as husbands', but six of them expressed fears of ineffectiveness, and eight cited their husbands' dislike of the method as a drawback.

The less than enthusiastic acceptance of condoms in present-day Japan, particularly among husbands, is a matter of common knowledge among family planning specialists and lay people alike. One study of contraceptive practice and attitudes, conducted by Yamanouchi Pharmaceuticals among 300 newlywed Tokyo wives, found that about 35 percent of the wives and 60 percent of the husbands were dissatisfied with their experience with the method.[2]

For Japanese couples, the positive features of condoms stem from two aspects of their availability: the convenience with which they can be purchased, because of the saturation of marketing outlets, and the ease with which their mode of action can be understood, given the greater need for some form of explanation and guidance that other methods require. Interviewee wives were most likely to mention convenience as a positive feature of condoms, with terms like "quick and easy" (*tebayai*) or "ready" (*tegaru*). Among the husbands who

[1] These responses are reminiscent of the reactions of husbands in Rainwater's American working class sample, who expressed "a kind of resignation about the method"; 1960:153.

[2] Kon 1973:114-15.

stated specific desirable features, the "reliability" (*kakujitsu*) of condoms was foremost. The interviewees' feelings of security probably resulted from their easy comprehension of the condom's mode of action, as one of the wives interviewed (a 32-year-old junior college graduate) specifically mentioned. A few who mentioned simplicity as a positive point could have been referring to either availability or mode of action.

Part of the acceptance of condoms must come from the knowledge that so many other couples are using them—a few informants initially referred to condoms as "that thing that everybody's using." Health safety was also mentioned, although it did not figure as prominently as the availability-related features of condoms. (Three of the women interviewees and one husband mentioned it.) Door-to-door condom saleswomen have also observed that using the adjective "harmless" (*mugai*) increases the effectiveness of their sales pitches. Japanese couples can obtain condoms effortlessly and feel confident about using them without instruction. Nevertheless, these same people dislike having to use them: the result is the seeming contradiction in which an informant cites "convenience" as a positive point of condoms and then goes on to describe them as "troublesome."

THE UNFAMILIAR MODERN METHODS

The Japanese consumer does not necessarily turn to condoms because of an aversion to the health risks that accompany modern methods, appearances notwithstanding.

The health issue does make oral contraceptives the most controversial family planning method in Japan. Male informants uncharacteristically volunteered their opinions on this method more than on any other except the condom. Both men and women expressed the fear of side effects from continued use, and the idea of having to ingest a synthetic drug on a daily basis seemed particularly objectionable. Some of this sentiment stems from media's decidedly negative treatment of the pill; two of the wives in the interviewee group made specific reference to media warnings against pill use. Recent incidents involving death or deformities from synthetic drugs, mentioned in Chapter 3, have further deepened a fear of side effects from oral contraceptives.

Despite these negative sentiments, objections to the pill's safety are neither widespread nor deeply rooted. A question in the 1975 Mainichi Survey, "Do you think there is a need for the pill?" was asked of those respondents who claimed familiarity with the method. Some 32 percent answered in the affirmative, and another 43 percent answered that they did not know.[3]

Indecision about the pill was also evident among the expectant women in the 14-city survey mentioned in Chapter 3; over a fourth of those who said they knew about the pill also responded that they did not know if they would like to try it themselves when next faced with the need to use contraception.[4] Then, too, if dislike of the idea of chemical contraception were in fact a strongly held feeling, there would be no need legally to prohibit the pill. Ironically, a few family planning specialists, like Tangezaka Urako of the Association for Family Life Research, oppose legalization of the pill for contraceptive use because they fear it would become too popular; Tangezaka claims that Japanese couples might all rush to use the legalized drug, thus endangering many young women for whom pill use is contraindicated.

Distrust of the pill is probably fueled by unfamiliarity and ignorance. This response is exacerbated by the nature of contraception itself, involving as it does health, sexuality, and fertility, three areas of life that are prone to generate anxiety; as a result, unfamiliarity is more likely to engender negative, rejecting attitudes than if these three issues were not involved. Informants expressed vague fears and unfounded hazards in their discussions of pill side effects, as opposed to the substantiated dangers. Although they frequently expressed a fear of ill effects of the pill because of its effects on female physiology, both men and women were inclined to mention general

[3] Mainichi Shinbunsha 1975:35.
[4] Satō et al. 1977:37.

health, sterility, cancer, or the possibility of deformed off-spring after discontinuing pill use instead of citing scientifically implicated ailments like thromboses. The comment of one interviewee housewife (a 34-year-old high-school graduate) also suggests the link between unfamiliarity and distrust: "I feel insecure about the pill when I think about its effects on the body. And I can't believe that by taking one tablet that it works." The prescribing doctors' reassurances were sufficient to allay any fears among the few informant wives who did rely on the pill.

Female informants were less negative about IUDs, and those who were familiar with the method expressed opinions that were more factually oriented. These differences may reflect the greater number of IUD users than pill users, since more informants referred to the experiences of friends or friends' hearsay information about other IUD users.

Here as well, however, there may be considerable indecision and ignorance about the method; in the expectant mothers' survey, 30 percent stated that they did not know if they would want to try the method once the need for contraception arose. Over a fourth of the women who claimed no interest in trying the method said they did so because they did not know enough about it.[5] Convenience and effectiveness were the attractive features for women who were positively oriented toward the IUD. More often than not, however, informants having an opinion on the method found the IUD unattractive because of the cost and discomfort of yearly replacements as well as word-of-mouth reports of bleeding or uterine injuries among users.

The number of informants with opinions regarding contraceptive sterilization was limited because few who had not reached their desired family size had given any thought to the method. A few informants expressed the feeling that it was "unnatural" (*fushizen*) or objected to its irreversibility. A typical theme in discussions of sterilization was the fear that a

[5] *Ibid.*:38.

traffic accident or some such tragedy would leave a sterilized couple childless and unable to bear more children.

Sterilization seemed to be the method that inspires the most misunderstandings—an observation that doctors and family planning counselors corroborated. Typical of mistaken ideas was the fear of loss of energy or vigor, especially in the case of vasectomy; the possibility that vasectomy could cause enervation and decrease work energy and motivation seemed particularly distressing to those having reservations about the procedure. Confusion with the effects of castration was common; men considering vasectomy expressed the concern that it would decrease or destroy libido, and one interviewee who had had a vasectomy had been asked by close friends if the operation had brought about the lack of hair on his legs.

There are other reasons to doubt that the Japanese have rejected modern contraception on the basis of their fear of possible side effects. Japanese women do not necessarily believe that the safety of contraception should take precedence over effectiveness. In addition, "safety versus effectiveness" is not an either-or issue for many Japanese women; rather, the effectiveness of a contraceptive method can increase its safety, because ineffective contraception necessitates abortion—itself a source of risk to health. When women in the survey sample were asked a multiple-choice question about the most important quality that they would want in a contraceptive method, those who opted for effectiveness outnumbered respondents more concerned about health by two to one; the distribution is reproduced in Table 5-1. The significance of this response is limited, of course, by its hypothetical nature. The results merit attention, nonetheless, not only because the distribution of responses points strongly to concern about effectiveness, but also because so few respondents were unable or unwilling to register their opinions.

Women's complementary perception of safety and effectiveness is illustrated by the relationship between their opinions on contraceptive safety and the method they actually use: users of modern methods were significantly more likely to

TABLE 5-1

Distribution of Responses to a Question Regarding
Priority of Contraceptive Method Features,
in Percentages, Tokyo Area Clinic and Hospital Sample,
1975-1976

"If you were to choose a contraceptive method, what would
be the most important quality?" (One answer only)

	Percent
Safety to my health	31.2
Safety to my husband's health	3.0
Complete (failure-free) contraception	62.5
No answer*	3.3
TOTAL	100.0
(N = 635)	

* Includes women checking more than one response or indicating
inability to decide.

place first priority on safety.[6] Similarly, a fourth of the women
in the expectant mothers' survey who expressed an interest
in trying pills or IUDs gave the methods' "safety" as their
reason.[7]

INDICATIONS OF THE UNAVAILABILITY
OF MODERN METHODS

Contrasts between modern and traditional contraceptive method
users suggest that availability plays an important role in determining whether or not Japanese couples choose medical
methods. The cost of modern methods poses an important
limitation on their availability. The couples in the questionnaire survey who used modern methods were more likely to
have higher incomes, a statistically significant association that

[6] Statistically significant results were obtained when using a Chi
Square test.
[7] Satō et al. 1977:38.

held true regardless of length of marriage or wife's educational level.[8] It would be very difficult for an informant to admit that a certain contraceptive method has a cost that places it beyond the couples' reach. Informants did not discuss the prices of various methods, with the exception of one 33-year-old interviewee wife, who cited the low cost of condoms as a point in their favor. Husbands in particular would find it hard to say that they could not afford a medical method. In one instance, a young husband whose job was subject to frequent layoffs expressed a strong interest in the IUD, but claimed that his wife would object to having to see an Ob-Gyn in order to obtain it. His wife was also interested in the method, but she did not object to the necessity of seeing a gynecologist in order to have it; rather, family finances did not permit it, especially since her husband had recently been talked into buying about $100 worth of condoms by a door-to-door saleswoman.

The reluctance of health-care specialists to promote modern contraception also seriously limits the availability of those methods. The contracepting wives in the questionnaire survey were significantly more likely to be using a modern method if a specialist had provided information on the method currently used.[9] This relationship is hardly surprising, since it reflects the activities of family planning service providers at six of the eight questionnaire distribution points. The specialists who cooperated in conducting the questionnaire study were particularly active and innovative in family planning activities, unlike their colleagues at small private hospitals

[8] Statistically significant results were obtained using a multiple regression of a modern/traditional dummy variable against the following six variables: wife's educational level, husband's income, length of marriage, number of marital abortions, husband as source of information, and professional as source of information.

[9] Statistically significant results were obtained using a multiple regression of a modern/traditional dummy variable against the following six variables: wife's educational level, husband's income, length of marriage, number of marital abortions, husband as source of information, and professional as source of information.

who provide abortions. (Hence the strong association between professional information and modern method use, whereas no association emerged between number of marital abortions and professional information source.) This association also suggests, however, that Japanese specialists can promote the acceptance of modern methods. There are other indications of this possibility as well. The Japan Family Planning Federation's 1969 report on over 4,500 IUD users found 48 percent claiming they accepted the method on the basis of a doctor's recommendation.[10] Six of the 22 couples interviewed were relying on medical methods, but in 5 of these 6 instances the method was suggested by a physician; none of these 5 couples had decided beforehand on the specific methods they had adopted.

PERSONAL INFORMATION CHANNELS

Japanese couples rarely receive information on contraception through their face-to-face networks of close friends or kin. There are no subrosa folk networks for family planning information that could obviate the need for professional guidance or supplant it. Many Japanese, among them the sex researcher Muramatsu Hiroo, believe that when local community organization was transformed by economic development and urbanization during the last century, various human relationships and institutions that ensured the transmission of sex information disappeared and have yet to be satisfactorily replaced.[11]

Family members rarely provide information on contraception for either men or women in present-day Japanese society. Inter-generational transfer, such as from mother to daughter, is especially low. Only one interviewee, a 25-year-old wife, reported a family member as a source of information for the method she was currently using; in that instance an older sister who had married some years before had told her about con-

[10] Nihon Kazoku Keikaku Renmei 1969:13-14.
[11] Muramatsu 1974.

doms. The two women had an unusually close relationship, partly because they had lost their mother at an early age. The low degree of communication with family members is corroborated by the Mainichi Survey's multiple choice question about sources of information about contraception, in which "parents" received 2.6 percent of responses, "siblings" 2.7 percent, and "other close kin" 3.5 percent.[12] By contrast, 76 percent of respondents in a 1973 family planning survey of English and Welsh mothers reported discussing contraceptive methods with another family member.[13] The near-absence of inter-generational transfer of information is probably due in large part to the small number of couples in the parental generation who had practiced contraception in their own marriages.

Non-kin personal networks sometimes provide useable information for Japanese women, but not often: only 14 percent of the survey respondents using contraception cited friends or family members as an information source, a figure that resembles the 17 percent who mentioned friends in the 1975 Mainichi Survey.[14] Perhaps the most important limiting factor is the simple fact that couples using condoms are in the great majority, so relatively few women have experiences with other methods that they can share. Certain tendencies also act to limit the contribution of communication with friends and acquaintances, chief among them the embarrassment and repression evidenced by women when discussing matters related to sex and reproduction. A related tendency is the widespread reluctance—if not inability—of Japanese women to discuss contraception and related topics freely with one another until they have become mothers. This can cause a somewhat subtle but ironic cross-cancelling effect with generational differences, in which older women having more conservative attitudes

[12] Mainichi Shinbunsha 1975:32.
[13] Cartwright 1976:74; only 6 percent identified relatives as their most helpful source of information, but this figure represents a recent decrease resulting from increased reliance on health professionals.
[14] Mainichi Shinbunsha 1975:32.

(including reticence about discussing matters related to sex) are nevertheless able to discuss fertility limitation more easily than younger women who have yet to begin their childbearing careers.

Husbands constitute the single most relied-upon personal source of information on contraception for Japanese women. Even though the majority of questionnaire survey respondents was drawn from among patients at facilities having family planning counseling services, "husband" was their single most reported source, with 47 percent of currently contracepting wives claiming their spouses as one of their sources of information for the method they were currently using; 30 percent claimed they relied on their husbands *only*, a figure nearly equal to all of those who relied on a professional or paraprofessional source alone or in combination with other sources. In the 1975 Mainichi Survey, husbands ranked second only to magazines, with 23 percent of the women claiming their spouses as a source.[15]

The Japanese wife's dependence on her husband usually results from her lack of personal resources for obtaining contraceptive information elsewhere. The tendency to rely on husbands is stronger in the earlier years of marriage. Among questionnaire respondents the relationship between length of marriage and husband as an information source was significantly negative.[16] A number of interviewee wives commented that they had relied on their husbands for the choice of their first contraceptive method because they did not know of any themselves.

It is doubtful that very many wives who claim their husbands as an information source are successful communicators who have consulted with their spouses on matters of mutual importance. In the questionnaire survey, wives who were using medical methods instead of condoms were much less likely to have relied on their husbands as a source of information for

[15] Mainichi Shinbunsha 1975:32.

[16] Statistically significant results were obtained when using a Pearson correlation of the two variables.

their current method, either alone or in combination with other information sources. (Two-thirds of the wives relying on condoms named their husband as an information source, in contrast to 11 percent of modern method users.) Those wives who stated that professionals constituted an information source for their current method were even less likely to include their husbands as a source, a relationship that was statistically significant.[17] Although it was possible for questionnaire respondents to cite both husband and medical or paramedical specialist as information sources, only 3 percent did so. These results, in conjunction with interview accounts, suggest that a pattern of joint effort and information sharing for family planning is rare among Japanese couples.[18]

Male informants who identified a personal source of contraceptive information stated that schoolmate friends had taught them about condoms at some point since their early or mid-teens. Aside from this one channel of information, there is no personal source of contraceptive information for men for any other method, despite the fact that so many Japanese women rely on their husbands for the selection and use of contraceptive methods.

It is difficult to state with any certainty if Japanese men have more ease of communication among themselves than do women in the treatment of the topic of contraception. There are circumscribing conditions to which men, too, must conform. Work-place society places limits on the content of discussions involving personal matters. The appearance of normalcy in one's private life presented to fellow workers appears

[17] Statistically significant results were obtained when using a Chi Square test on a cross-tabulation of the variables for presence/absence of husband as one source of information and presence/absence of professional as one source of information.

[18] Anthropologist Linda Perry provides a similar observation based on her field research conducted among families in an Osaka suburb in the early 1970s (personal communication); a typical response among wives who were disillusioned with their husbands' contraceptive performance was to act unilaterally, procuring a female method from a local physician without consulting their husbands.

to be of great concern, particularly among white-collar informants who claim that evidence of "deviation" (*itsudatsu*)
can damage career goals. Coupled with this concern is the
unavoidability of the close association with the same co-workers throughout one's career. If there is a co-worker who is
disliked, these considerations can intensify fears that unfavorable information might later prove damaging to workplace status. One example of this situation involves a 39-
year-old engineer who works in a small firm with 28 other
employees, two of whom he dislikes but with whom he must
keep a day-to-day working relationship. He declined to answer co-workers' probes about how he and his wife have been
limiting their fertility after the birth of their third child. Although she now has had a contraceptive sterilization, he re-
pelled co-workers' inquiries by half-jokingly replying that they
had given up sex, because he feared that his disliked work-
mates would create the rumor that he had forced his wife into
having the operation.

Men who feel they are unable to confide in co-workers are
not necessarily cut off from all communication on contraception; they may also have confidants among friendships formed
during adolescence. Such friendships are few and difficult to
maintain, however. In an 11-country youth survey conducted
in 1972, nearly a fourth of the Japanese respondents stated
that they had no close friends of either sex, in contrast to a
range of 3 to 15 percent for Sweden, France, West Germany,
England, and the United States.[19] Mass migration to large
urban centers by the young in the postwar period has separated childhood friends by the time they reach their early
twenties. Another cause of friendlessness is the pressure to
achieve in entrance examinations, which necessitates social
isolation for many middle-class youths.

Even among men who feel they are able to discuss sexual
matters candidly with work-mates there is no guarantee that
a flow of information capable of contributing to knowledge
of contraception will result. Since such talks are often confined

[19] Sōri-fu 1973:110.

to joking and anecdotes rather than to an exchange of personal information, it is difficult for a topic such as a couple's problem in choosing a desirable contraceptive method to arise spontaneously. More important still, however, is the lack of variety in experiences with different methods among the discussants; like their wives, few men are in a circle of acquaintances having experience with a variety of methods. One good example of these points is a 29-year-old manager in wholesale distribution of paper products (a college graduate) who stated that he finds no trouble at all in discussing sex and contraception: "It's actually something you can talk about with anyone because it's a common element in everyone's life and everyone's interested." He and his wife are using condoms only, and he reported that all but one of his married friends also use the same method, the exception being one couple relying on douche. When asked for his opinions on methods other than condoms he declined to discuss the topic, saying, "My wife knows more about contraception than I do."

COOPERATION AND CONTROL

The widespread adoption of condoms among Japanese couples cannot be explained by the husbands' desires to assume responsibility for contraception. If anything, the quality of husbands' participation in family planning casts doubt on the appropriateness of the condom's preeminent position among contraceptive methods. Open opposition to contraception from husbands is rare, but the use of condoms invites ample opportunity for less overt noncompliance.

Clinicians reported that a lack of cooperation from husbands poses a familiar complaint among women patients. Clinical observations cannot substitute for statements about couples in general, of course, since the patients may not be typical of all wives. It is noteworthy, nonetheless, that male noncooperation has been a problem which Japanese wives present to Ob-Gyns and family planning counselors. Family counselor Fukazawa Michiko stated that, in her experience, it has been the wives' most frequent complaint concerning contraception, and the Ob-Gyn Maruyama Kazuo observed in his newspaper article on family planning among young couples in large apartment complexes (*danchi*) that he has heard many complaints about uncooperative husbands.[20] Specialists also observed that the problem of the husband's failure to cooperate typically emerges when he returns home drunk.

A direct question to Japanese spouses of either sex about the issue of cooperation in their own family planning experience would offer little in information on the subject because husbands and wives are loath to reveal any signs of discord in their marriages. The need to present an appearance of normalcy (referred to as *tatemae*, as opposed to the actual state of affairs, *honne*) is an extremely strong theme in Japanese social relations, to the point where the Japanese themselves believe it a feature unique to their culture. Wives suppress their remarks about disagreements because they would reflect poorly on the ability to maintain marital harmony. Japanese husbands would also be reluctant to report their own noncooperation, since it would reflect badly on the couple's relationship and also stand as a tacit admission that self-indulgent sexual gratification could exert a strong pull on their conduct.

Interviewee wives' comments did reflect poor male cooperation, although almost all of these instances were imbedded in discussions of liked and disliked features of the condom rather than in any direct questions about cooperation. Their husbands' dislike of condoms was the most frequently cited disadvantage of the method, a complaint that signaled an inability to get thorough and consistent compliance. The Japanese husband's noncompliance in condom use can take on a passive cast. Two wives reported applying their husband's condoms for them, but this in no way constituted a part of erotic foreplay; one wife only did it when her husband returned home intoxicated, and the other because her husband would not do so himself despite her own dislike of applying it. (Contrary to occasional claims that Japanese couples have

refined applying condoms into an erotic art, I have not encountered any instances of wives who apply their husband's
condoms as a part of foreplay, nor do Japanese family planning counselors and literature generally promote the idea.)

Coitus interruptus among Japanese couples may also represent male noncooperation, although that judgment requires
an investigation of the individual couple's circumstances and
the process by which they end up relying on withdrawal.
Family planning counselors hold a negative view of the man
who practices it, a few labeling the act "male insolence" (*otoko
no gōman*). Since condoms are so readily available, they assume that such men are avoiding condom use, contrary to
their wives' wishes for the stronger sense of security that condoms offer.

It is difficult, however, to separate individual instances of
the husband's noncompliance from cases of genuine collusion
between husband and wife when they rely on withdrawal,
particularly if the wife does not communicate her feelings
about the practice. Two interesting contrasts appeared among
interviewee husbands reporting the use of coitus interruptus.
One husband (a 43-year-old college graduate) had rejected
his wife's half-joking request that he have a vasectomy since
she had experienced three abortions since their marriage. When
asked if his use of withdrawal bothered his wife, he replied:
"Well, it's not exactly a matter of minding or not—it's more
a matter of being in the mood and not thinking about it at
the time. It's only afterwards that there's any worry about
pregnancy." His wife had expressed anxiety about withdrawal
failure in her interview, and he interpreted her suggestion of
vasectomy as dissatisfaction with the methods they were then
using. A younger husband (a 29-year-old high-school graduate) also said that his use of interruptus was a spontaneous
matter, but when asked if his wife disliked it he replied, "She
doesn't say anything but I can tell from the way her body
reacts. It's different at those times." Unlike the older husband,
he was actively interested in finding contraception more effective than the condom, which they were then using. His wife

said that, if anything, he was the more conscientious about contraceptive failure, "to the point of being nervous about it."

The sexual involvement of both partners may be very hard to distinguish from the man's self-centered desire for unhindered gratification in cases of condom nonuse. Nevertheless, given the greater obstruction to the male's satisfaction posed by condom use and the greater tendency of Japanese men to complain about it, we should suspect that a large proportion of such instances of condom misuse indicate noncooperation. The same can be said for the practice of applying the condom after intromission (sometimes shortly before orgasm), a practice that informants acknowledge and that some family planning specialists believe is widespread.

Aside from their use of condoms, Japanese husbands do not take a prominent part in couples' family planning efforts. Family planning educators reported that it was difficult to involve men in their programs. Nor does male initiative in family planning appear in the ratio of female to male contraceptive sterilizations; the Mainichi Survey of 1977 (the first year that contraceptive sterilizations were recorded by sex) indicated a ratio of three female contraceptive sterilizations to every vasectomy.[21] This is more than double the ratio of 1.3 female sterilizations to each male sterilization in the United Kingdom and higher still than the ratio of 0.9 in the United States, countries where condom use is far lower.[22]

The task of obtaining condoms typically devolves to wives. Both men and women buy condoms at drugstores, but female customers buy in larger volume, probably out of a greater desire to avoid running out of supplies. Home sales of condoms are geared to selling to housewives, as are supermarket sales, in which condoms are placed in the midst of feminine

[21] Calculated from figures in Mainichi Shinbunsha 1979:42.

[22] The ratio for the United Kingdom was calculated from figures in Cartwright 1976:14; the United States ratio was calculated from figures in Ford 1978:266.

hygiene products. Much of the advertising for condoms is also geared to women; the most frequently used medium is women's magazines.[23] Although the Yamanouchi survey of Tokyo newlywed couples found over twice as many instances of husbands purchasing as wives,[24] this pattern may be unique to the first year or so of marriage. Among the 12 husbands in the intensive interview study who claimed current condom use, 8 stated that their wives purchased their contraceptives.

The lack of enthusiasm for conception control among Japanese husbands means—practically by definition—that they have less desire to avoid pregnancy than do their wives. Among the interviewees, wives were far more likely than husbands to mention fear of ineffectiveness as a drawback in condom use. (Six wives specifically mentioned a fear of condom failure, in contrast to only two husbands, neither of whom was married to one of the six.)

There are other indications as well that Japanese men are more likely to welcome births than are their wives, and less likely to fear unwanted pregnancies. Large-scale surveys have found Japanese husbands both more inclined to want more children and to want them sooner than do their wives. According to results from a 1970 nationwide survey, husbands of two-child families who wanted more children outnumbered wives in the same category by 30 percent, and, among three-child couples, by 60 percent.[25] When a 1973 government survey of newlyweds asked both partners when they wanted their first child, 52 percent of the husbands said "as soon as possible," in contrast with 45 percent of the wives.[26] Among the interviewee couples, the husbands tended to give a smaller figure than the wives for their ideal time interval between births.

The husbands' motivation to avoid induced abortion, unlike their wives', is dampened by their ability to pay for the op-

[23] Ando 1976:121.
[24] Kon 1973:115.
[25] Calculated from figures in Kōsei-shō 1972:27.
[26] Kōsei-shō, 1974:22.

erations. Among the questionnaire survey participants, women whose husbands had higher incomes were progressively more likely to have had a greater number of induced abortions, a significant relationship that held regardless of length of marriage. A few Ob-Gyns believed that the expense of an induced abortion serves as a major impetus for husbands' cooperation in contraception: evidently the reverse also applies. The relationship is not due to the wife's increased spending power; although a third of the wives in the sample held paying jobs, there was no statistical connection at all between the amount of the wife's income and the number of abortions that she had received.[27] (Nor does the phenomenon result from a greater tendency to have a live birth among couples with less money, since those with higher incomes also have more children.)

Japan's family planning specialists agree that younger men are more cooperative. Family planning counselors who were active in the early postwar period promotion of contraception state that today's husbands are far more cooperative than men were twenty-five years or so ago. Two family planning counselors who began in the immediate postwar period recalled the problem of husbands who forcibly removed their wives' diaphragms before intercourse. Older men today, according to family planning specialists, are more likely to be willful, selfish, or indifferent, although estimates of the critical age vary somewhat. Among interviewees and other informants as well, age appeared related to husbands' cooperativeness in family planning, in the direction posed by the family planning specialists. The wives of men over 35 years of age seemed to have the most difficulty in exacting compliance in condom use. The wife of a 36-year-old heavy equipment salesman (both are college graduates) reported that in the past he had attempted to remove the condom once applied but she had dissuaded him, and she still fears that he might try again.

[27] Results were obtained when using a multiple regression of the total number of marital abortions against the following five independent variables: length of marriage, husband's income, wife's income, wife's educational level, and husband's educational level.

The contrast between Japanese men's behavior today and in the recent past may condition lower expectations among Japanese women. The result is a minimal definition of cooperation, such as the one held by a 29-year-old grade schoolteacher with a husband the same age: "I suppose my husband's cooperative. After our first child was born and we saw how easily I got pregnant, he told me to go talk to someone about it."

Despite all of the indications that Japanese husbands are not particularly suited to the demand for cooperation that condom use poses, there remains the issue of control: do couples choose condoms because wives prefer to leave control of the method to their husbands, and do husbands insist on that prerogative?

Wives who prefer that their husbands assume control are in the minority. The survey questionnaire asked wives about their own preferences for the locus of control, providing three alternative answers: (1) "[A method] I can use myself without having to rely on my husband"; (2) "One I can leave to my husband's care rather than myself"; and (3) "It makes no difference to me." Only 23 percent chose the second answer indicating the desire for no part in applying conception control. The third response poses some difficulty for interpretation since respondents include wives who have achieved a genuinely cooperative relationship with their husbands in contraception as well as women with a passive or indifferent approach. This answer was chosen most often, with 38 percent of respondents claiming no special preference. However, about an equal proportion (37 percent) expressed preference for control.

The limited availability of female methods in Japan may have subtly affected this distribution of responses; some respondents may not have accepted the idea of their own control as a realizable alternative because they have no real-life referents for such a concept. More importantly, a breakdown among contracepting wives suggests that there are women who desire control but are relying on a method that is controlled by their husbands. The relationship between desire for control and actual contraceptive roles among current contraceptors in the questionnaire sample has been cross-tabulated and appears in Table 5-2. The "couple" category is composed of those who are concurrently using both a male and female method, which is in almost all cases the rhythm method and condoms.

Nearly half of those who claimed they wanted control were actually relying on their husbands for cooperation, and over a fourth were currently using a method entirely under the husband's control. These women accounted for 17 percent of the total of currently contracepting wives in the sample. By contrast, only 6 percent of those wanting their husbands to take charge were actually using a female method. Users of female methods also constituted the smallest group among those claiming no preference in method control.

This preponderance of male method and shared control method users does not arise because of the husband's insistence upon method control; there are no indications that Jap-

TABLE 5-2

Method Control Preferences Among Currently Contracepting Wives by Type of Method Actually Used, in Percentages, Tokyo Area Clinic and Hospital Sample, 1975-1976

	METHOD PREFERENCE		
	Wife's Control	*Husband's Control*	*No Preference*
Female	54.8	6.0	24.9
Male	27.7	60.3	38.5
Couple	17.5	33.6	36.7
Total	100.0	99.9	100.1
(N)	(166)	(116)	(169)

Total percentages may not equal 100.0 due to rounding.
(Chi Square = 85, df = 4, p < 0.0001)

anese men are so intent on controlling their wives' exposure
to pregnancy that they prefer condoms despite their dislike of
the method. The possibility of a spouse's secret extramarital
sexuality is a matter of concern for both Japanese husbands
and wives, but it is doubtful that men prefer condoms and
coitus interruptus as part of a strategy of sexual control over
their wives. No male informants referred to the issue of control
as a positive feature of male method use. Men who would
choose a male method in order to maintain control probably
exist, but it would be extremely unusual for any Japanese
husband to state explicitly such a strategy. Other means of
immediate control are probably far more effective guarantees
of the wife's fidelity, among them constraints on her time alone
away from other family members and the husband's power
to make life unpleasant for her were she to have an extramarital affair that was discovered. One midwife with extensive
experience in providing diaphragms did relate stories from the
past in which the method precipitated strife because it facil-
itated the wife's extramarital affairs or provoked the husband's suspicions. Other family planning counselors have in-
terceded on behalf of wives using diaphragms to reassure
suspicious husbands, but such cases were infrequent.

The major problem area in the Japanese male's approach
to marital contraception, as family planning counselors see it,
has not been the desire for control of pregnancy. Rather, it
has been the husband's indifference, or an assumption that
pregnancy is a woman's concern. For such husbands, of course,
the issue of control is irrelevant. In extreme cases, husbands
disregard contraception entirely because it concerns reproduction, which is the wife's responsibility. Fukazawa Michiko
offers as example an irate husband who complained to her
that his wife failed her responsibility by becoming pregnant.
He did not know what contraceptive method she was using.
None of the interviewee husbands expressed this attitude, but
a few Japanese males in less structured settings did feel that
since women are the ones who experience pregnancy and have
children it is only natural that they should be more concerned
about contraception than are men.

ADOPTING THE FIRST METHOD

Condoms are almost universally the first method that Japanese couples adopt. Among contraceptors in the questionnaire sample, 89 percent of those married for one year or less were relying on condoms (either alone or in conjunction with other methods). The greater probability of reliance on condoms in the early years of marriage is also suggested by the Japan World Fertility Survey's cross-tabulation of methods by wife's age, in which condom use decreases consistently from 100 percent among wives under 20 years of age to 70 percent among contracepting wives between the ages of 35 and 39.[28] A 1976 countrywide survey of 2,300 couples who had used contraception at marriage found 87 percent using condoms.[29] Since these figures are cross-sectional, they present a synthetic depiction of the effects of time in marriage (i.e., a sample of women of different ages at one time, as opposed to historical accounts). Greater concentration of condom use in the early years of marriage is also indicated, however, by retrospective data in the interview sample; only one couple had not relied on condoms as their first contraceptive method. (In that case, the wife's Ob-Gyn provided her with an IUD immediately after the second of two births in the span of ten months.)

As the discussion of male versus female control over contraception suggests, there are no widespread, explicit shared understandings about family planning responsibility among present-day Japanese couples. When asked which marriage partner should assume responsibility for choosing a contraceptive method, Japanese spouses would typically respond by saying that the decision should be a joint one reached by discussing the matter together. In the case of their own choice of contraceptive method, however, these individuals found it difficult to describe how the decision actually took place. This seemed particularly so when discussing the couple's first contraceptive experience. The phrase used most often by interviewees in relating how they settled on their first marital con-

[28] Figures calculated from Kōsei-shō 1976a:33.
[29] Ogino 1976:35.

traceptive method was "somehow or other" (*nan to naku*). If one partner was identified as the person who decided, it was typically the husband. These observations reiterate the findings of the Yamanouchi newlywed study, in which 45 percent of the contracepting wives answered that their method was chosen "somehow or other," another 23 percent saying that their husbands chose.[30]

A few informants described the decision-making process by saying that their method was chosen "naturally" (*shizen ni*). This usage of the word *natural* as something effortless or allowing for passivity is a recurrent theme in informants' discussions of family planning. In two instances of this usage, wives were explaining that their husbands had had prior experience with the method before their marriage (in one case condoms, the other, interruptus); thus the couple did not need to expend any effort to choose since the husband merely continued using the method he had used before. In another instance, the husband of a wife who had initiated condom use after she purchased them from a condom saleswoman also described the couple's decision as one that took place "naturally" instead of indicating that the choice was his wife's, probably because he did not want to admit that she had assumed initiative in the matter.

The highly vague phraseology used by interviewees to describe how they arrived at their choice of contraceptive methods is noteworthy. It may indicate an attempt to dissemble, in some cases, but it is more probably a sign of difficulty encountered in actively pursuing some form of conception control. Ambiguity regarding the allocation of initiative and responsibility and a lack of knowledge about alternative forms of contraception both contribute to difficulty in deciding on and procuring a method for preventing pregnancy. The actual scenario for those couples who gave vague answers about how they chose their first method began, in all likelihood, with the wife hinting at the need for conception control; the husband,

[30] Kon 1973:116.

by virtue of his knowledge of condoms, then chose and procured the contraceptives himself or told her about them and told her to get them. This pattern explains the high degree of exclusive reliance on husbands for contraceptive information, despite the fact that they are in no way specially qualified for that role: the Japanese husband assumes leadership by default.

Japanese couples begin using contraception later in their life cycle than do their counterparts in the United States; comparing nationwide surveys, 58 percent of currently married white women in the United States who were between the ages of 25 and 29 years in 1970 had used contraception before their first pregnancy, in contrast to fewer than 30 percent of Japanese wives of the same age in 1971.[31] The delay is partly related to the late age at marriage that prevails in Japan, where couples who marry later are more likely to begin childbearing right after marriage. Three-fourths of wives under 20 years of age in 1974 reported using contraception before their first pregnancy, and, among wives who had had no pregnancies, about 43 percent of those between age 20 and 24 were currently using contraception, in contrast to 34 percent of those women five years older than they.[32]

RHYTHM, THE GREAT ESCAPE FROM CONDOMS

As mentioned in Chapter 1, Japanese couples tend to use condoms together with one or more other traditional contraceptive methods. Of 305 condom users in the questionnaire survey, 46 percent (140) reported using two or more methods. The method most often used in conjunction with condoms is rhythm. The large number of rhythm method users in Japan can be mostly accounted for by multiple method use; in the questionnaire sample, only 10 of the 133 respondents re-

[31] U.S. figures are from Westoff and Ryder 1977:58, and are for women who married between the ages 20 to 24; figures for Japan are from Muramatsu n.d.:5.

[32] Kōsei-shō 1976:30, 152, 156.

porting rhythm use (7.5 percent) had specified that it was their only current contraceptive method. (Figures based on World Fertility Survey statistics show that nearly three-fourths of rhythm method users are concurrent condom users, but the original statistics do not identify the proportion of couples using rhythm as their sole means of pregnancy prevention.)

The concurrent use of condoms and rhythm offers Japanese couples a respite from the relentless demands of proper condom use. There are basically two ways in which couples can make use of more than one contraceptive method concurrently: when the methods are used together on each occasion, their application is referred to as *combined use*; when one method is used on some occasions, another on other occasions, the practice is termed *alternate* use.[33] Alternate use involving rhythm and condoms would mean that condoms are used in the fecund portion of the menstrual cycle, and no method is used during "safe" days; conversely, combined use of rhythm and condoms would mean that the couple uses condoms during the infecund part of the cycle and abstains during midcycle. (The dichotomy also applies to methods used independently of coitus.) Combined use of the rhythm method and condoms is the more cautious approach, but it limits opportunities for sexual intercourse to the frequency allowed by rhythm only, which is decidedly low. Among women in the United States, for example, those who rely on rhythm report the lowest coital frequencies among contracepting women.[34] (There were too few women in the questionnaire sample using rhythm only to enable a reliable comparison of coital frequencies.) Alternative use of the two methods increases opportunities for coitus (and could conceivably encourage male cooperation). Pregnancy rates may also be lower than if the couple were to use rhythm only,[35] but the effectiveness of the

[33] Christopher Tietze provided the convention and terminology in a personal communication of April 21, 1980.

[34] Westoff 1974:138.

[35] Liskin 1981:48-49.

practice does not equal the protection offered by consistent use of barrier methods.

According to Ob-Gyns and family planning specialists, most Japanese couples use condoms and rhythm as alternate methods. In the course of my research, I encountered only two couples who combined the methods (i.e., periodic abstinence with condom use during infertile periods), one of them in the interview sample. The mean monthly coital frequencies of rhythm and condom users reflect alternate method use as an attempt to escape the direct impediment to sexual gratification posed by either condom or rhythm when used alone. Table 5-3 compares mean coital frequencies among the survey participants by the three categories of contraceptive control. Reported coital frequencies for this group do not fall below the figures for male method users; indeed, for wives between the ages of 25 and 34, mean frequency approaches the figure for coitus-independent methods.

If Japanese couples alternate use of condoms and other nonmedical methods to minimize their obstacles to sexual gratification, we might expect a higher coital frequency among those couples using more methods concurrently. Such a relationship appears to be the case among the traditional method users in the questionnaire sample who reported their coital frequencies; a slight but significant positive correlation emerged between number of methods used and frequency of sexual intercourse.[36]

Attempts to elicit information from interviewees regarding multiple method use met with reticence, probably because the object of multiple use was to diminish hindrances to sexuality rather than to increase contraceptive effectiveness. The most direct expression of preference for rhythm as a means for avoiding condoms came from a 26-year-old wife (a technical junior college graduate), who said that omitting condoms immediately after menstruation gave her "a certain really good psychological feeling." The adjective *natural* also made its way

---

[36] Statistically significant results were obtained using a Pearson correlation of the two variables.

TABLE 5-3
Mean Monthly Coital Frequency* Among
Currently Contracepting Wives by Age and Type
of Contraceptive Method, Tokyo Area Clinic
and Hospital Sample, 1975-1976

	Mean Frequency, by Age			Number of Women, by Age		
	< 25	25-34	35-44	< 25	25-34	35-44
TOTAL USERS	9.8	7.9	6.7	65	298	94
Method Categorized by Relation to Coitus						
Coitus-independent	10.6	8.9	7.4	10	78	43
Coitus-dependent	9.6	7.6	6.1	55	220	51
Method Categorized by Partner Control						
Female	10.6	8.9	7.4	10	87	45
Couple	9.7	8.4	6.1	18	91	21
Male	9.6	6.9	6.0	37	120	28

* Interval midpoints for response categories in weeks were multiplied by a four-week month.

Reprinted with the permission of the Population Council from Samuel J. Coleman, "The cultural context of condom use in Japan," *Studies in Family Planning* 12, no. 1 (January 1981): p. 32.

into informants' discussions of their reasons for using rhythm. The term, when used to describe rhythm, meant "no feeling of using something" (*shiyōkan ga nai*), an implicit contrast with the obtrusive presence of the condom in intercourse.

PATTERNS OF UNWANTED CONCEPTIONS

Although a large proportion of Japanese couples have adopted contraception—a proportion comparable to that of many Western countries—the quality of Japanese contraceptive practice is questionable. The way in which Japanese couples adopt traditional methods and adapt them to their sexuality casts doubt on their ability to reap a high level of protection, and certain indicators of their family planning performance lend further substance to the suspicion.

In Japan, the extent to which married women rely on induced abortion is the most important indicator of how effectively couples are adopting and using contraceptives, particularly in the early years of marriage. As Chapter 1 noted, about seven of every ten abortions in Japan take place among married women, in contrast to the Western pattern, where married women constitute a minority among abortion patients.

Equally noteworthy is the way in which Japanese couples integrate abortion into their childbearing years: in addition to using abortion for limiting, in which a couple resorts to abortion after they have reached their intended number of children, Japanese couples use abortion to postpone their first birth and to maintain a certain length of time between the births they intend to have, a practice called *spacing* births. In the questionnaire sample, 21 percent of the women with childbearing experience had had at least one marital abortion followed by a live birth. Among all of the wives married at least three years, 18 percent had experienced at least one abortion in their first three years of marriage. If we look at the questionnaire respondents' reported abortions which occurred in the five years immediately before the survey was conducted (excluding wives married less than that length of time), we find that over half (33 of 65) were followed by live births.[37] Since the questionnaire sample is composed of women who have not ended their fecund years (average age is 29.5), it

[37] Limiting abortions to those occurring in the last five years minimizes selectivity bias; see Rindfuss, Palmore and Bumpass 1982.

underrepresents abortions to women limiting their family size. On the other hand, however, there is probably some understatement of abortions preceding births, due to an inability to recall or to a desire to conceal them.

Other sources also point to extensive use of induced abortion to space births after marriage. In the nationwide survey conducted in 1969 for the Office of the Prime Minister, a fourth of the women married less than three years reported one or more abortions.[38] The national-level aggregate figures for abortion by age, presented in Table 1-1 in Chapter 1, also suggest a high degree of reliance on abortion among recently married women, given that average age at first marriage for women in that year was 24.9. A Tokyo Ob-Gyn's clinical study of about 1,300 induced abortion patients found that 17 percent of the married sample were newlyweds, and nearly half (47.5 percent) of all marital abortions had taken place in the first two years of marriage.[39]

Nor do induced abortions represent the sum total of unwanted conceptions, since informants' accounts of contraceptive failures in early marriage and Mainichi Survey data indicate that young couples are more apt to carry an initially unwanted pregnancy to term than abort it. In the 1975 Mainichi Survey, 59 percent of currently contracepting wives aged 25 to 29 said they would give birth in the event of a contraceptive failure, in contrast to only about 25 percent of wives aged 35 to 39.[40]

Although about half of newly married couples want to begin childbearing as soon as possible, the rest have some very specific reasons for wanting to wait, ranging from a desire to enjoy life as a couple for a while to very pressing financial considerations. Since employers usually either dismiss working wives who become pregnant or put them in less remunerative employee categories, young wives with jobs often

[38] Naikaku Sōridaijin 1970:17.
[39] Miyamoto 1973.
[40] Okazaki 1977:143.

want to avoid childbearing for a while, usually until they have saved a certain amount of money. Family planning specialists believe that postponement of first births among wives who want to keep their jobs longer is the foremost source of abortions of first pregnancies. The extremely tight housing situation in metropolitan Japan makes it imperative for young couples to avoid childbirth when they live in an apartment complex that does not allow children. Informants provided ample accounts of all of these situations in their own lives as well as in their friends' experiences. A minority of these couples had used contraception or/and abortion, however; more typically, both partners assumed that becoming parents would take some time, were unpleasantly surprised at how quickly a conception took place, and resigned themselves to becoming parents sooner than they had anticipated.

Condom use in alternation with rhythm accounts for a substantial part of unwanted conceptions in Japan. Almost all of the Tokyo area Ob-Gyns questioned on the subject identified alternate rhythm and condom use as the greatest source of contraceptive failure resulting in induced abortion. Although the questionnaire survey did not investigate contraceptive methods used at the time of failure, wives in the interviews attributed 5 of their 14 unwanted pregnancies ending in induced abortions to alternate use of condoms and Ogino rhythm and another 4 to failure to apply condoms. (The remainder resulted from use of no method, or rhythm method used alone.)

Despite the widespread use of periodic methods and their extensive coverage in magazines and family planning education, many couples have not been applying the methods correctly. Doctors and midwives consistently reported widespread ignorance of the Ogino rhythm method, where knowledge was substituted by simple rules like "one week before the period and one after are safe." Family planning educators refered to this as "half-baked Ogino" (*ii kagen no Oginoshiki*). The evaluations of popular knowledge of rhythm offered by family planning workers may have overemphasized ignorance while downplaying other causes of rhythm failure.

Nevertheless, evidence of incorrect applications of safe period methods was common among interviewees. Two of the wives in the interview sample had measured their temperature for the BBT method by placing the thermometer under their armpits. (Axillary temperatures are far too inaccurate for identifying the minute temperature changes associated with ovulation. Both women had since stopped using the method.) Two other couples were omitting condoms "right after the period," and three more were also using crude rules of thumb that were not based on calculations. (In one case, "one week before and after menstruation," another, "one week after," and, in a third case, "five days before and after" were reported.) None of the husbands claimed the ability to calculate the rhythm method, although one (a vasectomy recipient) said that he used to calculate it in the past with his wife.

By the same token, a thorough and correct knowledge of condom use among Japanese men should not be assumed, despite the widespread use and its accompanying familiarity. Some users among informants were uncertain about the point in intercourse at which the condom had to be applied. One user, a 36-year-old high school graduate in a white-collar occupation who complained that condoms were too long for him, was applying them incorrectly by completely unrolling them before application.

THE SWITCH TO MODERN CONTRACEPTION

Although condoms are the universal first contraceptive method for Japanese couples, subsequent years of marriage bring an increasing shift away from condoms to modern medical methods. Figure 8 plots methods among wives using contraception by the number of years they have been married, with methods grouped by condoms only, jointly controlled traditional methods (almost entirely condoms and rhythm), and modern medical methods. According to the survey results, the process takes place within the first six years or so of marriage. Only 11 percent of the women using contraception in their first year of marriage have adopted a modern method, but the figure

Figure 8: Type of Method Used Among
Currently Contracepting Wives by Length of Marriage,
Tokyo Area Clinic and Hospital Sample, 1975-1976

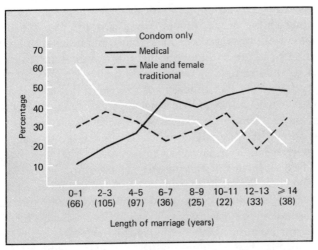

Reprinted with the permission of the Population Council from Samuel J. Coleman, "The cultural context of condom use in Japan," *Studies in Family Planning* 12, no. 1 (January 1981): p. 35.

rises to nearly half (45 percent) among respondents married more than five years.

The simplest explanation for the lower rate of modern method acceptance during the early years of marriage is that couples are postponing or spacing births, so the need for contraceptive effectiveness is not felt as keenly as when the couple later begins to limit family size. Indeed, six or seven years of marriage typically marks the point at which most Japanese couples have attained their intended number of children. As one family planning counselor observed, it is at that point that the wife feels a "sense of urgency" which inspires the search for more effective contraception. This cutoff point for childbearing among many couples results from men's anticipated income changes. In the mid-1970s, a Japanese man marrying at the average age of 27 would anticipate a steep decline in income some 28 years later, with retirement at the age of 55; thus, the couple has only some seven years or so for childbearing, because any children born to them afterward would still be in college (under age 22) and economically dependent when their father's earning ability drops. Among wives, a desire to avoid protracted child-raising obligations, sometimes because of an intention to return to the work-place, also stimulates an early end to childbearing. Between small family size (average fertility was about two children per woman in the early 1970s) and an early end to childbearing, Japanese women's fertility undergoes a sharp drop once women enter their 30s, as the age-specific fertility rates graphed in Figure 9 show. (Late age at marriage and extremely low rates of premarital illegitimacy hold down birth rates in younger age groups.)

Although length of marriage does have a statistically significant effect on the choice of modern contraception that acts independently of other variables, including husband's income level and even the number of living children,[41] this factor does not adequately explain the switch to modern methods, given the extent to which married women in Japan rely on abortion in the early years of their marriages; the timing of births as well as their number is of great importance to Japanese wives, and pills or IUDs would spare them from much of their use of induced abortion if only they would adopt these effective pregnancy preventives earlier in their marriages. The shift to modern contraceptives also represents couples' trials and disappointments with traditional methods that have resulted in both induced abortions and ill-timed births. As Chapter 4 stated, contracepting women in the questionnaire sample who had experienced induced abortions were more likely to be using modern methods over traditional ones. The relationship holds regardless of length of marriage, but it completely dis-

[41] Statistically significant results were obtained when using a multiple regression of a modern/traditional method dummy variable against the following 7 independent variables: wife's educational level, husband's income, length of marriage, number of marital abortions, husband as source of information, professional as source of information, and number of living children.

Figure 9: Comparison of Birth Rates per 1,000 Female Population
in Five-Year Age Groups

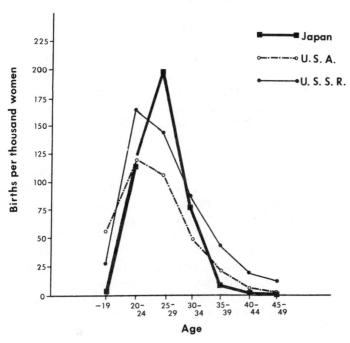

Gross Reproduction Rates	
Japan (1974):	0.990
U.S.A. (1974):	0.904
U.S.S.R. (1973)·	1.182

Source: Calculated from figures in United Nations 1976:582-83, 589.

appears when a more statistically powerful determinant of
modern method use, the number of contraceptive failures experienced since marriage, enters the equation.[42] This means

[42] Statistically significant results were obtained when using a multiple regression of a modern/traditional method dummy variable against

not only that many of the abortions that promote modern method selection result from contraceptive failures, but that the experience of unwelcome pregnancies carried to term has also provided additional impetus to abandon traditional contraception.

The wives who shift to modern contraception have become more independent of their husbands in family planning matters as their marriages mature. As the last chapter noted, women who have been married longer are somewhat less likely to rely on their husbands as a source of family planning information. The wives in the questionnaire survey who used modern methods were especially unlikely to have received any information from their husbands; indeed, as mentioned earlier in this chapter, reliance on a specialist (which was positively related to length of marriage) had a mutually exclusive relationship with the husband's information, despite the option in the questionnaire of indicating that both sources (as well as others) were used simultaneously. With the accumulation of contraceptive failures, wives also became somewhat more likely to state a preference for a contraceptive method over which they themselves could hold control.[43] The process was neatly summed up by a midwife who found some wry humor in the switch to modern methods; when she first saw the graph that became Figure 8 she laughed, and said, "Looks like she can't depend on him and has to do it herself."

Despite the significant shift in method choice among the sample population, modern method users comprise a small minority among those Japanese women using contraception who have been married for more than seven years or so; in

the following eight independent variables: wife's educational level, husband's income, length of marriage, number of marital abortions, husband as source of information, professional as source of information, number of living children, and number of contraceptive failures since marriage.

[43] Statistically significant results were obtained when using a Pearson correlation of the two variables. The preference for contraceptive control variable was recoded with a value of 1 for preference for own control, and 0 for all other respondents.

the mid-1970s, only about 10 percent of wives between the ages of 30 and 45 who were currently using contraception had chosen pills or IUDs, and fewer than 20 percent had ever used pills, IUDs, or sterilization. (The current use percentage of IUDs and oral pills in the major metropolitan areas is no larger than the nationwide proportion, either.)[44] The couples who have stayed with traditional methods have had to adapt to the dual disadvantages of traditional contraceptives, their interference with sex, and the insecurity that stems from their lower effectiveness. Older couples have responded in three ways: confining their contraceptive repertory to one traditional method and accepting the decreased sexual activity that accompanies consistent use, alternating condoms and rhythm and enjoying more opportunities for sex at the expense of effectiveness, or combining condoms and rhythm and experiencing maximum protection that also discourages more frequent intercourse. Neither single nor multiple method users among women in the questionnaire sample married eight years or more had the high frequency of intercourse seen among modern method users of the same age; this latter group had 8.1 acts per month, on the average, compared with 5.2 for single method users and 6.1 for multiple method users. The lack of a significant contrast between these latter two groups[45] probably stems from sizeable numbers of multiple method users who are combining methods for greater effectiveness; in contrast with younger couples using multiple methods, very few older husbands and wives would tolerate the greater possibility of a conception. They have responded by increasing effectiveness at the expense of sexual expression. (The multiple method users do not contrast with wives using only one traditional method in numbers of either contraceptive failures or induced abortions.)

[44] Current use figures calculated from Kōsei-shō 1976a:180; ever-use figures calculated from JOICFP 1977:135.

[45] Results were obtained using a t-test on the means of the frequency of intercourse values for single and multiple traditional method users married eight years or more. (Age averages in all three groups were nearly identical.)

Despite these strategies, adaptation to traditional contraceptive methods sometimes poses a cost to the older couple in unwanted pregnancies as well as in a diminution in frequency of intercourse. In 1975, there were 56,634 abortions reported for women between the ages of 40 and 44, which would mean 13.9 abortions for every thousand women in that age group; using Muramatsu's middle estimate of the actual number performed in that year among married women of those ages, the rate would be 64.2. (The United States rate for women over 40 in 1975 was 3.5.)[46] As these wives near their climacteric, many of them lose their contraceptive vigilance because they believe they are no longer capable of conceiving. The illusion of infecundity is fostered by a low coital frequency, or—ironically enough—by years of diligent contraceptive practice.

The research samples provided too few couples in the twilight years of their reproductive careers for an investigation of their contraceptive performance, but many Ob-Gyns and family planning counselors described the syndrome of assumed infecundity as a typical source of unwanted pregnancy among older couples. One of the interviewee wives, a 34-year-old girls' high-school graduate, poses an extreme example due to her relative youth, but her perceptions offer some substantiation of the descriptions offered by clinicians. She believed that she was sterile, even though she had given birth less than two years before the time of the interview, and she gave her age as one reason for her inabiltiy to conceive. Her exaggerated perception of her inability to conceive also stemmed from her misunderstanding of a doctor's diagnosis of a tipped (retroflex) uterus, but the couple's low coital frequency of about three times a month decreased the chances of pregnancy even though the couple was not making systematic use of contraception.

Abortions among women over forty years of age and the

---

[46] Figures were calculated using Kōsei-shō 1976a, 1975 Census of Japan, and Muramatsu 1978:95; the United States figure appears in Tietze 1979:49.

"syndrome of assumed infecundity" would both be far less frequent if couples relied more on contraceptive sterilization and if older women had a more sophisticated knowledge of their bodies. Like the difficulties that young couples experience in regulating their fertility, these problems highlight the poverty of family planning options provided in present-day Japanese culture despite that country's modernity and affluence. Some couples have broken out of the dominant pattern, however, and these couples differ from others in a number of important respects. Their example makes other Japanese couples' adherence to the unhappy status quo more understandable.

CHAPTER 6

Conjugal Roles and Women's Status

Taking the initiative to find an appropriate contraceptive method and then cooperating with one's partner for effective use can be difficult tasks in any culture. In Japan, not only is considerable effort required of the individual couple because resources for preventing conception are particularly meager; the nature of marital roles and women's low status combine to discourage successful responses to these challenges. The small minority of couples who have dealt with the problem most effectively stand apart by virtue of the wives' educational background.

CONJUGAL ROLE ORGANIZATION
AND CONTRACEPTION

The hypothesis that marital life-style may predispose couples to more effective contraceptive method adoption and use was developed and tested in the late 1950s and early 1960s in the United States by the sociologist Lee Rainwater.[1] His studies examined couples' organization of domestic tasks and activities as well as the nature of emotional interaction between spouses. Elaborating on a classification posed earlier by the British anthropologist Elizabeth Bott, Rainwater proposed a continuum for classifying couples in which conjugal role relationships ranged from jointly organized to highly segregated. In jointly organized relationships, tasks are carried out by both spouses at once or are executed by either partner at different times; leisure activities are shared, and couples exhibit a high degree of mutuality in their emotional interaction, including sympathy and an interest in those activities of the partner that are not shared, such as the husband's life at work.

[1] Rainwater 1965; cf. also Rainwater 1960.

At the other extreme are couples who have segregated their activities to the point of minimal sharing or interchangeability. These couples define their responsibilities in terms of the formal gender roles "husband/wife" or "father/mother," and their leisure pursuits are largely separate; empathy and interest in the other partner's concerns are minimal.

Between these two polar extremes stands the "intermediate" relationship that possesses a degree of role flexibility but preserves the basic allocation of labor by gender status. The degree of emotional interpenetration and communication, though higher than in segregated role relationships, does not attain the level found among couples having joint role relationships. Leisure activities conducted by both partners at a shared place and time but without interaction epitomize the intermediate role relationship: in these situations the husband and wife may be reading or watching television together, but they do not discuss their reactions with one another.

Rainwater found that those couples in joint role relationships used contraception most consistently and effectively; the results suggest that successful contraceptive adoption and use comes most readily to those couples who have more flexibility in their marital roles and a high degree of emotional mutuality. The relationship makes sense: effective use of contraception, especially with traditional contraceptive methods, is the quintessence of a task requiring the involvement of both parties, since the object—sexual gratification without conception—commands the concern and affects the interests of both partners. Since both partners have interests to protect and yet need the other spouse's cooperation on a consistent basis, a commitment to negotiation and skill in bringing about mutually satisfactory decisions is highly important. Such couples prefer working out problems together. Bott's study of conjugal roles in England found that couples who had many shared and interchangeable domestic tasks also placed importance on making decisions together.[2] In addition, couples who have had practice in joint decision-making become familiar with

[2] Bott 1957:54.

one another's response patterns and are more at ease in expressing their own desires, both of which are extremely important for coordinating behavior in an area that has high emotional stakes.

There were, however, class-related factors mentioned by Rainwater that could reduce the effect of conjugal role relationships on the quality of contraceptive practice. In the United States (and Great Britain), class status generally stands in a positive relationship with the degree of conjugal role integration; the higher the couple's social class, the more they resemble the joint type on the continuum. In Rainwater's study, there was a consistent increase in the proportion of couples in joint role relationships from lower-lower class to upper-middle class, and a decrease in segregated relationships to the point where they did not appear among middle-class couples.[3]

Most middle-class subjects in the study had received contraceptive guidance from specialists, and a large majority were using—as one would suspect, given such guidance—the diaphragm, spermicides, and the then recently introduced pill.[4] Reliance on Ob-Gyns reflects not only the couple's predilections but their ability to pay for the services of specialized private practitioners as well. The quality of the services—plus the availability of the pill—must surely have exerted an independent positive effect on the acceptance and optimal application of the methods provided. The availability of these services to middle-class couples probably explains the lack of a clear-cut relationship between good contraceptive practice and conjugal role organization in that group; the middle-class couples in Rainwater's study were more likely both to adopt more physiologically effective methods and to exercise more consistent application of their methods at an earlier point in marriage, regardless of whether their conjugal role relationships were joint or intermediate.

Since the time of Rainwater's research, developments in family planning in the United States have minimized the prac-

---

[3] *Ibid.*:56-57; Rainwater 1965:32.
[4] Rainwater 1965:216-19, 222-23, 297.

tical significance of conjugal role studies for issues in contraceptive practice; modern contraceptive methods that allow the separation of pregnancy prevention from sexual behavior have been made available on a subsidized basis to a large portion of the country's population, along with increasingly sophisticated and sympathetic guidance. In present-day Japan, however, conjugal role organization still affects contraceptive method adoption and use patterns, because the country lacks an active family planning program that provides modern contraceptive methods.

ROLE SEGREGATION IN JAPANESE CONTRACEPTIVE ADOPTION AND USE

The previous chapter's description of contraceptive method adoption in Japan points to a lack of integrated effort between husband and wife. Couples rarely adopt a contraceptive method through joint effort and information sharing between spouses. Few couples decide together on their first contraceptive method, even though their stated ideal is to share decision-making. Nor does a longer marriage encourage more pooling of effort. As was noted, women who have been married longer are also less likely to rely on their husbands as a source of contraceptive information; his role as information provider is *replaced* rather than supplemented by other sources. The tendency for couples to allocate the responsibility for contraception to one partner or the other is also reflected in the term used by informants to designate the partner responsible for contraception, -*makase*, meaning that it is left entirely up to the spouse named. (*Ottomakase*, for example, means entrusted to the husband.)

The deficiencies in contraceptive practice among Japanese couples resemble those of American couples with segregated conjugal role relationships in Rainwater's study. In both instances, family planning is marked by delayed adoption of contraception, ineffective use after a method is first adopted, and deficient cooperation from husbands. The resemblance extends further: husbands and wives in present-day Japan lead their marital lives with a high degree of gender-based task specialization, separate activities, and a relatively low degree of emotional interdependence and communication.

THE JAPANESE CONJUGAL DIVISION OF LABOR

The casual Western observer of Japanese home life typically gets the impression that the husband takes little part in domestic tasks. The impression has been corroborated by a time-use study conducted in ten Euro-American countries and Japan; Japanese men ranked lowest, in both absolute amount of time spent in household tasks and errands as well as in a ratio of men's to women's hours of housework. Japanese men averaged 24 minutes of weekly time spent in household tasks and errands as opposed to an overall average of 83 minutes for men in each of the other countries investigated. As a ratio of women's housework, this represents one hour for every 10.8 hours of women's housework time, in contrast with ratios ranging from 2.3 to 5.4 for the other countries studied.[5] In a survey published by the Japanese government from the same period (the early 1970s), over half of the wives questioned claimed that their husbands gave them no help at all.[6] In the questionnaire survey, 36 percent reported "practically no help" from husbands.

When men do participate in household tasks, it is most typically taking out and putting away bedding quilts and pads (*futon*). Some husbands tidy up one area of the dwelling from time to time, such as the couple's bedroom or the husband's recreation area if the home has one. There is very little in the way of shopping or kitchen tasks performed by husbands. Many have one or two favorite dishes that they are able to prepare, but their repertoire does not include cleaning the kitchen area afterward. Washing and ironing of clothing are

[5] (Calculated using figures in Keizaikikaku-chō, 1973a:60.) Data for the ten Euro-American countries in the study—the United States, West Germany, France, Belgium, Hungary, Czechoslovakia, Yugoslavia, Poland, Bulgaria, and the Soviet Union—were gathered in 1965-66; Japanese data were gathered in 1972.

[6] Cited in Fujin Chōsakai 1974:221.

tasks that are most rarely performed by husbands. With the exception of "Sunday carpenter" home repairs, the husbands' household task participation is confined to very simple, brief activities.

The low level of domestic task sharing and interchangeability between spouses also applies to child-raising activities. Husbands are absent from the day-to-day activities of child-rearing, a separation that is evident from the time their children are born. Few men are present at the hospital when their wives give birth; they are either at work or at home (presumably resting for work, given the late hour of many births) when they receive the news of their children's birth. In one study, only a fourth of the 210 husbands of women delivering in a Niigata Prefecture hospital were at the hospital when their children were born. Almost all of the rest were either at work or home.[7] It is also common practice for the wife to return to her family of origin to give birth and remain with them for 6 to 12 weeks in order to recuperate and receive infant care help from her own mother, in part because husbands do not help by assuming a larger share of household chores.

The most typical form of father-child interaction is to bathe together, although many husbands say that they return home from work too late for that. Taking children to a nearby park is another such activity. Interestingly enough, interviewee fathers were inclined to identify these activities as assistance to their wives in domestic tasks as opposed to shared recreation or interaction with their children. It is not unusual for a father to help his older children with their homework, but such help rarely takes place on a regular basis.

More often than not, husbands explain their non-participation in domestic tasks by pointing to their economic support of the family and the long hours that their jobs require, or they simply state that work leaves them too tired to do anything after returning home. Their claims of long work hours are validated by the international time study referred to ear-

[7] Murayama 1976.

lier; Japanese men ranked highest in hours devoted to work in comparison with men in the other ten industrialized countries.[8] In the interviews, as well, it was not unusual for husbands to report work-days beginning with departing from the home before 8:00 a.m. and ending with their return at 8:00 or 9:00 p.m. Staying overtime and putting in extra hours at the work-place is an extremely common occurrence, as well as working on Saturdays. Long commutes from home to work-place and back also extend the husband's absence; average one-way commutes in the Tokyo area are over an hour.

Both husbands and wives tend to evaluate the man's performance as husband primarily in terms of his dedication to his work and his ability to support his family. A study of family role expectations conducted by Koyama Takashi et al. found Japanese wives' strongest expectation toward their husbands to be "enthusiasm for work"; the converse, her cooperation in economic matters, is lowest among husbands' expectations.[9] The centrality of the husband's role as economic supporter of the family also figures prominently in marital quarrels; according to one newspaper survey, titled "A Collection of Tabooed Words That Depress Husbands," invectives like "Your pay's low," "You haven't got the wits to succeed" (*kaishōnashi*), and invidious comparisons with the salaries of other husbands rank highest on the list.[10]

Child-raising responsibilities are highly concentrated on the individual mother in Japanese society. Because of increased urbanization and fragmentation of families into nuclear units in the postwar period, women have lost both the assistance and expertise of mothers and mothers-in-law. At the same time, however, there has not been a compensatory increase in participation from husbands. Substitutive child care is particularly scarce in Japan. Day-care facilities for children are at a premium.[11] Baby-sitting is infrequently practiced; ac-

[8] Keizaikikaku-chō 1973a:54-55; Keizaikikaku-chō 1976:105-07.
[9] Koyama 1967:102-03.
[10] *Sankei Ribingu* 1976c:12.
[11] Fujin Chōsakai 1974:234-42; Yamashita 1974:20, 188.

cording to informants, women are very reluctant to assume responsibility for looking after someone else's child.

Certain child-raising obligations also intensify the amount of energy and attention required of the mother. Pre-school-age Japanese children experience few restrictions on behavior; their freedom to roam and explore is kept from reaching destructive (or self-destructive) limits by the ever-attentive mother, who is prepared to intercede at the critical moment or else to keep the child distracted with innocuous interests, as opposed to disciplining the child against initiating such behavior in the first place. Educational functions performed by mothers are quite extensive. In Japan, a larger part of the responsibility for the quality of education falls on each child's family, as opposed to the public sector. Public expenditures on education below the university level are relatively low compared to the United States and Europe.[12] Schools present mothers with numerous demands to outfit their children correctly, supplement their classroom education, and participate in parent-teacher conferences. A woman who excels in this capacity is labeled an "education mama" (*kyōiku mama*), a familiar expression for the zealous mother who takes every step possible to assure her children's entry into the best possible college (which in turn assures attractive employment possibilities). If a child succeeds academically, non-family members assume that it is due in large part to the mother's efforts.

The centrality of childbearing and child-raising to the Japanese wife's life expresses itself in demographic facts and opinion surveys as well. The percentage of couples who do not have children is surprisingly small. In 1974, only 4.7 percent of ever-married women between 30 and 34 years of age had not given birth to at least one child,[13] in contrast to 10.5 percent of American women in the same category in 1976.[14] An even smaller proportion of Japanese women claim that they intend to remain childless; among both married and un-

[12] Monbu-shō 1976:145; Yamamura and Hanley 1975:106.
[13] Kōsei-shō 1976b:16.
[14] U.S. Bureau of the Census 1977:34.

married women surveyed, the figure ranges from 1 to 3 percent.[15] A comparable figure for all women under age 35 in the United States in 1976 would be 10 percent,[16] although this figure does reflect a recent swelling in the ranks of American women intending to remain childless. Japanese women most frequently respond to opinion survey questions on the activities they find worthwhile by citing their children,[17] and numerous commercials and advertisements in Japan's mass media depict mothers and children enjoying various products together.

There are other indications of the considerable emotional investment in childbearing. My own impression from discussions and review of the media is that infertility receives more attention and provokes more anxiety in Japan than in the United States. In one newspaper item, for example, local police authorities attributed the suicide of a 29-year-old housewife to her despondency over an inability to bear children.[18] The importance of childbearing also manifests itself in feelings of competition with other mothers and insecurity regarding one's own ability to raise children correctly. Such insecurity can assume in new mothers a morbid condition known as "child-raising neurosis" (*ikuji noirōze*), characterized by profound depression. There are no reliable estimates of the frequency of occurrence of this disturbance, but a few of the Ob-Gyns interviewed take special care in observing new mothers who show signs of despondency.

The intensive responsibilities and energy demands of child-raising on the individual Japanese mother also figure heavily in women's decisions to abort for the purpose of increasing the time interval between births. Most interviewee wives who had had induced abortions stated that caring for an infant made them too tired or too weak to undergo the birth of another child. Medical social workers also observed that ex-

[15] Kōsei-shō 1978:43; Mainichi Shinbun 1979:10; Yuzawa 1971:50.
[16] U.S. Bureau of the Census 1977:14.
[17] Fujin Chōsakai 1974:102, 108-09, 317.
[18] Mainichi Shinbun 1975b.

haustion from infant care was a major reason among wives
for seeking abortions.

Leisure activities in Japanese marital life also conform to a
more segregated pattern of role relationships. Japanese couples typically choose leisure activities that may allow a common locus for activity but do not involve interaction. According to time use surveys, a larger part of free time is spent
in viewing television and in resting than in other industrialized
societies.[19] A few of the interviewee husbands and wives reported that they enjoyed listening to music together. Women
tend to choose hobbies that are either an extension of their
housework activities, like sewing or shopping, or cultural classes
in flower arranging or traditional music. Men's favorite sports
activities, fishing and golf, are not shared with their wives.

Japanese couples with children rarely set aside time for
leisure as a couple only. A 1973 government-sponsored survey
of married couples in Japan and in ten other countries (six of
which are industrialized) ranked Japan lowest in the percentage of couples reporting that they went out for recreation
together without their children. A third of the parents of junior-high-school children surveyed in 1971 by the Asahi newspaper claimed that they never went out as a twosome without
their children.[20] Among the interviewees, shared outings for
most couples were all but confined to shopping trips accompanied by their children. Vacation travel almost invariably
proved to be the most enjoyable activity as a couple for both
partners, but such outings were rare; those that extended over
more than one day were confined to major holidays once or
twice a year.

Even when the couple is at home, ostensibly engaging in
leisure activity, the prevailing segregation of roles by gender
limits the degree of genuine recreation in their time spent

[19] Keizaikikaku-chō 1976:109-10.
[20] Both studies are cited in Fujin Chōsakai 1974:390, 104, 106.

together. The 11-country time use study found a telling contrast in the time wives spend in housework on weekdays and
on Sunday: housework time generally decreased in the Western countries studied, but in Japan it actually increased.[21] The
group conducting the study interpreted this phenomenon as
the Japanese wife's desire to "demonstrate" her diligence in
housework to her husband. There is also an alternate interpretation, more in line with my own observations made during
visits to Japanese homes: on Sundays and holidays, when
husband and children are home, the wife spends more of her
time seeing after their needs, in particular serving them meals
and snacks. This explanation also gains support from housewives' statements obtained in a study on leisure–time use,
such as "I'm busy all day long [on Sundays and holidays]
fixing food for my husband and child" (a 35-year-old college
graduate with one son), and "I'm all the busier because I'm
constantly attending to keeping my husband company" (a 42-
year-old high-school graduate with two children).[22]

When husbands do take off more time from work and spend
it at home in the prevailing style which makes continuous
demands on their wives' services, wives are understandably
ambivalent about—or even, in some cases, openly opposed
to—their husbands' use of their home for recreation. The label
"my-home type" (*mai hōmu taipu*, phrased using English loan
words) for the husband who spends more time at home derives
its pejorative ring from this image of indolence, as well as the
attendant supposition that the husband lacks ambition and
industriousness.

EMOTIONAL INTERACTION AND COMMUNICATION

The segregation of conjugal role relationships acts to sub-
merge spouses' individual personality differences beneath a
uniformity imposed by the themes of husband as breadwinner
and wife as housekeeper and mother. This effect was exhibited

[21] Keizaikikaku-chō 1973b:50-51.
[22] Fujin Chōsakai 1974:375, 378.

most vividly in the intensive interviews, when spouses were asked what they liked most about their partners. Wives consistently referred to their husbands' dedication to work and their dependability in that capacity, well over and above reference to shared interests or personality traits they found appealing. More often than not, husbands referred to their wives' homemaking skills and their ability to handle domestic matters smoothly and without any problems. Typical of such husbands is a 38-year-old section chief at a major corporation, who said, "I can just leave the whole household to her and she'll take care of things well." A few husbands referred to their wives' personality traits, a favorite term being "bright" or "cheerful" (*akarui*). These men, however, were unable to elaborate or give specific examples of the expression of this personality trait; basically, they seemed to look to their wives for a pleasant and relaxing atmosphere at home, free of interpersonal problems.

The forms of address that spouses use for one another also indicate the subordination of personalities to formal roles. It is not uncommon for husbands and wives to call one another by parent terms like "*papa*" and "*mama*." A questionnaire survey of Tokyo area apartment complex (*danchi*) couples in their 20s and 30s found that these forms of address were the most frequent, outnumbering first names or nicknames.[23]

Another typical theme for both spouses that emerged in response to the question of most-liked traits in their marriage partners was essentially the absence of a negative trait: the propensity for expressing dissatisfaction. These responses signal a high degree of emotional autonomy—if not a certain kind of emotional territoriality. The 33-year-old wife of the section chief (like her husband, a college graduate) said, "I like it that he doesn't gripe." Husbands said of their wives that they were "not bothersome" (*urusakunai*). Maintaining this kind of modus vivendi appears an important element in the Japanese marriage. As a response to the casual discussion question to husbands of how they like their wives' cooking,

[23] *Asahi Shinbun* 1976b.

one is apt to hear, "I eat it all and don't complain." When asked about how household chores were allocated in her home, one 35-year-old housewife (a junior-high-school graduate) replied that her husband did none, saying "In return for not complaining [to me] he doesn't give me any help."

The extent of verbal communication between Japanese husbands and wives is legendarily low, in part because of other features of segregation in conjugal roles; since there are fewer shared or interchangeable activities and experiences in Japanese conjugal role organization, there is simply less to coordinate and comment upon, and this, too, means fewer occasions for communicating. Then, too, greater emotional autonomy also results in a lower volume of verbal exchange. Another explanation offered by some informants has some validity also: the high degree of homogeneity in Japanese society, which extends to husband and wife relations, brings about shared understandings, in turn obviating the need for communication. (There is a term for such "unspoken understanding," *ishin denshin*.)

De-emphasis of the emotional, affective component of marriage in Japan is also reflected in—and perpetuated by—the practice of arranged marriage, which accounted for about a third of new unions in the major urban centers in 1973.[24] The process contrasts starkly with the emphasis on personality factors that lies behind dating in the West, especially in the United States, where the institution has been widespread since the end of World War I.[25] Since the pair brought together by arranged marriage are introduced by a third party and have minimal interaction before making the decision to marry or not, the criteria for their choice of a marriage partner cannot give much attention to personality features. (Information passed from go-betweens to prospective spouses does include attention to the general issue of personality, but go-betweens' de-

[24] Kōsei-shō 1974:7.

[25] See Udry 1974:884-87 for a historical and functional account of dating in marriage partner selection.

scriptions typically take the form of rather stereotyped traits like "quiet and reserved.")

CLASS AND CONJUGAL ROLE RELATIONSHIPS

Although the comparison of conjugal roles in Japan and the West helps to explain Japanese couples' family planning style and performance, any contrast of family planning behavior by marital role type *among* Japanese couples would be severely limited by the much narrower range of conjugal life-styles in Japan than is seen in the United States, where Rainwater conducted his studies. If couples throughout Japan were to be classified in terms of conjugal role relationships, the distribution would have far less representation near the joint end of the continuum than it would have for a distribution of American couples. Of the 22 couples interviewed, only 2 displayed extensive integration in their relationship, despite the sample's preponderance of more well-educated interviewees in higher income brackets.

The reasons for the abbreviated range of role relationships in Japan lie in different effects of class status on marital lifestyle. Japan does, of course, have social classes. Income distribution in Japan does not differ much from the distributions found in Western countries,[26] and Japanese society has a wide range of educational levels and occupational statuses. Higher level occupations among Japanese men encourage *greater* role segregation, however, because higher occupational status brings more demands for work-related socializing and recreation. Responses to a questionnaire item asking how often husbands go out on late social engagements showed that men in the professions and upper levels of management had by far the highest frequency of outings; educational level and income were also positively related to the frequency of outings. (Both of these relationships were statistically significant, and the

[26] Keizaikikaku-chō 1975:33-34.

frequency of outings was unrelated to length of marriage.)[27] In addition, these men do not usually make their homes a place for recreation or a showplace of professional accomplishment outfitted with den or library. Their wives rarely if ever entertain business colleagues, and the home is only recently becoming a place to bring co-workers or professional acquaintances. Marriage counselors noted that the husband's job commitments which draw him away from domestic life assume their greatest intensity among white-collar workers at the chief clerk level (*kakari-chō*) and above who desire promotion.

Another factor that could hinder class-related differentiation in conjugal role organization applies to couples in the early years of marriage. Since incomes for men at higher educational levels do not appreciably rise above those for the less-educated until the employee enters his late 30s,[28] young couples with higher class backgrounds do not enjoy appreciably greater discretionary spending for shared leisure. By contrast, some older couples in somewhat lower social strata whose children are in high school or college appear to have a higher frequency of shared activities because of both their ability to afford travel and entertainment, and the fact that their children no longer require attention and supervision.

The incidence of arranged marriage in the higher social strata indicates a high proportion of segregated role relationships even among couples in the upper classes. There is no decrease in the proportion of arranged marriages among higher socioeconomic levels; if anything, there may be an increase (brides with higher educational levels living in large urban centers are slightly more likely to have marriages that were arranged),[29] and arranged marriages are popularly regarded as more respectable or higher-status than love-match mar-

---

[27] Results were obtained using a multiple regression of the variable for frequency of husband's outings with the following three independent variables: husband's educational level, husband's income, and length of marriage.

[28] Keizaikikaku-chō 1976:174-75.

[29] Kōsei-shō 1968:40.

riages. Some of these arranged marriages within the higher social strata may be made for the consolidation and perpetuation of family property (examples include the daughters of doctors with their own hospitals who hope to bequeath their facilities to a promising young specialist in the same field). Another function of the arranged marriage is to provide introductions to individuals who are not easily able to meet eligible members of the opposite sex on their own, and the young man on an elite career path typically finds himself in that situation; having entered the most desirable white-collar job via the top university, he is likely to have spent his entire adolescence in a cloistered existence studying for entrance examinations, thus excluding himself from interaction with women. Once he has entered the company or government bureau, his social life is centered around the work-place, with few opportunities for meeting members of the opposite sex (excluding office staff) and little skill and experience in handling such encounters with ease.

WOMEN'S STATUS AS A FACTOR IN FAMILY PLANNING

Women's status is an indispensable consideration for understanding a culture's family planning pattern. Most obviously, a woman's status—that is, her ability to command a favorable situation vis-à-vis men through her own influence or bargaining power—affects her ability to avoid unwanted pregnancies. A woman's independent efforts to meet her family planning needs also depend on her status, since higher status confers more self-confidence and initiative. The more self-reliant and independent a woman is, the more she will be willing and able to seek and use resources that, in feminist phraseology, give her "control over her own body."

The woman's status also plays an implicit part in shaping conjugal role relationships, which in turn influence the quality of family planning practice. The shared decision-making that marks joint role relationships can only take place when the wife has authority or bargaining power. By the same token, communication is a function of status when it concerns issues that directly affect both partners. The wider the differential in power, the greater the disincentives to communicate: where a favorable condition for one spouse who has much more power is also unfavorable for the other spouse, the more powerful party is satisfied and has no need to comment; the disfavored spouse is discouraged from making appeals because of the high probability of a flat refusal, which can only engender embarrassment and irritation. As the power differential lessens, the person enjoying the more favorable position becomes obligated to justify and rationalize, if not concede, and the person with the less favorable position is emboldened to make direct requests and proposals in a more open process of negotiation. Unless the petitioner stands a reasonable expectation of compliance, however, the issue must either be left as is or more subtle, roundabout techniques must be employed.

The husband's capacity for empathy—another diagnostic of conjugal role relationships—also reflects the woman's status, practically by definition: by participating in her feelings, her husband takes an important step toward helping her attain more favorable conditions for herself.

Women's status poses a particularly relevant issue for Japanese family planning not only because such a large part of responsibility for contraception falls to men by virtue of widespread condom use, but because some critical features of Japanese contraceptive practice suggest a low status position for women. Chapter 5 asserted that Japanese men do not give the high level of effort required for maximum condom effectiveness, nor are they inclined to accept vasectomies if the couple has reached their intended family size and has decided on sterilization. Both correct condom use and acceptance of vasectomy pose costs to husbands that their wives have not been able to override through greater bargaining power. Men's lack of more rigorous condom use results from their dislike of the method's dulling effect on sexual sensation. Resistance to vasectomy stems, in large part, from fear of the procedure itself; informants who had had vasectomies were often asked about pain by male friends, an observation which concurs with the clinical observations of the prominent urologist Kaneko Eiju, who believes that fear of the surgery itself is the greatest objection to the procedure among Japanese men.

Japanese wives assume a passive stance toward contraception, despite their personal stake in the issue. The most telling sign of female passivity lies in the way Japanese couples adopt their first contraceptive method: despite the consequences to the wife of unwanted pregnancy, she defers the matter to her husband and the couple end up using condoms. The young wife's lack of assertion also strikes Japanese family planning specialists as contrary to her interests. Commenting on the Yamanouchi survey of newlyweds, Kon Yasuo asked: "How can we understand the small number of cases where the wife proposed and determined the method? One would think that, since it is the wife who becomes pregnant, shouldn't she be more assertive about it?"[30]

Only after experiencing contraceptive failures do a noticeable proportion of women seek modern, female-controlled methods. Perhaps the younger wife assumes that, unless proved otherwise, her husband is competent and knowledgeable in all areas. To some Japanese family planning specialists, the women who leave contraception in their husbands' hands are responding to the principle of husbandly "leadership" (*shudōken*). This stance does not result from husbands who object to their wives' use of female contraceptive methods. The heart of the issue, rather, is the woman's inability to assume responsibility, which then makes the husband the "leader." Indeed, as we have seen, nearly half of those survey wives using contraception who indicated the desire for a method that they themselves could control were in reality sharing control with their husbands or giving it over to them entirely.

Japanese women also lack an ideology which legitimates female control of contraception. The prevailing view of childbearing described in Chapter 4, which pits the "child as gift from God" (*sazukarimono*) against the "child as personal

[30] Kon 1973:116.

product" (*tsukuru mono*), leaves no room for a positive depiction of the woman who individually decides on the number
and timing of her own births. Even Japanese feminists are
ambivalent about giving women such discretion. A guest ed-
itorial in the Mainichi newspaper, which linked birth control
to various abuses of motherhood via the "child as product"
mentality, quoted Yamada Mitsuko, one of the translators of
the American women's self-help book, *Our Bodies, Ourselves*,
wondering "whether the attainment of 100 percent effective
contraception really is such a good thing for humanity."[31]

Women's passivity in matters of reproduction might also
affect the acceptability of periodic methods of contraception
by virtue of two of their features which are unique among
contraceptive methods. First, they are based on the same principle as fertilization itself; the same concept can be—and
sometimes is—used by Japanese wives to maximize their chances
of conceiving. Second, contraception based on phases of the
ovulatory cycle lacks the volitional element required of other
female methods, in that the calendar or BBT graph "tells" a
woman if unprotected intercourse is safe or not. As one medical social worker observed, the matter is entrusted to the
"dictates of Nature" (*shizen no setsuri*, also translated as Di-
vine Providence), and the results, including pregnancy, are
beyond one's control. The women informants who were using
the rhythm method described it positively as "natural (*shi-
zenteki*), a term that has extremely strong appeal in descriptions of contraceptive method attributes. The word apparently
applies because it highlights the fact that rhythm and BBT
operate in a natural cycle as opposed to the action of chemicals, but the nuance of letting nature take its course also
pertains. (Recall, for example, how some interviewee spouses
described their choice of their first contraceptive method as a
"natural" happening.)

Japanese women also engage in a negotiating style that is
symptomatic of low status. The low degree of communication
between Japanese spouses could be the result of an imbalance

[31] Itō 1976.

in power. The dynamic, as described above, probably lies behind the explanation of Japanese marital non-communication offered by a college-educated husband in his early thirties: "we already know too much."

As in other dimensions of conjugal life, wives' approaches to their husbands in family planning issues may rely on indirectness and manipulation. (Examples that I witnessed included a wife who understated the price of a household appliance to her husband in order to gain his consent and then paid the difference from her own secret savings, and a wife who first applied for and obtained a part-time job before asking for her husband's approval to work.)

Two of the wives in the interview sample had attempted to negotiate a family planning issue with their husbands using indirect approaches. In both cases the wives wanted their husbands to have vasectomies. One, a 37-year-old high-school graduate, had suggested vasectomy to her husband, the 43-year-old college graduate introduced in the last chapter. She broached the subject as a joke, however, saying "now it's your turn," laughing as she spoke. The "turn" referred to the three induced abortions that she had had since marriage, between two live births. By laughing, she partially defused the assertiveness of her remark, leaving a face-saving avenue for herself if he were to reject her suggestion, which he did; the husband felt that switching to vasectomy or any other method was "not particularly necessary."

The second wife was more successful. (She was 41 years old, a high-school graduate, and he was a 49-year-old with a prewar commercial school education who had become successful in an advertising and public relations firm.) When she became pregnant after the couple's last wanted birth, she told her husband that it was necessary to abort the pregnancy because the conception resulted from intercourse when he was drunk, which meant risking a mentally defective child. Then, after consulting with her Ob-Gyn, she chose a urologist who was very zealous in promoting vasectomy; her husband went to him for a "discussion" and left with a sterilization.

Empathy is an important factor in the sequence observed

by Ob-Gyns in which wives who have experienced induced abortions investigate the method and persuade their husbands to accept it, using the fact that they had to undergo surgery themselves as an argument. According to one doctor, the men who accept are "husbands who dote on their wives" (*aisaika*), who dislike the idea of their wives undergoing surgery.

Empathy—or the lack of it—could be playing a part in another important aspect of family planning in Japan, the maintenance of an adequate time interval between wanted births. The husbands interviewed did not share their wives' intensity of concern about spacing births. When wives in the interview sample were asked what in their opinion was an ideal length of time between births, their most common answer was three years or "two to three years," accompanied by vivid description of the energy demands of care for infants not yet toilet trained. The possibility of children born within a year of one another (for which there is a term in Japanese, *toshigo*) was roundly rejected as a "horrendous" child-rearing demand. (The word typically heard was *taihen*, also meaning "awful" or "immense.") Wives were also concerned that children spaced too far apart (over four years) would be unable to relate to one another as siblings and play together, which would in turn increase the burden of parental attention. Another theme was the desire to avoid prolonging the most difficult years of child-raising by waiting more than three years.

The husbands, on the other hand, tended to give figures for ideal intervals that were shorter than their wives'. The content of men's responses strongly suggested that they were not able to recognize the undesirability of a conception within two years of childbirth with the conviction displayed by their wives. Fewer husbands mentioned the work demands than did their wives, and their reasoning typically lacked detail. In the case of one couple with a child 20 months old, the husband (a 29-year-old college graduate) said he had no reasons for the birth interval that he gave except that he knew it was his wife's opinion. The more explicit men's answers involved the effects of nearness of age on the children's relationships with one another as siblings, an issue that also attracted the attention of their wives. Wives, however, were much more likely to talk about such personality development problems in terms of their significance as extra parental child-raising demands. These observations complement the statements of a few family planning workers that men fail to cooperate in contraception because they lack a sense of the importance of adequate birth spacing.

THE IMPORTANT FACTOR OF EDUCATION

Education is an important determinant of women's family planning performance not only because it enables the understanding of different contraceptive methods and their proper use, but also, more significantly, because it provides higher status for women. In modern industrialized societies, education confers marketable skills and assets and thus increases the woman's economic power. A more diffuse but nonetheless important effect is the enhancement of the personality traits of assertiveness and self-reliance, because the individual woman has learned to assimilate information and to exercise initiative in assessing problems and solving them independently.

These effects of education on women's status are indeed discernible in present-day Japanese society. The most tangible contribution to status is the labor market, where industrial wage scales not only are higher for those women with more education, but also rise consistently with age for employees with education beyond high school, unlike the downward drift that working women with less education experience once they enter their 30s.[32] The Japanese themselves commonly believe that higher education makes women less passive and compliant. When asked about their intentions for their children's education, some of the interviewees with daughters expressed the fear that college would make their daughters "obstinate" (*ijippari*). One interviewee whose wife has far less education than he (he is a 30-year-old college graduate but his 24-year-old wife's education stopped at junior high school) was the

[32] Rōdō-shō 1976b:5.

most explicit, saying that "If girls get too much education they don't want to get married." (Husbands who intended to provide college education for their daughters or give them their choice in the matter were married to women with college educations.)

The Japanese wife's educational level does significantly affect her family planning practice. Among the questionnaire respondents, higher educational levels afforded increasingly greater protection against induced abortion: those with the most education reported the fewest abortions, when length of marriage was controlled. There is also a hint about husband-wife status dynamics in the effects of his income and her educational level on frequency of abortion: wives with high educational backgrounds married to husbands with low incomes had the fewest abortions (again, regardless of length of marriage).[33]

More education also generates greater acceptance of modern contraceptive methods. Contracepting wives in the survey were progressively more likely to have adopted a modern method as their educational level went up, a relationship that maintained statistical significance regardless of the husband's income, length of marriage, and the number of contraceptive failures.[34] Mainichi survey results also show a tendency for greater use of the pill and IUD among women in higher educational categories.[35] In addition, Japanese wives with more education are increasingly more likely to begin contraception earlier in their marriages. In the 1975 Mainichi survey, only

[33] Results were obtained when using a multiple regression of the total number of marital abortions against the following five independent variables: length of marriage, husband's income, wife's educational level, wife's income, and husband's educational level.

[34] Statistically significant results were obtained when using a multiple regression of a modern/traditional method dummy variable against the following seven independent variables: wife's educational level, husband's income, length of marriage, number of marital abortions, husband as source of information, professional as source of information, and number of living children.

[35] Okazaki 1977:135.

8 percent of the respondents with a primary-school education reported that they began using contraception at the time of their marriage, but the figure rose consistently to over a third of the respondents with a university education.[36]

Wives with more education also exhibit more initiative in family planning. The choice of modern methods is the most important indicator of initiative, since the overwhelming majority of modern methods used in Japan today are women's methods. (In the questionnaire sample, only three wives had husbands with vasectomies.) There are other indicators as well, however, in both patterns of reliance on husbands and expresssions of initiative and responsibility. Wives with more education are less likely to rely on their husbands for family planning information. In the questionnaire sample, over half of the contracepting women with middle-school education or less stated that their husbands were a source of information; the figure dropped consistently to a third of those with a four-year college education. Contracepting wives in the survey sample who had more education were also more likely to express preference for a method of contraception that they themselves could control. (These relationships were also statistically significant.)[37]

WOMEN'S STATUS IN JAPAN

Unlike conjugal role organization, women's status measured in terms of educational level does offer enough variance among Japanese couples to allow comparison of family planning performance. The aggregate effects of women's status on Japan's family planning scene are minimal, however, because Japanese women have a much lower status in their society than do women in the West. Education, for example, has less overall

[36] *Ibid.*:133.

[37] Statistically significant results were obtained when using Pearson correlations of wife's educational level with husband as source of information and with preference for contraceptive control. The latter variable was recoded with a value of 1 for preference for own control, and 0 for all other responses.

impact simply because the proportion of women in Japan
enjoying a higher educational background is much smaller
than in the West.

Educational opportunities for women at the high-school
level and beyond have only recently emerged in Japan. As
Table 6-1 reveals, in 1970 the proportion of Japanese women
with an education beyond high school constituted a fraction
of the United States distribution, particularly among women
between ages 35 and 44.

Japanese women also possess less education than their
Western counterparts relative to men. Although almost half
(49.7 percent) of all high-school students in 1975 were female,
this is the recent result of a steady increase throughout the
postwar period; the proportion of female students shrinks to
less than a fourth for currently enrolled college students, giving
Japan the lowest ranking among the major nations of the
world.[38] This imbalance is also reflected in a 1973 government

TABLE 6-1

Educational Attainment Levels Among Women
in Two Age Groups in Japan and the United States,
in Percentages, 1970

	Jr. High School or less	*High School*	*Post- High School*	*Total*
Age 20 to 29				
Japan	37.2	52.1	10.8	100.1
U.S.	9.0	57.1	33.9	100.0
Age 35 to 44				
Japan	57.0	38.1	4.9	100.0
U.S.	20.3	55.8	23.8	99.9

Total percentages may not equal 100.0 because of rounding.

Sources: Calculated from figures in Japan, Office of the Prime
Minister 1972:117; U.S. Bureau of the Census 1973:7.

[38] Monbu-shō 1976:26, 44.

survey that found only 14 percent of mothers wanting their daughters to have a university education, in contrast to 49 percent for sons.[39]

Japanese women also have lower status in the labor market than their Western counterparts. Although Japanese women have one of the highest rates of labor force participation in the non-Communist world, over a fourth work for their families.[40] Female wage labor in Japan is still used mainly as auxiliary work, and is treated as a temporary labor force in contrast to the permanent male labor force, which assumes a pattern of lifetime commitment.[41] Women's labor is thus concentrated in unskilled forms of work with little opportunity for job skill development or advancement.[42] Women occupy about 6 percent of administrative positions in Japan, as opposed to 19 percent in the United States and 12 percent in France.[43] Even in the field of education, where well over half of all primary and secondary schoolteachers are women, only 3 percent of all assistant principals and 1 percent of all principals are women.[44]

My own observations of male-female interaction in everyday life also provide indications that Japanese women have lower status than their counterparts in the West. In the course of participant observation, I soon noted that male requests to females in such relationships as husband-wife, co-worker, and son-mother greatly outnumbered requests in the other direction (female to male), and also had a very high rate of compliance. Japanese women's deferential behavior is also noteworthy: they are reluctant to express opinions or participate in male conversations, and many have a characteristic motion of covering their mouths with one hand when laughing or expressing embarrassment, another sign of timidity. (This ges-

---

[39] Fujin Chōsakai 1974:122.

[40] Nihon Fujin Dantai Rengōkai 1975:11.

[41] Akamatsu 1969; Rōdō-shō 1975:13.

[42] Rōdō-shō 1975:12, 13.

[43] Calculated using figures in ILO 1975; cf. also Fujin Chōsakai 1974:81.

[44] Fujin Chōsakai 1974:81.

ture also occurs on rare occasion among young men who are unsure of their behavior or have difficulty expressing themselves.) In speech patterns as well, there are clear-cut differences in men's and women's speech which require women to use more elaborate deferential grammatical forms.

In the opinion of the Japanese of both sexes, as well, women have character traits that discourage independent initiative; informants described female personality as "passive" (*ukemiteki*) and lacking in "subjecthood" (*shutaisei*, a term succinctly defined by one Japanese psychologist as "the power to think for oneself, determine a course of action by oneself, and act independently").[45]

WOMEN'S STATUS IN THEIR MARRIAGES

If Japanese wives enjoy hegemony in their domestic lives, the criteria used to compare their status with women in other countries would be of limited validity for an explanation of family planning patterns in terms of low female status, since family planning is an inherently domestic activity. But the domestic sphere does not afford Japanese women their own domain of absolute authority.

Within the context of domestic life as well, Japanese women do not enjoy high status. In the arena of family finances, for example, a substantial proportion of wives defer to their husbands, despite the near-universal practice among husbands of handing over their unopened pay envelopes to their wives and then receiving their own personal expense money rather than subtracting it beforehand. The fiscal power for the wife that foreigners infer from this custom is illusory. More often than not the husband determines the amount of his pocket money.[46] More important still, because of the "bonus" system, husbands receive over a fourth of their yearly salaries in biannual payments, so regular pay envelopes do not represent much in the way of discretionary spending potential. When it comes

---

[45] Hirai 1976:28.
[46] See, for example, the survey reported in *Asahi Shinbun* 1976c.

to buying high-priced goods, the husband has the final say or the spouses decide together in a large number of cases. Research by a team of family sociologists led by Koyama Takashi found that the husband has the power of decision in about 40 percent of the 1,200 families surveyed,[47] and a Taiyō Kōbe Bank survey of over 1,400 wives between 20 and 30 years old found about 75 percent of respondents claiming that, "after discussing it together, my husband ultimately decides."[48] In terms of day-to-day decision-making regarding the family budget, the wife definitely makes more decisions, but these are in a capacity typified by Koyama and his colleagues as "assisting," or acting as "sub-leader."[49]

Another indication of the wife's subordination in the domestic realm arises in the issue of when she absents herself from the house (*gaishutsu*). If she is not present when her husband returns home from work, he may respond with irritation or outright anger.[50] His response reflects his need for her domestic services, since his complaint is usually that he has had no dinner—a demand that does not differ fundamentally from that of many husbands in the United States. The intensity of the restriction of wives' outings, however, is far greater in Japan. If and how often the wife is out after 6 p.m. is a matter of negotiation with the husband and is not left entirely up to the wife.[51] Wives who are seen alone in public in the late evening, when it is assumed that their husbands are returning home, are subject to criticism in the form of gossip.

Even data on hours of sleep portray a disadvantageous domestic interaction for Japanese women; in a near-reversal of

[47] Koyama 1967:49.

[48] Taiyō Kōbe Ginkō 1976:9.

[49] Koyama 1967:51.

[50] An intensive interview survey among ten Japanese housewives provides some vivid descriptions of the problem; Fujin Chōsakai 1974:379.

[51] See, for example, *Asahi Shinbun* 1976c; among a smaller proportion of couples the wife also has to negotiate for afternoon outings.

the European pattern, Japanese wives have less time for sleep
than their husbands. According to the international time-use
survey introduced earlier, unemployed Japanese wives had
almost one hour less sleeping time than the average for European housewives.[52] The disparity results from the wife's
duties and obligations, among them rising early to prepare
breakfast for the family and staying up at night to greet her
husband if he returns late.

As one might suspect, non-familial status factors may also
transform the woman's status within her home. A semi-profes-
sional occupation is one such influence; a study of Osaka
wives employed as schoolteachers found that their participation in various household decisions was more cooperative
and egalitarian, a result which the researchers credited to the
working wife's greater power relative to her husband's.[53]

The wife's level of education also affects authority patterns;
Koyama's research found that wives with more education were
more likely to decide on high-priced purchases, a phenomenon
that, according to the authors, reflected a "democratization"
or "modernization" of the family.[54]

A HYPOTHETICAL ADAPTATION

Can a wife with low status in a segregated role relationship
be an effective, independent agent in avoiding unwanted conceptions even if she does not have access to modern contraceptive methods? Such women may have existed in the past.
An industrial social worker in family planning counseling described some of her clients in the 1950s who chose the diaphragm as part of their domestic responsibility, out of a "spirit
of sacrifice" (*giseiteki seishin*) for their husbands. Their rationale was that they should spare their husband the added
worry and bother of fertility limitation because the men were
striving hard to support the family and were already burdened

[52] Keizaikikaku-chō 1973b:54-55.
[53] Fuse 1970:89-91; Kamiko 1965.
[54] Koyama 1967:50-51.

with cares about the family's economic well-being. These wives in effect concealed their use of a contraceptive from their husbands. (The social worker felt that their approach was a virtue, and criticized today's younger wives for leaving the entire matter up to their husbands.)

The self-sacrificing diaphragm user never was a prominent part of Japan's family planning scene, and it is doubtful that she could be today. Very few women romanticize their husbands' efforts for the family to the extent that they would undertake contraception on their own. The increased participation of Japanese women in the labor force during the postwar period has militated against that possibility because—as one might suspect—women's feelings of gratitude toward their husbands decrease when they themselves become working wives.[55] There is an even more fundamental reason, however, for the improbability of such initiative: Japanese women are held back from an assertive role in family planning by their sexuality, the final piece that we must now add to the seeming puzzle of traditional birth control in a modern society.

[55] Survey results reviewed in Fujin Chōsakai 1974:107-08.

CHAPTER 7

Sexuality

Sexuality in present-day Japanese culture profoundly affects the couple's ability to seek and effectively use contraception. The association between conjugal sexuality and family planning performance is fundamental: the goal of contraception is, after all, to allow sexual intercourse without conception. But human sexuality is subject to cultural variation, and, in the case of Japan, there are specific themes in female and male sexuality that pose obstacles to effective family planning behavior. These themes are natural concomitants to women's status and conjugal role segregation.

WOMEN'S SEXUALITY AND INITIATIVE IN CONTRACEPTION

Japanese women display an embarrassment in matters relating to sex that hinders their ability to seek and use conception control methods. Their resistance to the idea of going to an Ob-Gyn for the specific purpose of contraception is particularly noteworthy. Although the great majority of the interviewee wives favored unsolicited contraceptive guidance from doctors, four of them added that they would not want to make the special effort of going to a doctor's clinic or hospital to get it. One of the wives (a 37-year-old high-school graduate) suggested that it would be good to have mandatory guidance sessions, because "then I'd have to go even if it was embarrassing." Tsuboi Hideo, an Ob-Gyn who had studied the professional strategies of his Tokyo area colleagues, noted that there are women who prefer doctors with dual specialties in internal medicine or pediatrics coupled with gynecology because visits are less embarrassing. (Attracting the reluctant patient, however, is not a major motive for adding specialties.)

Family planning specialists are aware of women's resistance to making use of Ob-Gyns for contraception, and they, too, attribute it to the woman's feelings about sex. (There is also the possibility that women would not want to be taken for abortion patients, but specialists did not believe that that is a particularly important consideration.) Sexual embarrassment is evident in Japanese clinical procedures. Patients are typically draped for pelvic examinations so that the material completely separates the patient's field of vision from the physician. The patient's embarrassment can prevent her from cooperating with her doctor; two Ob-Gyns, one of them a university instructor, observed that patients would refuse to inspect the position of a properly inserted diaphragm or IUD string with their own hands when they were in the doctor's presence.

Women's embarrassment can also hinder their communication with Ob-Gyns. Women use pronouns and evasive expressions when discussing sexual topics. Menstruation, for example, is commonly denoted by the word *that (are)*. When combined with the Japanese language's potential for ambiguity, this tendency makes it very difficult for women to describe their problems to Ob-Gyns; one doctor candidly reported that when he has to ask his patients to be more specific they sometimes become flustered or even indignant. The availability of contraception without a visit to the doctor makes condoms more attractive to Japanese wives; successful door-to-door condom saleswomen claim that one of their most effective selling points is that a visit to the doctor is unnecessary. (Their other most effective arguments are that condoms are inexpensive and safe—hence the prospect of avoiding doctors is a benefit above and beyond the expense or fear of medical procedures.)

It may seem indicative of a sexually frank atmosphere to have women selling condoms door to door. On the contrary, however, the door-to-door sales strategy is a marketing adaptation to the embarrassment involved in buying contraceptives. As observed in Chapter 3, door-to-door commercial distribution of condoms was originally conceived as a strategy for bypassing the acute psychological discomfort experienced by drugstore customers making condom purchases. The women who do the selling are drawn to the trade by the lucrative commissions and incentives.

The saleswoman is an influential authority figure for the young mother or mother-to-be. Home sales companies recruit women who appear older and have children themselves, which has special appeal to the young urban housewife isolated from face-to-face information from older female family members in matters of child-raising and reproduction. Since these subjects generate considerable insecurity for her, she is open to the saleswoman's advice. Testament to this vulnerability are those cases where saleswomen arrange to sell the housewife up to four gross of condoms at once, or as many as 15 gross.[1]

The low use rate for intravaginal contraceptives in Japan is also due, in part, to female sexual inhibition. Physicians and family planning specialists universally agree that women reject diaphragms and spermicides because they dislike having to handle their genitals. The lack of promotion of female barrier methods is probably the single greatest determinant of their low use rates, but there are also other reasons to believe that Japanese women have strong inhibitions that prevent them from making greater use of these contraceptive methods. Very low use rates for mentrual tampons in Japan are one sign of such inhibitions. In the mid-1970s, tampons claimed only about 10 percent of the feminine hygiene product market in Japan, in contrast to over half of the United States market. Newspaper articles on the subject noted that Japanese women experience emotional resistance to tampon use in the form of anxiety about inserting something into their vaginas.[2] Japanese women also have a much lower rate for experience of masturbation than American women.[3] Recent figures for adolescents show a reported incidence of masturbation for Japanese females that is less than half the rate for United States female adolescents.[4]

[1] *Kazoku Keikaku* 1976b:5; *Sankei Ribingu* 1976a:15.
[2] *Asahi Shinbun* 1973; *Tōkyō Shinbun* 1975.
[3] Asayama 1975:98; cf. Kinsey et al. 1953.
[4] Nihon Seikyōiku Kyōkai 1975:116; Sorenson 1972:129.

The sexuality factor also helps to explain the independent effect of length of marriage on the choice of modern contraception; as the woman grows into her role of wife and mother, she feels more comfortable about seeking effective contraception. Conversely, the younger the woman, the greater her difficulty in going to an Ob-Gyn. High-school-age women have the greatest resistance to seeking gynecological services for any reason; some will avoid Ob-Gyns' clinics entirely and go to internists and generalists instead. Those who do go to an Ob-Gyn do not wear their school uniforms (standard dress for high-school students) because that would identify them as students at a specific school. Nor does the social legitimation of sex offered by marriage remove the inhibitions of the new wife or bride-to-be. A particularly striking example of the extent of their resistance to using gynecological hospitals as a source of contraception appeared in the Yamanouchi survey of newlywed wives, which asked the question, "What way of buying contraceptives poses the least psychological burden?" Of nine alternative answers offered, Ob-Gyn hospitals ranked last, behind supermarkets and drugstores.[5] In another study, Ogino Hiroshi explained the particularly low adoption rates of the pill and IUD among newlywed wives by pointing to "psychological resistance to contacting an Ob-Gyn."[6]

Motherhood, however, confers a sense of legitimacy to female sexuality. For women, childbearing is the touchstone of feminine sexual identity. Not to want children is "unwomanly" (*onnarashikunai*). A writer in the prestigious women's magazine *Fujin Kōron* summed the prevailing sentiment nicely:

How does a woman change when she marries and gives birth to children? . . . This statement of the problem itself is fundamentally mistaken. It is not how a woman changes, but the fact that through marriage and childbirth she becomes a woman for the first time.[7]

[5] Kon 1973:115.
[6] Ogino 1976:36.
[7] Kurahashi 1972:60.

The concomitant ideology concerning sexual behavior views pregnancy and childbirth as the most fulfilling object of female sexuality—a stance that many psychoanalysts in the United States assumed in the not-so-distant past. A number of female informants stated that visits to their Ob-Gyn became much less unpleasant after they were married for a while and had borne children. The relief they experienced stemmed from the social recognition of female sexuality by virtue of its association with motherhood. Mothers are also more emotionally free to seek effective contraception because they are not engaging in the denial of motherhood that lies implicit in contraception before childbearing begins.

The link between sexuality and motherhood expresses itself in the merging of childbearing and the romance of newlywed life. The popular expression "honeymoon baby" (*hanemūn bebī*) was coined for couples who experience conception immediately after marriage. A large marriage hall in Tokyo proudly advertises that, "50 percent of our brides have babies in the first year of marriage." (There is no stigma from suspicion that the conception was actually premarital.) Conversely, infertility fears can dampen sexual enjoyment for women in newlywed life. Four of the interviewee wives said that their sexual enjoyment improved after the birth of their first child; one of them (a 25-year-old high-school graduate) explained that the birth "reassured" her; to another (33 years old, also a high-school graduate), the birth brought her sexual satisfaction because she "settled down emotionally."

The wife's sexual enjoyment can affect her willingness to seek and use effective contraception: if she enjoys sex, she has an added incentive to do away with the fear of unwanted conceptions; if she dislikes sex, effective contraception poses a liability since it makes her more sexually accessible. Sexuality for the purpose of reproduction, however, makes up at most a tenth of sexual activity for Japanese wives of reproductive age, so the legitimating mantle of motherhood can go only so far in making them more at ease with sexuality.

The interviewee sample offered two instances of wives who would be reluctant to use modern contraception because it would remove an excuse for avoiding more frequent sexual intercourse. In both cases the couples had attained their intended family size. One wife (a 34-year-old high-school graduate) used rhythm as an excuse for avoiding sexual relations with her husband, although she did not actually calculate her safe periods. In another case where the wife did not share her husband's desire for a higher coital frequency (he is 36 years old, his wife, 33, and both are college graduates), she stated that she had rejected the pill because she feared the danger of side effects. However, she also said that her husband had intimated in arguments over his desire for more sex that the pill "might be better after all."

There were no expressions of preference for condoms from any wives because of the distraction that it poses to husbands or its physical barrier between the partners' genitals. (The latter characteristic of condoms was a source of appeal for the American wives in Rainwater's study who disliked sexual intimacy.) Interestingly enough, however, the three interviewee wives who said they disliked condoms because the method impaired their own erotic moods had also indicated that they derived a lot of enjoyment from sex with their husbands.

If a woman does not find fulfillment in non-reproductive sexuality, it is quite possible that she will be more conscious—and resentful—of the costs of effective contraception, particularly risks to her health: phrased simply, the woman's response at a subliminal level would be, "Why should I endanger myself for his pleasure?" Statements suggesting this sentiment emerged several times in conversations with female informants who expressed resentment that the health problems of both induced abortion and modern contraception, especially the pill, are "foisted off" on women (using the term *shiwayose*, which means shifting a burden onto someone or something else). Pronatalists have attempted to exploit the weakness of pleasure-oriented female sexuality in order to discourage women's acceptance of fertility limitation; the Seichō-no Ie's anti-abortion tract, for example, warns women that "when women deny their maternal essence, they become nothing more than the tools of men's pleasure."[8]

There are a number of signs that a larger proportion of Japanese women reject sexuality or derive less pleasure from it than do women in the West. Surveys conducted in Japan in the early 1950s, around the time that Kinsey's work on American women appeared, found that it took longer for Japanese women to experience orgasm in marriage than in the United States, and that the percentage of women who had not experienced orgasm after fifteen years of marriage was twice the United States figure.[9] Japanese sex experts believe that wives still face obstacles to the enjoyment of marital sex. The low rates of masturbation among young females also constitute important indirect evidence that Japanese women have inhibitions that retard or prevent sexual gratification in marriage.

Individual feelings about sexuality are complex and contradictory, so no one statement could ever sum up an individual's attitude. Nevertheless, the number of wives in the interview sample who expressed a rejecting attitude toward their sex lives was unexpectedly high. Six of the wives' discussions contained only unqualified expression of dislike. (No one was asked directly if she liked sex or not; the wives made these statements part of their responses to questions about coital frequency and whether they were satisfied with it, as well as to a question about the relative strengths of both spouses' libidos.) Rejection sometimes appeared in statements expressing the desire for a much lower frequency of intercourse than the couple was actually experiencing: "We have sex about once a week or ten days. . . . If it were possible, once a month would be fine with me" (a 34-year-old girls' high-school graduate). Eleven other wives expressed dissatisfaction in one form or another, in the form of complaints of tiredness, stronger fears of losing privacy than those ex-

---

[8] Taniguchi 1975:84.
[9] Asayama 1975:12.

pressed by their husbands, or claims of being more "indifferent" to sex (*tanpaku*) than their husbands.

Just as motherhood legitimates female sexuality, it also serves as a rationale for female sexual disinterest. A popular image of wives' sexuality portrays the woman with children as uninterested in sex because she no longer desires a conception. Among the interview couples, one of the sex-rejecting wives (the 34-year-old quoted earlier) commented, "Now that I've got children I haven't particularly felt like having sex." Other wives who reported that having children detracted from their interest in sex, however, attributed the decline to the demands of child-raising. Fatigue from child-raising and housework became a familiar theme in interviewee wives' discussions of sex; for many, tiredness generated resentment at their husbands' approaches. Muramatsu Hiroo believes that the mother's investment of energy in child-raising—particularly in the case of the "education mama" intent on her children's academic success—poses a major detraction from marital sexuality due to transfer and sublimation of her sexual drive. Among the interviewees, amount of sleep stood in a direct relationship with coital frequency that was statistically significant regardless of the wives' ages. Nevertheless, the presence of a child under age two had no significant effect on either total hours of sleep or on frequency of intercourse.[10]

WOMEN'S STATUS AND SEXUALITY

Differences in women's sexuality that result from higher status might be at work in the positive effect that educational level has on the choice of modern contraceptive methods. In the United States there are numerous indications that women with higher status (including higher educational backgrounds) de-

[10] The results regarding coital frequency were obtained from separate multiple regressions of frequency of sexual intercourse against wife's age and total hours of sleep, and wife's age and presence or absence of one or more children under two years of age. The zero-order correlation between hours of sleep and presence of a child under age two was negative but extremely weak.

rive greater satisfaction from sexuality.[11] The Japanese woman with more education might be enjoying a more positive attitude toward marital sexuality, which in turn would make her more favorably disposed to take the initiative in contraception.

Educational level does affect women's sexuality in Japan. Coital frequencies averaged from the questionnaire survey in Table 7-1 generally show a positive relationship with the amount of respondents' education. The effect remains and is statistically significant when husband's income and wife's age are taken into account.[12] For the women in the interview sample, more education appeared to contribute to more positive state-

TABLE 7-1

Mean Monthly Coital Frequency Among Wives by Age and Education, Tokyo Area Clinic and Hospital Sample, 1975-1976*

	Mean Frequency, by Age			Number of Women, by Age		
	25	25-34	35-44	25	25-34	35-44
Total	10.5	8.2	6.6	110	394	119
Junior high or less	8.7	7.4	5.1	14	65	37
High school	10.9	8.1	7.3	74	212	55
Junior college	10.3	8.0	7.7	19	79	13
College	11.3	10.5	7.0	3	38	14

* Interval midpoints for response categories in weeks were multiplied by a four-week month.

[11] See, for example, Kinsey et al. 1953:312-13, 354, 378, 544; and Westoff 1974:139-40.

[12] Statistically significant results were obtained when using a multiple regression of frequency of sexual intercourse against the following four independent variables: wife's age, wife's educational level, husband's income, and wife's hours of sleep.

ments about marital sex, but the relationship was not consistent; most of the five wives who were four-year college graduates provided negative statements like the following, from a 33-year-old housewife with two children:

> We have sex about once a week. Since I'm indifferent to sex (*tanpaku*) myself, that's fine with me. Sex was most enjoyable for me when I was first married—it was a new thing then. After our first child was born, I was very tired and not interested. Since then, even now, we both feel sex is a burden (*otagai ni mendō da*). I'd be concerned if we had none at all, but. . . .

Individual women's educations among the interviewees did not contribute more to their enjoyment of marital sexuality because an age-related counter-tendency in Japanese society blunted the effects. In the interview sample, all but one of the four-year college graduates were over age 30. Only recently have society-wide changes in women's status created a noticeable contrast in women's sexuality, in which more youth is accompanied by more assertiveness and candor in sexual matters. Japanese specialists varied somewhat in the age at which the contrast was most evident, but all of them placed the dividing line somewhere between 25 and 35.

Status-related contrasts in sexuality among women are muted still more, however, by the pervasive effects of their overall low status in present-day Japanese society. The disadvantages appear in many women's inability to demand—and get—more sexual gratification from their husbands. Prominent sexologists cite the husband's self-centeredness as a major reason for wives' problems in experiencing orgasm. In recent years women's magazines have taken up the issue of women's orgasm, an important step in exploring women's potential for sexual satisfaction in marriage. Nevertheless, the essential ingredient of male cooperation is still missing; with the rare exception of very young, highly educated couples, wives seek help from specialists for problems in marital sexuality alone. Therapists reported that they have difficulty enlisting husbands' cooperation. The decrease in time for sleep that Jap-

anese wives have relative to Western women must also exert
a negative effect on sexuality from lower status, despite the
presence of women who use late waking hours as a pretext
to avoid sex.

Japanese females enjoy much less latitude in sexual expression and activities than do males. Not only do a greater proportion of males participate in a variety of sexual activities;
among the experienced of both sexes, the males are more likely
to have started at an earlier age.[13] Among youths still in school,
nearly twice as many males have experienced sexual intercourse as have females by the age of 21 (28 percent, in contrast
to 16 percent); over three times as many males have mastur-
bated (92 percent, in contrast to 30 percent).[14]

Sexual inequality in the Japanese marriage reduces the acceptability of vasectomy to wives; some may be reluctant to
want the operation for their husbands because they fear it
will facilitate their husbands' extramarital affairs. Extramarital sex is far more frequent for Japanese men than for their
wives, and occurs more often than among European and
American men.[15] The husband's far greater mobility and the
accepted fact of his extended absence from home allow him
more opportunity. His power in the marriage limits the severity of the sanctions that his wife can impose. (As Chapter
5 stated, wives have far fewer opportunities for extramarital
sex, and far harsher consequences at the hands of their spouses
if their affair is discovered.)

Both Japanese men and women see vasectomy as a great
facilitator of extramarital liaisons. Spontaneous reference to
the subject of extramarital affairs (*uwaki*) in discussions of
vasectomy was nearly universal among male informants. Although a few men said that their wives or friends' wives were
opposed to vasectomy for fear of facilitating their husbands'
extramarital sex, it would be very difficult for a wife to admit
such concern about her own husband, since it would contra-

---

[13] Nihon Seikyōiku Kyōkai 1974; Asayama 1975.
[14] Nihon Seikyōiku Kyōkai 1974:160.
[15] For a comparison of survey results, see Asayama 1975:107-09.

dict the image of a harmonious household and her ability to hold her husband's attentions. Women do discuss the danger of vasectomy as an encouragement to extramarital affairs, however, and one of the interviewee wives whose husband had had a vasectomy was warned by her friends that it would lead to infidelity.

MALE SEXUALITY AND INITIATIVE IN CONTRACEPTION

Japanese men also experience embarrassment at sexual matters, which prevents them from taking a more active role in learning about and acquiring contraception. A few family planning specialists offered the opinion that men are *more* bashful about sexual topics than are women. Family planning counselors with extensive experience in group instruction for couples described a strong reluctance to ask questions among husbands as well as among wives. Said one midwife, "Whenever I'd ask if there were questions there'd be no response— just dead silence." Another family planning instructor found that if she announced to her audience beforehand that she would answer questions after her talk as well as at any time before, her talk would proceed without interruption and the assembled group would all remain seated and motionless at the end of the session, everyone waiting for everyone else to leave so that individual questions could be posed in privacy. The door-to-door condom sales strategy arose to circumvent the embarrassment of male drugstore customers as well as females. A few married male informants stated that they preferred buying condoms from vending machines despite the greater expense because it was less disagreeable than negotiating a purchase at a pharmacist's shop.

Japanese men display signs of sexual repression, as do Japanese women. Exclusively male company does not allow a more relaxed discussion of sexual topics which, as noted in Chapter 5, typically consists of jokes and anecdotes. The joking spirit suggests anxiety; the typical setting, a men-only drinking session, suggests a spirit of taboo. Indeed, such discussions have a pejorative label (*waidan*, "filthy" or "smutty" talk), and there are sanctions against displaying undue interest or preoccupation in sexual matters; the man who initiates discussion of sexual topics runs the risk of being stigmatized as "no-account" or "shiftless" (*roku de mo nai*). Some middle class male informants expressed the belief that lower class men find it easier to discuss sex. The great majority of interviewee husbands, when asked if they had confidants for problems in sexuality or contraception, replied that they never felt a need for such discussions.

Embarrassment and anxiety over sexuality are intense enough to cause a dislike of complete nudity among Japanese men in the midst of members of the same sex. Most men take care to keep their genitals hidden from the view of fellow males when bathing together; the typical ploy is to hold a towel over the pubic area when walking, and leave it draped over the thighs when seated outside the bath. Japan's foremost business newspaper, the *Nihon Keizai Shinbun*, once carried an account of young men who moved out of their factory dormitory in order to escape from group bathing, and the article conjectured that there were "quite a few" young men suffering from "complexes" about their bodies.[16]

The key to understanding the embarrassment that sexuality poses to Japanese men lies in the social control of male sexuality in Japanese culture: indifference toward sexual matters is rewarded. Sexual identity receives more reinforcement from another source, the productive career. Men's occupations have an intimate symbolic link with male sexuality and sex-role identification; as the widely-displayed recruitment poster for the Tokyo Metropolitan Police Department proclaims, "Work's the Most Important Thing to a Man" (*Otoko wa shigoto da*). When work-place demands or work-related sociability take precedence over interaction with members of the opposite sex, it is an affirmation and not a denial of male sex identity. The male who treats romantic and sexual matters indifferently and concentrates his attention on work (or studies, if he is a stu-

---

[16] *Nihon Keizai Shinbun* 1973.

dent) is praised, and he is complimented on being "serious" (*majime*) or of "sound, staunch" character (*shikkari shita*). One example of this sentiment presented itself in a casual boast from a family planning worker about her son, an industrious man who attended night school in addition to his full-time job, and who had recently married: he had never looked at any of her books on family planning and sex. Narabayashi Yasushi, a prominent sex and marriage counselor, has observed that mothers who prod their sons into educational success instill negative thoughts about women into them, from fear that sex will become a distraction.

One depiction of sex in Japanese society that has gained currency among both Japanese men and foreign readers of shallow social commentary asserts that the Japanese recognize the legitimacy of sex as a human need, but keep it in its place; sex is, in a sense, taken in stride and enjoyed, but it is circumscribed by social obligations and duties, as opposed to the more pervasive control over sexual behavior exercised by religious guilt in the West. Some Japanese men also have voiced the opinion that, on the whole, they were less preoccupied with sexual matters than American and European men.

Aside from this expressed ideal of indifference, however, there are no indications that Japanese men are actually less interested in sexual matters than their Western counterparts. The use of sexual themes and sexually attractive women in the media and in advertising takes place to an equal—if not greater—extent than in the West. In Japan, however, men circumscribe their interest in sex by relegating it to the category of entertainment or pleasure; sexuality is made into a part of after-hours leisure. Sexuality and the entertainment world have an even closer association in Japan than in the West. The daily sports newspapers have a back page devoted to erotic advice columns and risqué serial stories. Late-night television offers the viewer strip-tease shows and reviews of pornographic movies. The foreign visitor who believes that these displays signify a relaxed and sophisticated attitude toward sexual matters, however, misses the important point that the context is male-oriented diversion. The word used for "pleasure" in "sex for pleasure" (*kairaku*) has a definitely pejorative association with hedonism, as well as nuances of selfishness and submission to base urges. This negative cast subsumed in the sex-as-pleasure orientation fits well with the attitude that the man dedicated to his work pays less attention to such matters, since they are essentially rather frivolous. The combination of sexual titillation in men's entertainment with penalties for an open interest in sex have created—quite predictably—a hypocritical bent, which Japanese men themselves have labeled with the slang expression "closet lecher" (*muttsuri sukebei*).

One other usage also suggests an essentially negative regard for sexuality; although used more frequently in the past, one still hears the term "animalistic" (*dōbutsuteki*) used as a description of sexual behavior, especially when referrring to a high frequency of sexual intercourse. The term even appeared in a professional publication, when a well-known Japanese demographer used it to refer to increased sexual activity among postwar Japanese married couples.[17] There are also still strong taboos on the public expression of affection in Japan. Although young people walk arm-in-arm with members of the opposite sex in a few areas in Tokyo, such as Roppongi and Harajuku, these places are small enclaves of worldly iconoclasts. Couples keep whatever feelings of affection they may have toward one another from the eyes of other individuals. Sanctions against expressions of affection were probably much stronger in the past, since the older the Japanese individual the greater the tendency to insist that matters of love and affection be kept secret (the term used is *himegoto*), but young people are not yet converted to the idea that acts which openly declare affection are justifiable, much less desirable. In interview material on youth attitudes toward sex gathered by Yuzawa Yasuhiko in 1971 and 1972, a college student expressed his revulsion at public scenes of affection by saying, "It's as shameless as dogs mating in the middle of the street."

There is yet a more concrete expression of the negative view

[17] Honda 1959:4.

of sexuality in Japan: side by side with the commerical exploitation of sex, there exists extensive censorship of sexually oriented materials. Views of pubic hair and genitalia, for example, are not allowed in motion pictures, much less on television programs. This censorship has its extremes; in 1975, customs agents at Tokyo International Airport confiscated a training film in gynecology from a Swiss pharmaceutical firm on its way to the University of Tokyo, because the film included views of subjects whose pubic hair was exposed. One reason for the censorship is the implicit fear that sexuality, if unchecked, could become a serious distraction to industriousness and maintenance of social order. Social commentators in the mid-1970s registered dismay at popular interest in sexual topics, using expressions like "sex chaos" (*sei no konran*) to impute a danger to the social fabric itself from sex in the media.

MALE PREFERENCES IN FEMALE SEXUALITY

Japanese male sexuality has another dimension that discourages the married couple's ability to seek and use effective contraception: a preference for repressed female sexuality, which results in the embarrassment and passivity that in turn vitiates wives' capacity to meet their personal family planning needs.

There are indications that many Japanese men dislike sexual assertiveness among women. Men typically assert that their own sex drives are stronger than women's and that they always enjoy sex. Occasionally one hears the saying that "a man's disgraced if he turns down a woman's favor" (*suezen o kuwanu wa otoko no haji*). At the same time, however, men display dislike and fear at the idea of a wife whose demands cannot be met, a "praying mantis wife" (*kamakiri fujin*; female praying mantises eat their mates). The hazards of a sexually demanding woman are also projected onto foreign women; more than one well-educated young Japanese man related the apocryphal story of the "friend-of-a-friend" whose marriage to an American woman ended in divorce because the wife was oversexed.

The two themes of the sexually ready male and the dangerous nymphomaniac coexist by virtue of men's encouragement of sexual passivity in women. Although the proportion of men who demand that their wives be virgins has steadily diminished in the postwar period, it still constitutes anywhere from a third to a half of respondents in opinion polls.[18] Those who do not require virginity may have a more comprehensive requirement for their wives-to-be, like the 34 percent of the male high-school students in Tottori Prefecture who stipulated in a 1973 survey that the woman need not be a virgin physically "as long as she is pure in spirit."[19] The young woman who has dated more than a few men is also definitely less desirable as a marriage partner. Many young men prefer wives who are naive and modest or even shy. A few of the husbands interviewed recalled that the most liked quality of the women they later married was their naivete (*seken shirazu* or *surete inai*).

There are also instances of women who have experienced sexual repression after marriage. When wives in the interview sample were asked which partner had the stronger sex drive, 12 responded that their husband's desire was stronger, but 3 of them (along with one respondent who declined an answer) gave indications that they were disappointed with their current frequency of intercourse or had been in the past but had since resigned themselves to less sexual activity. (None of these women had education beyond high school, and none were less than three years younger than their husbands.) Only two wives claimed that they had a stronger interest in sex. One of the two husbands involved stated that his own sex drive was stronger; the other agreed with his wife's appraisal of their relative interests, and later said that he opposed contraceptive sterilization for either of them (they had reached their intended

[18] Asayama 1975:101; Kon 1973:166.
[19] Kon 1973:166.

family size) because he feared it would make her more sexually demanding.

RISSHINBEN—THE "HEART" OF SEXUALITY

The dominant styles of male and female sexuality help to explain the difficulty that Japanese couples experience in allocating responsibility for family planning, in contrast to the relative ease with which they take up their other domestic roles and responsibilities; husbands' and wives' sexualities lack a basic congruence in goals that would make the coordination of family planning efforts much easier. Husbands are the initiators of sexual behavior and are more able to express an interest in sexual gratification than their wives, but marital sexuality also has direct consequences for reproduction, which is almost exclusively the wives' domain.

Japanese sexuality is still largely confined to this dichotomy of "sex for pleasure" and "sex for reproduction." A statement posed to elicit opinion in a 1971 survey conducted under the Office of the Prime Minister reflects this simple bifurcation: "The main goal of sexual intercourse is to create offspring and is not for pleasure (*kairaku*)."[20] Commentators also describe Japanese trends in sexuality as a turn away from reproduction toward "pleasure."[21]

A third and qualitatively distinct approach to sexual activity as expression of mutal love and affection would provide more common ground for couples to work out their family planning needs. The concept appeals to younger men and women (those under the age of 25 or so), but it has yet to become a familiar theme in Japanese attitudes toward sexuality, and the idea of sex as "communication" is all the more alien. Japanese sex specialists have recognized this tendency to place sex in a separate dimension from interpersonal relationships, and they have coined a term to describe it: "sex-without-a-heart-rad-

[20] Sōri-fu 1971:480.
[21] See, for example, the comments by Maki Shōhei in *Gendai Seikyōiku Kenkyū* 1973:27.

ical" (*risshinben no nai sekkusu*). The expression is a pun of sorts, based on the radicals (component parts) that make up the Chinese character for sex, 性 . The correctly written character consists of the radical for "life," 生 , together with the "heart" (*kokoro*) radical to the left, 忄 , meaning feeling, sincerity, or thoughtfulness. The heart radical connotes emotional involvement; hence, the expression describes sex without the emotions that would make marital sex an interpersonal dynamic.

THE DUBIOUS STATUS OF MARITAL SEXUALITY

The implications of "sex-without-a-heart" for family planning go beyond the difficulties that individual couples experience in coordinating their roles and responsibilities in order to obtain satisfactory contraception. Contraception means fertility-free sexuality, but married couples are subtly discouraged from attaining it by a prevailing disregard for sexuality as a component of married life that deserves recognition and nurturing. The simple proclamation of most Japanese commentators that "sex for pleasure is replacing sex for reproduction" should occasion some doubt about the respectability—if not the well-being—of marital sexuality in Japan, since sex for pleasure is a non-mutual, male-dominated approach that smacks of selfish hedonism. A more perceptive observation from Watanabe Kaku (Professor of Medicine at Keiō University) holds that

> Even though we now live in an era where we can have sex without giving birth to children, no one has been educated for it in that form . . . although sex and the reproductive function have been separated, the problem men and women face is that the only moral interpretation assumes the creation of children. . . .[22]

This moral void concerning the status of marital sexuality without procreation contrasts strongly with the treatment of

[22] Quoted in Aoki 1976:132.

sexuality in the West, where various Christian sects formally approved non-reproductive sexuality in marriage many years ago. The Lambeth Congress of Anglican Bishops, for example, declared in 1930 that sexual intercourse is as important for marital love as for procreation; some thirty years later, the Second Vatican Conference adopted the same stance.[23]

In the past (roughly speaking, before World War II) conjugal love was antithetical to the principles of Japanese family organization, which emphasized loyalty to parents and continuity through male heirs. Parents chose a bride for their son on the basis of the woman's potential for serving family interests, including her fecundity, and families that paid much attention to the issue of mutual attraction between the prospective spouses were a distinct minority. The young bride's full membership in the family often depended on proving her fertility; one practice, especially prevalent in the rural areas, was to delay registration of the marriage until the wife had had a live birth. An old saying—still widely quoted—held that "the bride who bears no children leaves after three years" (*yome shite sannen, ko naki wa saru*). When love became an issue, it was typically as a threat to the functioning of the family: unmarried young men and women formed attachments to individuals whom they could never marry, or, if they were already married, created liaisons that threatened the well-being of the family. Nor was a strong bond of affection between husband and wife desirable, since it could subvert the vertical tie between parents and son, a key relationship in the organization of the traditional family.

Conjugal sexuality for both men and women in the old family system emphasized—as one would imagine—reproduction to the exclusion of pleasure. For husbands, sexual intercourse was a duty to produce offspring, summarized in the expression "obligatory fuck" (*giri man*). Pleasureful sex was extramarital. The married woman thus faced another challenge, that of keeping her husband from straying and dissipating his attentions—and wealth—elsewhere, particu-

[23] Polgar 1977:179.

larly since the children of extramarital alliances were legally recognizeable. The grandmother of one informant from a middle-class family in Yokohama had once described her own efforts: "I was taught to get up before my husband did, dress in a completely wrinkle-free kimono, and arrange my coiffure so that there was not a single stray hair. I was competing with *geisha*." She was also taught to thank her husband after sexual intercourse. Women were also encouraged to resign themselves to their husbands' extramarital affairs by consoling themselves with the impersonal, contractual aspects of their legal and social status as wives (referred to as *tsuma no za*).

The monumental social change in Japan in the last half century or so has resulted in strong inter-generational contrasts in sexuality; as mentioned before, younger women are less inhibited than their mothers. Men, too, have shed some of their sexual dominance. Far fewer couples live in multi-generational households, and those who do share life with their parents on a far more equal footing.

Despite the changes in women's status and the rise of the nuclear family, however, Japanese marital sexuality has not converged with the Western pattern, just as segregated conjugal life-styles have persisted across the class spectrum. A theme from the traditional family remains: the subordination of conjugal love to other functions of the family unit, the most noticeable of which is child-rearing. The proliferation of nuclear families does not necessarily mean the preeminence of the conjugal bond; although it is widely said in Japan that marriage is now "couple-centered," the sentiment refers to freedom from subordination to elderly parents and not to a shift away from the old emphasis on parent-child ties over the husband-wife relationship.[24]

Japanese couples still find it difficult to assert their conjugal companionship and sexuality over lineal, parent-child ties. Not only do children have a predictable presence in the couple's outings, as noted in the last chapter; they literally come

[24] This point has been put forth and developed by the family sociologist Masuda Kōkichi (1969:14).

between the spouses in seating on public conveyances or when walking abreast. Commericals also depict parents separated by their children. Many couples still share their sleeping rooms with their younger children, although parents have been putting children in separate sleeping quarters at an earlier age in recent years.[25] Only about 22 percent of the questionnaire survey couples with a child under four years of age sleep separately as a couple.

The act of creating a private space for sexual activity may be difficult to accept even if the children already sleep separately; some couples are quite ambivalent about locking their children out of their sleeping room. In one discussion with a public health instructor in his late twenties, for example, I posed the scenario of the American parents who closed their bedroom door on weekend mornings (together with the children's tacit understanding that entering was taboo); his reaction toward the parents was that they were "selfish" (*wagamama*).

The most dramatic example of the precedence of the parent-child tie over the conjugal relationship develops when a newlywed pair who enjoy a high level of shared leisure activities experience an unwanted pregnancy. The decision of whether or not to keep the pregnancy can generate a crisis if the wife is undecided and the husband favors an abortion, fearing (with justification) the loss of his companion to motherhood. Older relatives—and the family planning establishment, if a midwife or family planning counselor is involved—will oppose the husband by criticizing his stance as selfish and accusing him of trying to "monopolize" his wife.

The demands of being parents are not the only centrifugal pull on conjugal sexuality; while the traditional family no longer turns the husband away from conjugal love, the workplace makes a claim on his time and energy that can detract substantially from his participation in a fuller marital sex life. In interviews and discussions, both men and women identified the husband's job-related fatigue as an obstacle to marital

[25] Caudill and Plath 1966; Mizushima 1975; Morioka 1973.

sexual activity. Four of the interviewee husbands, ranging in age from 25 to 43, said that their frequency of marital intercourse would be higher were it not for exhaustion from work. According to Japanese sexologist Muramatsu Hiroo, the problem is aggravated by commutes on crowded trains for two or three hours every day. Muramatsu also pointed to the social demands of the husband's work group as a drain on libido, likening the company work group to a "social hothouse."

Some wives express disappointment at the slack in—or complete loss of—their husbands' sexual attentions because of their commitment to work. A social worker at a large electronics firm described a fairly recent phenomenon among couples having infrequent intercourse because of the husband's long work hours: a few of the wives angrily reject their husbands' sporadic advances, saying "You're not married to me, you're married to the company." Japanese social scientists have conjectured that the vicarious success of the "education mama" in her children's accomplishments offers her a "psychological consolation" for a lack of communication with her husband,[26] a lack that would almost certainly encourage libidinal transfer to child-raising. Narabayashi Yasushi is more explicit: sexually frustrated wives channel their interests in their sons' success. One older, Western-educated mother observed wrily: "We have no Oedipal problems here in Japan—there's no competition from the father."

Women's inability to gain equality in the sexual politics of their marriages also frustrates the development of sexual love. Wives still assume a one-sided burden of responsibility for the quality of marital sex, as evidenced in their solitary searches for help when sexual problems arise. The danger of husbands' extramarital affairs plays a subtle but pervasive part in wives' feelings of responsibility for an active marital sex life. A subconscious concern for holding on to a husband could account for the "quota mentality" toward frequency of intercourse among wives that the marriage counselor Fukazawa Michiko

[26] Fujin Chōsakai 1974:115.

described and criticized as a mechanical approach to sexuality that lacks mutuality and emotional content.

THE SEXUALITY OF THE SERVICE PROVIDERS

Sexuality in present-day Japanese culture poses another problem for family planning; the feelings and attitudes about sex among the specialists prevent them from promoting contraception more effectively. The ability to discuss sexual aspects of reproduction spontaneously and in detail is indispensible to effective contraceptive instruction. As an extreme example of the dangers of inadequate communication, there was one case in Tokyo at the time of this research in which a patient given contraceptive pills was inserting them in her vagina.

It is doubtful that any doctor would reply in the affirmative if asked directly about difficulty in discussing sexual matters with patients. However, there are instances where doctors have expressed their own discomfort in such situations. One Ob-Gyn with his own hospital who graduated from medical school in 1941, after commenting on the greater frankness displayed by his patients under age 50, was then asked if he thought it was a good trend and if he appreciated the difference. After a brief pause he replied with a laugh, "Well, I was born in Meiji society myself [before 1912, but in this context meaning pre-Shōwa], so I sometimes feel like my older patients." Another private practitioner, a few years younger and more direct about expressing his difficulty in discussing matters related to sex, noted, "In my family it was considered highly improper to discuss food and hunger, elimination, and sex. No one ever brought up such matters."

Most doctors in private practice are in the higher age groups that are the least communicative about matters relating to sex. The average age of hospital-operating Ob-Gyns in Tokyo is about 53.[27] Generational differences in sexuality may also be at work in shaping Japanese specialists' attitudes toward elective sterilization. As described in Chapter 3, doctors typically

[27] Tsuboi 1975:324.

share with family planning administrators a negative view of contraceptive sterilization. Since older individuals in Japanese society have a greater tendency to regard reproduction as the primary—if not sole—purpose of marital sexuality, sterilization strictly for contraception conflicts with their feelings about conjugal sex. Doctors and administrators in the upper echelons of the family planning organization who teach family planning instructors and write texts on birth control are also in the higher age brackets—hence the warning that appeared in the advice book for working women quoted in Chapter 3 that sterilization could make marital sex "hollow."

Given the advanced age range of Ob-Gyns in private practice, one might suspect that they would prefer to reinforce the sexual mores of their generation on younger women. One indication of this tendency lies in the negative attitudes that some Ob-Gyns express about menstrual tampons; they justify dissuading unmarried women from using them by pointing to the danger of a ruptured hymen.[28] Japanese feminists who have counseled young women in self-examination and have conducted marketing research on tampons cite the attitudes of health care specialists as one reason for low tampon use rates; the basic attitude of Ob-Gyns, they claim, is that the only object that should enter the vagina is the husband's penis.

Japan's medical schools do not offer formal training in human sexuality or family planning. An indication of a need for more information among Ob-Gyns comes from the Kantō doctors' survey; although the questionnaire form was anonymous, seven respondents put their names on the form and requested to hear the survey results, which Satō attributes to a very low level of communication among doctors relating to sex and related subjects, as well as to the absence of education in human sexuality and family planning.

The orientation toward motherhood found in Japan's family planning programs stems from an inability to recognize the existence of non-reproductive sexuality, as well as the preponderence of older maternal child health specialists in the

[28] *Tōkyō Shinbun* 1975.

ranks of these organizations. The sentiment that contraceptive sterilization does not rightfully belong in the family planning armamentarium persists in the movement's leadership. Similarly, their definition of family planning does not include the use of contraception before childbearing begins, even among married couples; regardless of how long a couple has been married and using contraception, "family planning" does not begin until they have their first child.[29]

The sexuality of Japan's family planning movement gives its orientation and activities a decidedly old-fashioned flavor: in the words of one disgruntled Western-trained Ob-Gyn, Japan's family planning establishment is "strictly Old Country (*naniwabushi*)." The commitment to reproductive sexuality might also explain the movement's promotion of periodic methods of contraception; because instruction in these methods necessitates little more than a description of the female reproductive cycle, it affirms the priority of reproductive potential.

Perhaps Japan's family planning leadership also finds an appeal in the maternity-oriented approach to sexual issues because it offers social respectability. For the Japan Family Planning Association, the controversial topic of sex education for adolescent females falls under the rubric of "maternal health guidance," despite the fact that childbearing is some twelve years in the future for Japan's nascent women.[30]

The discomfiture at non-reproductive sexuality within Japan's health care and family planning establishments has resulted in a gap in information and guidance for today's young couples that cannot be filled by their peer group or by the parental generation. Where the specialists have fallen short, the commercial media have carved out a niche, however, in an attempt to fill an information vacuum that excites their profit motive. Magazine articles and television programs on

[29] *Kazoku Keikaku* 1976a:5.
[30] There has been some mild criticism of the maternal health approach within the family planning establishment, however; Negishi 1976.

sexual topics appeal strongly to their Japanese audience, not only because of intrinsic interest and a dearth of alternate sources of information; in a society where there are few channels of communication on sexual topics, individuals can look at television programs and read magazine articles in privacy and anonymity.

The desirability of commercial media activity in family planning and sex education is undercut by the very reasons for its involvement. The media stepped in where informed professional activity was absent, which means—as Chapter 3 argued—minimal professional control on the accuracy of the material offered. Of at least equal damage, however, is the entertainment media's way of presenting sexual topics sensationally. Valid information must come from a source that is perceived as "sincere" or "serious"; the treatment of sexuality and related matters in the mass media is commonly regarded as suspect since it smacks of appeal to vulgar curiosity (referred to as *kyōmi honi*, whereas a serious treatment is *majime*). As a result, many Japanese read these articles avidly but may still be somewhat at a loss when it comes to discerning authoritative, dependable sources of information among the articles that they read. In their efforts to increase readership appeal, publishers have recently placed articles on sexuality alongside articles dealing with contraception, a trend that has reduced even more the perceived reliability of the information presented. These problems in the media approach to family planning education probably underlie the observation made by Kon Yasuo that, "the flood of information from weekly magazines, women's magazines, and television hinders correct judgment, and has a contrary aspect of aggravating insecurity."[31]

Similarly, the mass media pose a liability for the serious specialist who wants to disseminate information to a broad audience. Ob-Gyns on university faculties expose themselves to criticism from colleagues if they appear on commercial

[31] Kon 1971:21.

television to discuss contraception. Individual sex specialists have become popular figures, but each has enjoyed only a passing popularity, and the price has been ostracism from the professional community of specialists, if not credibility in the public eye.

CHAPTER 8

Four Couples

Generalizations about a society always cut across a melange of unique individual differences—even when the generalizations are about the Japanese, a people very homogeneous in culture. Rapid social change has generated noticeable age-related differences in marital life-styles that cross-cancel or accentuate the effects of each couple's social status and affluence, and individual life histories and personality differences add their own flavors to each couple's way of going about life together. As a result, no couple is completely typical. At the same time, however, it is these same husbands and wives who face common problems of fertility limitation, and their responses fall into the aggregate statistical patterns which make up Japan's unique fertility limitation scene; it is, after all, couples who have abortions, not fertility survey data sets.

I offer the following profiles of some of the interviewee couples in order to give the reader a feel for the fusion of individual idiosyncracies with the larger cultural themes that influence the Japanese couple's approach to family planning. The non-essential details of these marriage portraits have been modified to help protect the interviewees' anonymity, and all names are fictitious.

AFFLUENT BLUE COLLARS: THE IMAIZUMI COUPLE

Imaizumi Sumie and her husband, Toshio, live in a two-story house in a new housing development on the northwest side of Tokyo. Married for a little over twelve years, they have two children, an 11-year-old boy and a 5-year-old girl. Sumie is 33 years old, and Toshio is 36. The house, where they have lived for four years, is rather spacious by urban Japanese standards. Each child has a separate bedroom, and the downstairs has a modest drawing room that Toshio has made into his own den. The small front hallway is dominated by a stand which displays a two-foot tall geisha doll in a glass case.

Toshio is a semi-skilled worker at a large chemical processing plant that hired him after he graduated from high school. He gets up at 5 a.m. on workdays, for his commute is an hour and a half. Toshio does not particularly enjoy associating with his fellow workers, and he goes drinking with them only about once every other month. Recently he has been working overtime a lot, however, so it is not unusual for him to return home around 9 p.m. His personal recreation consists largely of home electronics projects, listening to music, and occasional reading.

Sumie had been working in the same plant when she met Toshio, but she left her job within a few months of their marriage because she had become pregnant. She has been a full-time housewife and mother since then. The children's education is her major preoccupation, to the point that she feels anxious about their academic success and exhausted from her own efforts. Sumie's own education ended when she finished junior high school.

Toshio limits his household help to straightening out his den occasionally. On rare occasions when Sumie is ill he prepares meals, but his cooking repertory is limited to a few very simple dishes like fried eggs. (Sumie told her interviewer that she was satisfied with that level of help; he told me that she was not.) He also bathes with his children, and helps them with their homework in mathematics.

The Imaizumis go out together only on shopping trips to buy specific items, and their children usually accompany them. Sumie does not particularly want to go out more often because she feels fatigued from child-raising. She does not share her husband's enjoyment of music, so the two do not listen together.

Toshio feels that his interest in sex is stronger than his wife's, and she concurs. Her own statements about sexual intercourse were extremely negative: "Once a year would be fine with me—I hate sex, and the less of it there is, the better."

She feels, though, that her husband doesn't like sex that much, so he isn't especially dissatisfied. They have sexual relations about three times a month, which is a little less than half the figure for wives Sumie's age who are using contraception. Although the children have separate sleeping quarters, the daughter occasionally sleeps with her parents.

The couple began using condoms when they were first married. Sumie said her husband introduced her to the method. Toshio said, "It wasn't a matter of either of us choosing, we just kind of decided on it. But my wife is the more interested of the two of us." Sumie has had discussions with a midwife whose services were provided as an employee benefit by the chemicals plant, and she has many discussions about child-raising with friends from school days. Sex, however, is rarely a topic. Toshio said that he has never confided in relatives or workplace friends about contraception or matters related to sexuality: "I have no reason to, since there's nothing that really bothers me."

Within seven months of their marriage, Sumie became pregnant; both partners attributed the conception to a torn condom. When they had married, the Imaizumis had planned on saving money to build a house before having children. Sumie explained their reason for keeping the pregnancy: "We were already married, so having a baby was just a matter of course (*tōzen*)." Giving birth meant that Sumie had to leave her job, but Toshio's parents in nearby Saitama Prefecture offered the couple lodging with them and child-care help. (Three years later they moved into a company-owned apartment.)

After their first birth, Toshio and Sumie began using condoms again. Their next pregnancy was planned, and it occurred almost six years later. Sumie said she waited until her son was four years old before discontinuing contraception because she was entirely responsible for taking care of him, and morning sickness during her first pregnancy had left her bedridden for days on end. (Toshio said they waited for "economic reasons.") They have been using contraception since their second birth, and neither partner wants more children.

The couple is still using condoms. Although Sumie said that

she has "entrusted control" of contraception to her husband (*otto ni kontorōru o makasete imasu*), some time after the second birth she began calculating her cycles, using the Ogino method, and she now refuses to have intercourse during her fecund period. Toshio dislikes buying condoms because it is "too embarrassing"; Sumie buys them from the midwife at the chemicals plant. Although Sumie had no likes or dislikes about condoms that she wanted to express in her interview, Toshio cited two advantages: condoms were "easily available" and a "sure method with no failures." The disadvantage of condoms, however, was that "feeling nothing is better." Sumie said that she did worry "somewhat" about contraceptive failure, and that although she wasn't especially confident about their current contraceptive regimen, neither did she think about it much. Both partners reported that they had not had any contraceptive failures, other than the torn condom, and neither spouse anticipates any. In the event of a conception, they would rely on induced abortion.

The Imaizumis fit into one pattern among couples who have completed their families; they have opted for an effective combination of traditional methods instead of modern contraception, and their low frequency of intercourse helps to assure that they will not have to face an unwanted pregnancy. Sumie's relatively low level of education and the couple's experience of only one unwanted conception also militated against an eventual switch to moderns, as did the guidance of a midwife who was probably promoting condoms and the Ogino method.

On a deeper level, however, the marked segregation of conjugal roles in this marriage has also contributed to the Imaizumis' contraceptive status quo. Although Toshio's personality runs counter to the popular image of the group-oriented Japanese worker, he has not sought companionship with his wife, either; his leisure activities are solitary, his help with domestic tasks and child-raising minimal. Sumie, for her part, was the most intense "education mama" in the interviews, and her rejection of sexuality one of the most unequivocal.

Just as this husband and wife do not approach sexuality as

a way of sharing, neither have they worked out a way for more satisfactory contraception despite Sumie's concern about failure and Toshio's dislike of the condom's tactile sensation. Their emotional separation and their desire that the other partner handle contraception is illustrated by their responses to the question of whether they had ever considered another contraceptive method. Toshio mentioned that his wife had tried foaming tablets, but "she said they felt terrible so we stopped." Sumie did not mention the foaming tablets, but she did relate that she had suggested vasectomy to Toshio some two years after their second child was born; according to Sumie, he had rejected the idea because the operation was too painful.

YOUTHFUL MIDDLE CLASS: THE ISHIDA COUPLE

Ishida Shigeru was 27 years old when he met 25-year-old Kataoka Mayumi, the woman who was soon to be his wife. They met in a very atypical way for prospective Japanese spouses: they noticed one another on the same suburban station platform waiting for trains, felt a mutual attraction, and started dating one another. Now, some six years later, they live in an apartment with three rooms and a kitchen dinette in a suburban town about six kilometers from Nagoya. They have two sons, ages four and two.

Shigeru is a college graduate in business economics, and he works in consumer research for a medium-sized advertising company. He enjoys his work, and he enjoys associating with his officemates. Shigeru believes that after-hours social drinking with fellow workers provides an important opportunity for solving personnel problems, but he also said that he is "too busy" for more than two or so late night outings per month. He usually returns home from work between eight and nine p.m. His favorite hobby is fly casting, and the living room walls of the Ishida home display mounted specimens of his finer catches.

Mayumi is also a four-year college graduate. Her major was French, and she has applied her education by translating French fashion magazines and cook books at home. Her income supplements housekeeping expenses and clothing, but she values her work more for offering her a chance to exercise her abilities outside of housework and for giving her "ongoing contact with the world."

Shigeru has also encouraged her to value her part-time career. Mayumi appreciates her husband's regard for her work, which she regards as compensation for his own late work hours: "My husband also thinks highly of my work, so I'm not irritated if he works late or spends a whole night on the job."

Shigeru's household tasks are minimal. He puts away the family's bedding (*futon*) a few times every week, and he occasionally cooks dinner on Sundays and holidays but does not clean up the kitchen afterward. His child-care activities are limited to watching the children when his wife goes out on errands alone. Mayumi would like more help with cleaning, particularly since the children create more cleaning jobs but are still too young to help. Mayumi also mentioned that she would like help with the laundry, but that she doesn't really mind doing it all herself.

The family goes shopping and on walks together every Sunday at nearby temples and parks during the younger son's waking hours, but Shigeru and Mayumi practically never go out together as a couple. Both partners said that before their children were born they had had a high frequency of shared leisure activities, and they both look forward to the time when they can once again enjoy leisure together as a couple. Mayumi said that she would like to use babysitters if they were available, and just recently their children were accepted at a local nursery school. This allowed the couple the chance for a day trip to a nearby vacation spot, for which Shigeru took vacation time from work.

Shigeru expressed a desire to preserve a romantic element in their marriage. He was critical of Japanese wives who lose interest in sexuality because they have turned their attention and energy toward their children. Mayumi, however, had some very negative things to say about sexual intercourse: "I don't like it that much—it's a bother (*wazurawashii*). I've got too much else that concerns me." She also reported that her husband expressed dissatisfaction that they had little time to relax alone together after the birth of their second child. Her translating work also kept her up at night—and out of his arms—when their children were in their infancy. She reasoned that her husband has a stronger libido than she by noting that she had never approached him for sexual intercourse. Men in general, she believes, have an "animalistic instinct (*dōbutsu-teki honnō*)" that makes them more sexually desirous. The couple's present coital frequency is about ten times per month, nearly half again as high as the figure of seven for contracepting women between the ages of 30 and 34 in the questionnaire sample.

Both spouses claimed one another as their only conversation partners for matters of sexuality and contraception, and both also relied on books for information. Shigeru said that he would like to see a freer atmosphere among men in which such matters could be discussed, but he had never discussed these things with fellow workers because "there never was an occasion for it."

The Ishidas began using condoms when they married. Shigeru said that he selected the method after reading about it in a book, but Mayumi made the purchases from drugstores and door-to-door saleswomen. The couple avoided using condoms when Mayumi thought her menses were approaching, but the risk-taking resulted in an unwanted pregnancy. In Mayumi's own words:

> When we were first married we were both working and we wanted to enjoy life as a twosome. Also, we were thinking we wanted to be able to put away some savings, but a child was conceived a little sooner than we'd planned. I guess it happened early enough to call it a "honeymoon baby." When I knew I was pregnant I thought, at last it's come (*tōtō yatte kita*). I'm not young, I'll give birth. I wasn't disappointed. I think my husband probably wasn't either.

After the birth of their first child the Ishidas resumed condom use, but they also alternated with Mayumi's casual rhythm
method. Within two years their second son was born. He was
Mayumi's second pregnancy and he, too, was unplanned, but
both partners said he was more welcome than the first pregnancy. (The birth interval was about a year shorter than the
wife's stated preference.) Within the next two years, however,
Mayumi underwent two induced abortions, both resulting,
again, from omitting condoms during what the couple had
hoped was an infertile part of Mayumi's cycle. After the birth
of the second son they had decided that they wanted no more
children. Mayumi said she was willing to keep the pregnancies,
but her husband did not want more children. Shigeru said
that he would want one more child were it not for their cramped
housing and the exorbitant cost of more living space. Shigeru
convinced her of the need to abort, given the shape of the
family economy, she said, so she underwent the operations
"without resistance."

Soon after the second abortion Shigeru had a vasectomy.
Both spouses claimed that they researched the method in books
on family planning and then suggested it to the other partner.
Mayumi, however, gave a more detailed account of how she
read up on various medical methods and then suggested the
method, and Shigeru's discussion dwelled more on how he
chose a urologist at a large hospital. Shigeru was also well
versed in his knowledge of the law relating to sterilization.
Despite her negative statements about marital sexuality, Mayumi also said that, thanks to the vasectomy, she had gotten
to the point where she could enjoy sex. Although neither of
her abortions had left physical or emotional after-effects, sexual intercourse gave her strong anxieties about pregnancy,
particularly when her menses were later than usual.

The Ishidas displayed a degree of initative in contraception
that is rather unusual among Japanese couples. The way in
which they researched vasectomy highlights the contribution
of their educational backgrounds to their solution of their
family planning problems. Despite their education, however,
they had started their marriage no better off than couples

having a lower class status, even though they had wanted to postpone childbearing. By Western middle class standards, the length of time that they tolerated a selection of methods that was inappropriate to their sexuality is remarkable.

The Ishida couple also presents an interesting blend of modern themes familiar to the West, together with characteristically Japanese influences on marital life-style. Shigeru respects his wife's work and welcomes it as something that will make her a socially more interesting person, and both spouses explicitly attach great importance to shared leisure and a romantic element in marriage that should not be completely displaced by child-raising. Mayumi welcomes Shigeru's companionship, and she derives considerable pleasure from her professional activity. In these ways the couple appears very progressive; their ideals represent a youthful new wave among conjugal life-styles. Nevertheless, the husband's work and the demands of child-raising exert familiar pulls on the couple's life together. Shigeru enjoys his job as well as the after-hours socializing involved, and Mayumi's work is, in her own words, a happy compromise for his absences. His long hours at work probably account for his minimal domestic assistance as well as for her acceptance of his lack of help. The lack of baby-sitting or other child care had reduced their activities as a couple to virtually nil.

More noticeable still are Mayumi's negative comments about sexuality, which were unexpected, given her educational level and her enjoyment of her husband's company. For his part, Shigeru's account of their selection of family planning methods hinted at a desire to maintain the appearance of a leadership role as opposed to genuine cooperation in selecting a family planning method. (He was reluctant to mention that his wife used to purchase their condoms, and it looks more likely that she had actually proposed vasectomy to him than vice versa.) Perhaps, had Mayumi been more accepting of sexuality and Shigeru less committed to a traditional male leadership image, they could have met their contraceptive needs at an earlier point in their marriage.

OLDER MIDDLE CLASS: THE MIYAMOTO COUPLE

Miyamoto Yutaka is 43 years old, ten years older than Ishida Shigeru. Like Shigeru, he is a college graduate, but his wife, Mariko, is six years younger than he and her education ended when she graduated from high school. They live in a newly developed community some distance from Osaka with their two daughters, ages 16 and 10. Their home is very commodious, especially by Japanese standards: resembling a California semi-ranch style house, it boasts seven rooms. Every family member has a separate room, and the husband's mother lives in an adjoining unit with its own kitchen and bathroom. The rooms are elegantly furnished, and they display Mariko's successful efforts at interior decorating.

Yutaka works as an executive for a large textile fibers manufacturing corporation. His greatest pleasure in his work is the "strong team spirit" among his work group, and he gets along with them well. Although his work ends around 5:30 in the afternoon, Yutaka prefers to stay longer, and he also enjoys drinking with friends "as a way of avoiding rush hour." Since his commute home takes nearly an hour and a half, he usually arrives home between 10 and 11 p.m. Mariko explained that since her husband's work is managerial he goes out for social drinking often. Mariko does not object to his late return home, but when they were first married 17 years ago, he was addicted to playing mah jongg and she complained about that often. He quit playing when he was in his late 30s because, in his words, "you have to stay up really late in order to play a good game and my body just can't take it any more." Yutaka's current favorite leisure activity is golf, and he usually plays on Saturdays and Sundays if the weather is agreeable.

Yutaka does not perform any household tasks, although he used to wash dishes occasionally and put up the family's bedding. The family now has beds which Mariko makes up, and Yutaka believes that the couple's older daughter can provide whatever help he does not. Yutaka does not provide childcare help, either. He sees a role for himself as provider of help for his children's educational development, but he does not mind if both daughters' educations stop with high school.

Mariko has not worked outside their home since she married. Before then, she was an office worker at the Hiroshima branch of the company that employs Yutaka. Yutaka worked there as well, and the couple met one another at their workplace just as the Imaizumi's did. Both partners gave the same remarkably bland account of their reason for choosing one another for marriage: there were very few single members of the opposite sex in their office. Nevertheless, Yutaka recalled that they dated "very often" before they married, seeing movies and drinking tea together. Lately they have been going out together as a couple, primarily to visit acquaintances or shop. Yutaka said he encourages Mariko to get out of the house because it is "psychologically good for her." Mariko explained that their children do not accompany them because the children don't like outings with their parents.

Mariko's youthful and stylish appearance belies her embarrassment at discussing sexuality. She declined to estimate the couple's current coital frequency, and she worries about sexual privacy despite the spaciousness of their house. Mariko said that she began to enjoy sex more after the birth of her first child, and that in her late 20s her interest in sex temporarily surpassed her husband's, because she had fewer child-raising tasks and he was becoming more tired from increased work demands. She ended her comments on sexual compatibility by quipping that her husband returns home so late that he must be having affairs.

Yutaka recalled that he was very anxious about his ability to father a child when he was newly married. He declined to state who of the two is currently more sexually interested, observing instead that "it depends upon our individual moods." His estimate of the couple's frequency of intercourse was six times a month, which is close to the mean figure of about seven for survey respondents in Mariko's age group who were using contraception.

The Miyamotos did not use contraception after they married. Yutaka said he wanted a child as soon as possible, and he felt that Mariko did too. Mariko said she was "very surprised" when she became pregnant four months after their wedding. After that pregnancy, which resulted in the birth of their first daughter, they began using condoms. Yutaka proposed the method, but Mariko made the purchases via a neighborhood druggist at greatly reduced prices. He could not recall how he had learned about condoms, but he conjectured that friends had told him about them when he was single.

The couple practiced contraception for two years after their first birth. Mariko calculated her cycles using the Ogino calendrical method, and the couple omitted condoms during infertile intervals. Mariko blamed that practice for her three consecutive pregnancies that all ended in induced abortions within the two-year period. The pregnancies were too soon after the first birth for her, she explained, since she had to contend with infant care. Yutaka did not oppose her wish to end the pregnancies; according to Mariko, his response was one of resignation. When I asked Yutaka about the best length of time between births he said, "Our daughters are too far apart in age—three years apart would be best . . . they'd be closer to one another if their ages were closer together. But the question isn't number of years, it's the family economic situation."

When they suspended contraception because they wanted another child, the Miyamotos experienced difficulty in achieving a viable pregnancy; over the next two years they had two spontaneous abortions. They consulted a doctor, and Mariko also began calculating her cycles, using basal body temperature in order to optimize her chances for another conception. Her efforts were rewarded with a second daughter a little over six years after the birth of their first.

Yutaka said that he wanted a son and was willing to try again, but his wife was opposed. They resumed condom use, alternating with basal body temperature. Some five years since, however, their supplier went out of business, and Mariko has not found another source for condoms. For the last four and a half years they have been substituting interruptus for condoms, but have maintained the practice of unprotected inter-

course during the infertile periods that Mariko calculates, using BBT. Both partners are now certain that they want no
more children.

Neither of the Miyamotos particularly likes condoms, but
Yutaka was more explicit in voicing his dislikes. He laughed
when I asked him what he thought the advantages were, and
after probing, responded that, "They prevent pregnancy and
that's it." He dislikes the way that condoms "completely destroy the mood" of sex. Mariko said that condoms were "simple" but that they weren't safe. Early in their marriage, when
they were living in a large apartment complex, Mariko received an announcement from the local health department
that diaphragm fittings and instruction were available. She
wanted to go but felt too embarrassed, and she still occasionally thinks about the possibility of using a diaphragm. She
is also uneasy about the effectiveness of their present use of
interruptus. Yutaka's attitude toward interruptus has been
described in Chapter 5; he is also the husband in Chapter 6
who rejected a half-joking suggestion from his wife that he
obtain a vasectomy.

From the standpoint of need, Mariko is a good candidate
for a modern female method of contraception, but her embarrassment appears to be her greatest obstacle to obtaining
it. Mariko is the woman in Chapter 7 who suggested that
visits to gynecologists or public health centers for contraception should be compulsory, because that way she could overcome her embarrassment and go. And although she still thinks
about getting a diaphragm, her embarrasssment has held her
back since the birth of her first child. She is not completely
convinced that she is still fecund, which poses another disincentive to seek better contraception. Nevertheless, she dis-
trusts the couple's current contraceptive methods. Nor does
she regard abortion casually, although she would have to
resort to it again if her present methods fail; Mariko is the
woman described in Chapter 4 whose three abortions gave
her progressively greater feelings of guilt and unaccountable
pains in her abdomen that have persisted over the years. Mariko also felt that although husband and wife should both

"think about" contraception, the wife has to be more concerned because "it's the woman who gets pregnant."

Perhaps a higher educational background would have helped Mariko muster more initiative for contraceptive guidance, because in certain other respects she does resemble women who have chosen modern methods; she has experienced a number of contraceptive failures, her husband is in a high income bracket, and she has been married well over six years. But the most powerful determinant, exposure to professional advice, is still absent.

The Miyamotos' family planning history and their current contraceptive status clash with their affluence and cosmopolitan appearance, but not with the nature of their conjugal role relationship. Their approach to childbearing and fertility limitation bears the marks of a segregated relationship, in which the husband's concerns center on his ability to sire children, sexual gratification, and economic constraints on family size, but omit a recognition of the consequences of unintended pregnancy to his partner. His lack of concern for contraception, her inability to persuade him to accept vasectomy, and her own passivity in sexual matters point to an inegalitarian dimension that is also typical of segregated role relationships. Both partners claimed that the married couple should act together to take care of contraception, but their own family planning history does not approach the expressed ideal.

The partnership bears signs of segregation in other areas besides family planning; Yutaka's late-night returns home, his non-participation in domestic tasks, and both partners' pallid recollections of their reasons for marrying stand out in particular. During her interview, Mariko referred to her husband as "papa" (*papa*), another indicator of role segregation. The Miyamoto couple's weekend outings together without their children contradict the segregated pattern, but these events result partly from the couple's stage in their life cycle and their affluence. Yutaka no longer has pressing work demands or youthful ventures into mah jongg, and the children have grown independent of Mariko. If outings require money, they have it. Beneath the Western-style appearances, however, an older form of marital life-style still asserts itself, and it has affected the most intimate areas of this couple's life together.

ANOMALIES: THE KONDO COUPLE

Tanaka Hiroko was 29 years old and had a six-year-old daughter by her previous husband when she met Kondo Kazuo, who was then 26. (Her first husband had died in an auto accident some four years before.) They met three years ago, and, like the Ishida couple, in a public place that they both frequented—in this case, a Chinese noodle lunch counter. Hiroko and Kazuo have been married for two years and live with Hiroko's daughter in a two-room apartment with kitchen and bath in one of Kyoto's downtown neighborhoods.

Hiroko is a free-lance interior decorator for homes and restaurants. She graduated from a two-year arts junior college and, until recently, drew for an advertising agency. Kazuo is a sculptor. He came to Kyoto to work as a jewelry maker after he graduated from high school in Toyama Prefecture (a rural prefecture northeast of Kyoto). Some four years ago he quit his job, however, because it gave him no time for sculpting. Since then he has been doing various kinds of temporary and day labor, most of it manual, in order to provide support while he pursues his art. Kazuo wants to contract his sculpture to a gallery in a few years, when he feels his work has matured.

Both partners enjoy their work very much, but their income varies considerably, depending on whether or not jobs come in. Their combined incomes are below the average incomes of urban Japanese households. Since Kazuo does not work at one place, work-related outings after hours are not an issue. He has a few close friends who are also artists. Although he would enjoy drinking with his friends, he does not because it would pose a burden to family finances. His hobbies happily coincide with his family's needs in their present economically straitened circumstances; he likes to make items of furniture and clothing, in line with his personal philosophy of self-sufficiency.

Kazuo provides extensive household help when Hiroko's

work schedule gives her long work days away from home. At those times he cleans house—including the bath—cooks, and washes the family laundry. Although Hiroko said that she is quite satisfied with his help, Kazuo mentioned that there are times when she has expressed dissatisfaction; they have argued over it, he said, but the result is to work out an agreement with no hard feelings remaining for either of them.

Kazuo had some difficulty in telling me that their child was Hiroko's by a previous marriage, but he emphasized that he wants to treat her as his own. He enjoys giving her lessons in sculpting and baseball, and he mends her clothes. He and Hiroko have both taught her to help with cooking and laundry, and she is responsible for keeping neat the smaller room of roughly 80 square feet.

Hiroko and Kazuo share their outings as a couple; their daughter sometimes accompanies them, but lately she has preferred to stay at home. Their lack of money limits their activities to walks and only one trip a year for skiing. Like the Ishidas, they look forward to a future that will allow them more leisure activities together. Both partners said that the features of the other that originally attracted them are the same characteristics they like most today, and both described specific features of their spouse that reflect a high level of emotional mutuality. His favorite qualities that she possesses are her "unaffected, artless manner" (*tenshinranman*), her "pluck" (*yūki*), and her abilities as a good conversation partner. For her part, Hiroko says that she has always been attracted to his "kindness" (*yasashisa*); "I came to feel that I could walk through life beside him." She was also greatly relieved that her daughter has adapted smoothly to Kazuo's presence, and she appreciates the effort that he has made to gain her daughter's acceptance.

The couple's sexuality is also marked by a high degree of mutuality. Both partners said that the most enjoyable point in their marriage for sexual experiences is the present because they are learning one another's feelings. Hiroko finds that she can discuss sexual matters with her husband, whereas she felt she could not in her first marriage. Kazuo said he derives

pleasure from gratifying his wife through foreplay and "grad-
ualness" both before and after sexual intercourse; he is highly
critical of typical male sexuality, which he sees as inordinately
focused on penetration and rapid completion of sexual intercourse. Both spouses also claimed that they are pretty evenly
matched in sex drive, although Hiroko's interests may be
somewhat stronger; Hiroko mentioned that Kazuo is more
concerned about neighbors overhearing their lovemaking, and
he also mentioned that he sometimes doesn't feel well enough
for sex. When he is not interested in sex, however, they discuss
the matter until their feelings are resolved. Their frequency of
intercourse is about 16 times a month, in contrast to a monthly
mean of 7 for contracepting wives in Hiroko's age group.

The Kondos experienced an unwanted pregnancy together
before they had married. Although they intended to marry at
the time, neither felt ready for a child. Hiroko said she disliked
the idea of marrying because she was pregnant and felt that
when she gave birth it should be because she wanted to; Kazuo
felt they were ill prepared economically, not only in terms of
money available but also because he wanted to have clothing
and furnishings that they had made themselves for the child.
They decided together on an abortion.

The Kondos want to have a child together, but Hiroko does
not want one in the immediate future because she wants to
continue her career on a full-time basis. Kazuo, on the other
hand, is hoping that they can have one within a year.

The couple was not using a contraceptive method when
Hiroko became pregnant. After her abortion, the couple used
condoms. Neither partner could state specifically how they
had selected condoms originally, although Kazuo reported
subsequent conversations where they had discussed the alternatives but decided to use condoms. Both spouses purchase
them, but Hiroko buys them from a drugstore and Kazuo
purchases them from a vending machine when she asks him
to. According to Hiroko, a door-to-door saleswoman had
recently talked her husband into buying about a hundred dollars' worth of condoms (three gross).

The couple rarely deviates from condom use, although Kazuo applies them after sexual intercourse has begun. Hiroko said that she cannot rely on rhythm because her cycle is irregular, although she also reported omitting condoms when the couple makes love "right after" her menses end. Kazuo also reported sporadic use of interruptus; he is the husband whose assessment of his wife's reaction to the practice was contrasted with Miyamoto Yutaka's statements in Chapter 5. He is also one of the informants who, as related in Chapter 4, believes that Japanese men find it difficult to discuss abortion because their "selfishness" keeps them from considering the problem until they are confronted with an unwanted pregnancy.

Although neither partner particularly likes condoms, they have stayed with the method through a process of elimination. Both partners dislike the interruption that condoms pose to sexual intercourse. Kazuo also dislikes the dulling of sensation, and Hiroko does not trust the method's effectiveness. Nethertheless, Hiroko cited as positive points that condoms have a "simple mode of action" and pose no danger to health. Both partners distrust the pill's effects on female physiology. Kazuo also fears that pill use can cause deformed offspring. The Ob-Gyn who attended Hiroko's delivery had fitted her for a diaphragm, but Hiroko disliked using it, mostly, she said, because she disliked having to leave it in place after intercourse.

The Kondos were the only couple in the interview sample who were literally self-selected; after hearing about my research from a friend at a women's counseling center, Kazuo contacted me through the friend so that he could discuss his own family planning situation with me, find out what contraceptive method would be best for him and his wife, and perhaps also learn where to obtain it. (Both partners mentioned that they have friends with whom they can discuss sex and contraception.) Kazuo and Hiroko were seriously considering an IUD, but they were concerned about their ability to pay for one. Ironically enough, there was a clinic at a nearby medical school that was providing IUDs with copper as part of a research project for less money than Kazuo had paid for the three gross of condoms that the "skin lady" had sold him. After their family economy absorbed the cost of Kazuo's purchase, Hiroko went to the clinic for an IUD.

The most notable contrast between the Kondos' family planning efforts and those of more typical Japanese couples lies in the fact that this couple obtained a modern method of contraception before they had reached their intended family size. Kazuo's active role in finding more satisfactory contraception also stands out. Perhaps the underlying feature of the Kondos' marriage that is most responsible for both of these contrasts is Hiroko's status in the conjugal relationship: thanks to a strong egalitarian dimension, Kazuo is concerned about his wife's exposure to an unplanned pregnancy, which in turn has motivated him to search for more effective prevention. Then, too, his interest in creating a gratifying sexual experience for her could be contributing to her interest in finding a method that disrupts her sexual enjoyment less and makes her more sexually accessible to him.

Nevertheless, even the Kondos' fertility regulation history bears some features that are nearly universal among Japanese couples. Despite their initial mutual attraction for one another and the highly integrated role relationship that developed, coordination of contraception began at nil. The couple resorted to condoms despite their dislike of the method after the chastening experience of an induced abortion. Hiroko's rejection of the diaphragm despite her experience with its use is also noteworthy. Perhaps, in the earliest phase of their sexual relationship, both partners were locked into the larger culture's definition of roles and responsibilities; thus, Hiroko may have feared that she would displease Kazuo if she displayed some sexual sophistication by taking initiative, and Kazuo may have assumed a false authority that told him the risks of pregnancy were minimal. Then, too, the task of coordinating contraception may have been made more difficult because the relationship did not have the extra promise of stability that marriage provides. One wonders about the extent to which the Kondos' difficulties derived from insufficient availability of contraceptive information and services. Kazuo's fear of pill-induced deformities indicates the misinformation to which the couple has been exposed, and his victimization by an aggressive condom sales pitch accentuates an important point: the couple could have gotten more appropriate contraception with more adequate supervision, had their money spent on condoms gone instead into a well-organized clinical system staffed by trained medical personnel and operated with an aggressive outreach program.

It would be unwise at best to consider the Kondos representative of Japanese couples. Couples in which the wife has more formal education are unusual in present-day urban Japan. Most unusual of all, Kondo Hiroko, a widow caring for a young child, remarried with a younger man in his first marriage. She and her husband have a life-style with elements of frontier self-sufficiency and Bohemian independence that make these people anomalies in their larger culture. Their story, however, offers a valuable hint about the determinants of initiative in family planning: their mutuality in daily life and sexuality befits their positive approach to conception control.

CHAPTER 9

What Would Bring About a Change?

For Japan in the 1980s, fertility limitation technology and use pattern remain basically unchanged from the late 1950s. There has been a noticeable increase in couples who claim current contraceptive practice, from about 40 percent to 60 percent in the twenty years from 1959 to 1979.[1] The methods that they use remain the same, however, and the improvement in effectiveness dubious. As of 1979, 82 percent of couples in the Mainichi survey who had ever used contraception named condoms as a method that they had adopted, an increase over the 1977 figure of 79.

Nor has there been any great improvement in the extent to which the country's women make use of induced abortion. Although the absolute number of officially reported induced abortions has declined rather steadily since the peak years of the mid-1950s, with a 30 percent decline between 1965 and 1980, the figures behind the trend are untrustworthy. A remarkable demographic phenomenon of the mid-1960s highlights the unreliability of official abortion figures. The crude birth rate in 1966 dropped sharply to 13.7 from the rate of 18.6 for the year before because, according to folk belief based on the Chinese zodiac, female children born in that year (known as Fire and Horse, *Hinoeuma*) would make poor marriage partners. The dramatic drop in the birth rate attests to parents' anxieties about finding marriage partners for their daughters, but the official induced abortion figures for 1966 show the unreliability of the abortion trend line, because they show a *decline* of nearly 35,000 cases from the 1965 level. The decrease took place despite a greater exercise of fertility control among precisely those who would be more likely to rely on induced abortion, the rural, socially conservative sector of

[1] Mainichi Shinbunsha 1979:37.

society.[2] Muramatsu's estimates of actual abortion frequency, based on the age structure of the married population, show a decided drop in the ratio of abortions to live births between 1955 and 1960, but his 1975 estimate, based on the assumption of contraceptive effectiveness midway between his high and low extremes, results in a live birth to abortion ratio of 100:120, a figure that is higher than his estimate for 1965.[3]

Such stability invites an attempt at prediction: will the Japanese mode of family planning ever come to resemble the Western Euro-American pattern, and, if so, how and when? Forecasting any social trend is a risky proposition, and an area like family planning seems especially so, since so many different dimensions of social organization impinge upon it. Prediction, nonetheless, is the touchstone of explanation in the social sciences. My own interpretation of why the Japanese limit their fertility in the ways that they do identifies a number of factors that could reshape Japan's family planning scene. The next task is to elaborate on their meaning for the future.

DEUS EX MACHINA

Availability of modern contraception is the single most powerful determinant of the family planning methods Japanese couples choose. The evidence presented in Chapter 4 leaves little doubt that Japanese women prefer to prevent pregnancies rather than terminate them. If a family planning campaign like those in developing countries funded by foreign aid money were to take place in Japan, the response would reshape the country's family planning scene: Japanese couples would adopt medical methods of contraception if they were offered in a low-cost, comprehensive program involving positive promotion and instruction. The effects of income and professional sources of information on method choice, discussed in Chapter 5, substantiate this assertion, as do the positive responses

[2] See Azumi 1968; this argument was posed by Christopher Tietze and Sarah Lewit (1969).
[3] Muramatsu 1978:96; Muramatsu and van der Tak 1978:148.

of interviewee wives to the idea of contraceptive instruction from Ob-Gyns. Nevertheless, the point deserves reiteration not only because of its importance, but also because I fear that my explanation of how and why Japanese couples accept the family planning status quo will be misinterpreted as an apology for the present situation.

Even the promotion of intravaginal contraceptives in early postwar Japan had a demonstrable effect on user rates, despite women's strong resistance to handling their genitals—a tendency that was even more pronounced then than it is now. Low rates of intravaginal method acceptance were not always the rule in Japan; in the early postwar period, intravaginal methods were on a par with condoms in percentage of reported use experience. In 1950, 37.4 percent of couples having experience with contraception reported use of intravaginals (diaphragm, tablets or jelly, douche excluded), as opposed to 35.6 percent for condoms.[4] Midwives trained by Occupation personnel promoted diaphragms, primarily in the countryside; similarly, the manufacturers of spermicidal tablets conducted advertising and educational campaigns aimed at a rural as well as an urban market. The result as of the mid-1970s is a greater concentration of users of intravaginal methods among precisely those groups of women that would otherwise be the least receptive to them: older women with less education (by virtue of their generation) living in rural areas and small towns.[5]

Since Japan is a wealthy modern nation, the possibility of a family planning campaign sponsored by an international aid organization is the stuff of social science fiction. Barring that particular deus ex machina, where might we expect an effective force for change within Japanese society?

CHANGE FROM THE TOP DOWN

Since my research did not devote extensive attention to the government's role in perpetuating Japan's present forms of

[4] Mainichi Shinbunsha 1975:18.

[5] Kōsei-shō 1976a:180; Okazaki 1977:135; Population Problems Research Council 1970:110.

birth control, I invite my colleagues in political science to delve into that dimension of family planning in Japan. Nevertheless, I can provide a few observations of my own that have led me to believe that no force within the present governmental structure will bring about change in Japan's birth control picture.

First, the government's immediate concerns relate to the quantitative results of couples' fertility limitation efforts rather than the individual means. Since the end of World War II, the government's population-related concerns have centered on the economic and political issues associated with the population's rate of growth. Through much of this period, the government's primary worry has been excess population growth. And in terms of population dynamics, the availability of induced abortion has had much the same effect as would the widespread use of modern contraceptive methods. In the years since World War II, the Japanese have demonstrated an unparalleled ability to control their aggregate fertility; no other country can claim that it halved its birth rate in a ten-year period, as Japan did between 1947 and 1957. Today, Japanese fertility ranks among the lowest in the world.

Japan's reliance on induced abortion might also have an as-yet unrealized benefit for its population policymakers. Not only does a population relying extensively on induced abortion display a remarkable ability to limit its fertility: the removal of abortion from public access can also exert a dramatic upsurge in fertility that would not have resulted if couples were making use of a variety of effective contraceptive methods. The responsiveness of fertility levels to induced abortion policy may be behind the approval of abortion by Eastern European governments, who thus have more ability to manipulate national birth rates because they have not promoted contraception. After the Romanian government imposed severe restrictions on legal abortion in 1966, the crude birth rate shot up from 14.3 to 27.4 in the subsequent year; the pronatal effect on the birth rate persisted for some ten years after.[6]

---

[6] Berelson 1979.

The Japanese government has indeed attempted to restrict access to abortion a number of times, as Chapter 4 mentions. The government's anti-abortion moves crescendoed in the late 1960s and early 1970s, a time of rapid economic growth when increased school enrollment drove up the cost of young labor for the country's small and medium scale employers.[7] Since the time of the Arab oil embargo, rising inflation, and decreased growth, the government's moves to restrict access to abortion have dwindled.

Unless some constituency or interest group prods the government through its political power, the liabilities that the government would have to face were it to back a program of improved contraceptive services make such a move improbable. The Japanese people are still very aware of the prewar government's attempts to increase the population for its own ends; today, they are aware of the possibility that the government might promote population reduction as a panacea for chronic economic problems. At the same time, the sector of the economy that depends on less expensive domestic labor inputs would decry any openly anti-natal action, while those reluctant to pay for the new infrastructure necessitated by population growth would oppose pronatal policies. Because of the divisiveness and controversiality of government attempts—actual or imagined—to manipulate population size, the government has shied away from an explicitly labeled "population policy." (Its ostensible reasons for its move to restrict abortion have been social and moral.) The promotion of effective contraception, unlike many other government policies having a far-reaching effect on fertility, would be very visible and hence very vulnerable.

Another liability that would confront a government–sponsored program is the issue of contraceptive safety, despite the indeterminacy of safety criteria for contraception. The actual health safety benefits of the Japanese fertility limitation pattern are minimal relative to the Western assemblage of modern

[7] See Nagano 1973.

methods. Indeed, a case could be made for better overall health benefits from promoting modern methods, especially sterilization. In terms of mortality only, the differences in rates resulting from modern versus traditional fertility control regimens among women under 35 years of age in the West would be trivial if applied to Japanese women in the same age group.[8] First, very few Japanese women smoke, which would greatly decrease the danger of oral contraceptive use to that of the other methods. Second, younger Japanese women face a greater risk from birth-related mortality, which we should also take into account since a substantial portion of contraceptive failures to women in their early years of marriage result in live births. In the mid-1970s, Japan's maternal mortality rate was over twice the rates for the United States and England and Wales.[9] For women over 35 years of age, the safest alternative in terms of mortality is sterilization—especially if their husbands receive vasectomies, since the mortality risk from that operation is practically nil.[10]

Mortality risk is an extremely narrow criterion of contraceptive safety, of course, but public health specialists use it because non-fatal illnesses attributed to the various forms of fertility limitation differ so much in their nature, severity, and duration that they defy comparison on some sort of standardized basis. My own more qualitative evaluation of the healthiness of fertility control in Japan, which also takes into account emotional and sexual well-being, finds the system leaving wives less well off than if they had the benefit of choice between traditional and modern methods of contraception. In addition to the stress and trauma that individual women experience from inadequate conception control, one other health-related aspect of family planning stands as a strong argument for a government policy favoring the diffusion of modern contraceptive methods; the amount of health care money spent on

[8] Cf. Tietze and Lewit 1979:459.
[9] United Nations 1979:312-15.
[10] Tietze 1978:55.

abortions in Japan every year represents a diversion of medical resources, including trained personnel, away from health problems such as maternal mortality.

Nevertheless, in the politics of birth control, as in personal decisions regarding contraception, health is never an unalloyed issue. It is not the evidence attaching specific health risks to specific modern contraceptive methods that discourages a government stand in greater favor of modern contraceptives, so much as all of the unresolved conflicts over Japan's future population size, the role of women in society, and the social control of sexuality. In this context, a unilateral declaration of safety from the government is highly unlikely. If and when a more positive government stance toward modern contraception emerges, it will most likely result from a more positive approach to effective contraception taken by either of the two political forces that can reshape public opinion on contraceptive safety: doctors or consumer organizations.

CHANGE FROM SERVICE PROVIDERS

There are no reasons to suppose that the organization of Ob-Gyns licensed to perform abortions will spontaneously take up the promotion of medical methods of contraception. The organizational makeup of the Maternal Protection Association favors inertia: the *sine qua non* of membership is, after all, the ability to perform safely a dilatation and curettage. The status of these operations as a fee for service procedure whose price is regulated by the professional organization and not by the government provides a powerful incentive to ignore modern contraception.

A few Ob-Gyns do criticize the volume of abortions that their colleagues perform. The critics are usually Roman Catholic doctors opposed to all forms of birth control, or specialists with advanced foreign training or professional activity who compare Japanese practices unfavorably with the Western emphasis on contraceptive guidance. The latter group is sensitive to foreign professional criticism like that which appeared in a 1972 book on abortion technique written by specialists in the United States:

> My only negative reaction to Japanese gynecology was in their handling of contraception. Gynecologists do not consider it part of their practice. There is no attempt at counseling and no effort to dispense contraceptives. The problem is totally ignored.[11]

It is doubtful, however, that this handful of critics has the degree of political leverage within their organization that could effect a change. Younger doctors may be more amenable to promoting modern contraception than their older colleagues because they are less repressed in their attitudes toward sexuality, but this factor alone is probably insufficient because the opposing factor of abortion profits is more powerful.

There is always a possibility that physicians could monopolize pill distribution in the future. If so, they could not only effectively select and monitor oral contraceptive users, but also enjoy the profits that would accrue from prescribing the medication and then providing it from their own dispensaries. By law, physicians can dispense their own medications only under exceptional circumstances, but the practice has grown considerably in the last ten years and has proven quite lucrative.[12]

Generally speaking, medical guilds rarely if ever initiate a change that is socially controversial, and Ob-Gyns are less innovative still because sexual mores are involved.[13] As attested by the description in Chapter 2 of Ob-Gyns' problems surrounding abortion consent forms, gynecologists in Japan have a rather tenuous hold on respectability. Were they to undertake the promotion of modern methods, their vulnera-

[11] Neubardt 1972:137.
[12] *Asahi Shinbun* 1976a.
[13] See, for example, James Reed's interesting account of the American medical community's self-imposed separation from the country's birth control movement in its early years; Reed 1978.

bility would stem from the profitability of modern contraception (real or imagined) to their practices—the same Achilles heel in their public image that attaches to their abortion services.

Ob-Gyns may inadvertently spur demand for effective contraception through their pricing policies. Induced abortion has grown quite expensive since the mid-1960s. If gynecologists also attempt to keep their fees for modern methods in the range of one first trimester abortion per year per patient, however, no great shift in method use patterns will emerge from the current abortion price trend: those with higher incomes will have abortions followed by modern method use, while the less affluent will exercise greater caution with traditional methods at the expense of sexual gratification.

Japan's family planning organizations will probably not become a driving force for change toward increased modern method use, for the same reasons that they have not assumed that role so far. The fact that the family planning organizations rely very heavily on condom sales for their operating expenses restricts their willingness to innovate in the range of contraceptive methods that they could provide. Also, modern methods require the services of doctors, but the family planning organizations are unable to form effective liaisons with them because their members rarely benefit from a system of referrals and coordination of services with Ob-Gyns. As noted in Chapter 3, the services of midwives and of doctors overlap, and thus compete: midwives provide condoms, and a few offer diaphragms and home deliveries, whereas doctors control abortion and modern contraceptive methods and provide hospital deliveries.

The exclusively maternal health orientation of Japan's family planning movement has bought social respectability at the expense of an ability to respond to the needs of women who fall outside the category of young mother. These other groups of women have been growing as Japan enters the 1980s. They include young unmarried women exposed to pregnancy, newly married working women who need to postpone their first births in order to hold their jobs, and women who have attained their intended family size and would benefit from permanent contraception. Perhaps younger midwives and public health nurses will want to respond to these women's needs, but an effective response through the existing family planning organs would require an accompanying source of revenue for counseling and an effective system of physician referral. Solution of the referral problem would depend on the doctors' responses to requests for cooperation; solution of the funding problem would ultimately depend, barring adequate government subsidy, on women's willingness and ability to shed their passivity and literally make an investment in their sexual and reproductive well-being.

CHANGE FROM THE BOTTOM UP

If a change toward greater use of modern contraceptive methods does come about, it will in all likelihood originate in the organized efforts of those who have the most to gain from such a trend: married Japanese women. A contraceptive revolution might occur without organized effort, through a gradual increase in demand through greater individual use of the clinics and private practitioners offering modern methods. I doubt, however, that such a quiet evolution could change family planning to a significant degree, since the legal and economic barriers decribed in Chapter 3 (including adverse media treatment of modern contraception) would have to come down before any significant shift in method use patterns could develop. Be that as it may, the same social trends that would encourage a gradual increase in demand from individuals would also spark activity of a more organized political nature.

The ability of Japanese women to organize effectively around political and economic issues of immediate importance to their domestic roles is not the ultimate stumbling block; rather, it is their ability to take part actively in issues that involve their sexuality. Housewives form the backbone of the consumer movement in Japan, which has mustered a number of impressive victories in the postwar period. Nevertheless, the reform of gynecological care and contraceptive services has remained beyond the reach of consumer group activity. Various women's organizations have worked to oppose the government's attempts to restrict abortion availability, but they have waged these battles under the argument that economic hardship makes continued dependence on abortion indispensable. This stance, which portrays Japan's women as frustrated mothers who would otherwise prefer to have more births, is a far cry from the fundamental argument in support of contraception that women need the effective separation of sexuality from fertility without fear of trauma.

Feminist groups have taken up the issue of contraception, but they have so far failed to change the family planning status quo because of their size, membership and tactics. These groups, which are explicitly geared to pressing their demands through political confrontation, have not enjoyed the broad base of membership that housewives' organizations can claim. They are perennially hampered by inadequate funds and organizational instability. Their membership is largely confined to younger unmarried women, which severely limits their ability to establish rapport and credibility with married women, and their statements on contraception are couched in a rhetoric that does not provide answers to the specific dilemmas married women face. These shortcomings, together with confrontational tactics, make feminist groups prime grist for media caricatures. Japanese feminists are also deeply divided on the issue of pill safety, which further vitiates their efforts at reform of family planning.

Women's groups formed explicitly for the reform of contraception are not necessarily doomed to failure, but their opportunity for success depends on an ability to avoid the pitfalls and weakness that have so far hampered feminist attempts at improving family planning. One key to effectiveness lies in the early participation of married women who cannot be labeled by the media as deviants and then be summarily dismissed from serious attention. And the involvement of married women in turn will depend on their ability to overcome their inhibitions regarding sexual matters—the same inhibitions that currently prevent individual wives from generating more demand for modern contraceptives.

The description of Japanese women's sexuality in Chapter 7 follows an underlying tenet: although the emotions and attitudes that shape the expression of human sexuality are complex and often subtle, they are determined to a great extent by women's status and the functions of sexuality within marriage. Perhaps by looking at the related trends in women's status and marital role organization, we can assess the chances for a less passive female sexuality, and, with it, an eventual movement for more effective contraception.

Since women's educational level has a positive effect on their acceptance of sexuality, we should expect a trend in more education for women to result in less sexual inhibition and passivity. There is one other change in women's status that could also exert a far-reaching and pervasive influence on women's sexuality: a higher level of employment in positions that are fulfilling and remunerative enough to compete with the roles of housewife and mother. This trend would weaken the emphasis on the maternal role in Japan, which generates a sexuality that is quintessentially passive. In addition, if women contribute to their household economies substantially and on a long-term basis, as opposed to the current rule of low-paying work with high turnover, their improved bargaining power in the marital relationship could extend to more compliance from husbands in the area of sexual gratification as well, which would in turn encourage more assertiveness in sexual matters.

Greater integration of roles in Japanese marriages would also contribute to less female sexual inhibition; if the companionate element grows, so would the importance—and hence, legitimacy—of sexual compatibility and mutual enjoyment. Changes in men's workplace participation patterns may prove equally critical to a shift in marital life-style. In one form or another—as after-hours socializing, extra work, or complaints of tiredness from work—men's jobs preempt time and energy for shared activities with their wives. Chapter 6 mentioned men's very high degree of workplace socializing that extends into after-hours recreation, often in the form of drinking. Larger private organizations put together occasional overnight outings to hot springs and other recreation areas. Private corporations provide their employees with a variety of recreation facilities and clubs, the larger the organization, the greater the number, variety, and quality.

In addition to requiring long work hours and providing attractive leisure activities, personnel policy at the workplace discourages conjugal companionship by making gestures of interest in one's wife and family definite liabilities to the man's workplace reputation. The classic issue is whether or not the husband notifies his wife in advance of late arrival home from after-hours socializing with colleagues or overtime work. A weekly newspaper's informal survey investigating the wife's common complaint of "Why don't men say when they're coming home?" elicited this response from a 32-year-old bank employee:

> Unless you're a newlywed, something like an indiscreet phone call gives the mistaken impression to co-workers and superiors that you don't have your "house in order." What's more, if I called regularly then they'd probably get all the more suspicious about my behavior.[14]

In one instance found among my informants, a 28-year-old employee of a business consulting firm called home only when he was sure he could not be overheard by fellow employees. The importance to employers of molding male employees' marital lives around the company or government bureau also explains the common practice of discouraging marriage for younger employees until a number of years on the job have passed and company-oriented habits have become entrenched.

There is reason to believe that the workplace is relinquishing some of its influence on men's lives, and that the trend will

[14] *Sankei Ribingu* 1976b.

continue. The slowdown in the rate of growth in Japan's economy inaugurated by the 1973 oil crisis has made overtime less profitable for Japanese companies because of higher energy costs and reduced demand for products. Decreased growth has also meant that corporations have fewer managerial positions to offer the swelling ranks of highly educated candidates born in Japan's postwar baby boom. At the same time, workers have attained increased discretionary spending power, and have come to enjoy consuming a greater variety of goods and services that has resulted from the development of domestic markets. The Japanese want the time to enjoy this affluence. In a multinational survey of workers under age 25, conducted by the Office of the Prime Minister in 1977, more young workers in Japan expressed dissatisfaction with work hours and holiday schedules than did their Western European and American counterparts.[15]

With fewer demands and fewer rewards coming from the workplace, Japanese men's private, non-work existences will take up a large share of their lives. This trend may not necessarily suffice to bring about a more companionate function in their marriages, however. Japanese men might not be drawn to seek more companionship from their wives if their workplace social network remains intact and active, albeit in an attenuated form. Perhaps a shift from the present employment pattern of low job turnover to a more open labor market would stimulate men to look for emotional resources in the their marital relationships, since a higher rate of turnover would inevitably bring a more impersonal atmosphere to the workplace.

Should men turn to their families for both the enjoyment of consumption activities and the emotional gratification that the workplace had previously afforded them, there remains the question of whether their wives will resist the trend or try to create more companionate, egalitarian roles. If women's status remains low, wives will probably opt for the more

[15] Naikaku Sōri Daijin 1978:64.

familiar segregated style. There is no special regard or esteem for domestic activities in Japanese society, nor do Japanese women themselves regard their household tasks as particularly important.[16] Nevertheless, unless wives enjoy more bargaining power, they cannot hope for genuine assistance and cooperation in domestic life. In the typical segregated Japanese conjugal role relationship, the wife prefers that her husband absent himself from home life for perfectly understandable reasons: her servant role requires her to see to his comfort when he is at home rather than to share equally in leisure activities. The Japanese husband who does not help regularly with household tasks also creates more work for his wife on his occasional sallies into her domain. When he takes over cooking, the kind of assistance he demands from her means as much work as if she were to prepare the food herself; when he gives his attention to the children, he indulges their desires in ways that she would not, which undermines her authority. In addition, when she depends entirely on her husband's career for her own economic security and well-being, she will encourage him to spend time away from home with his work group because it solidifies his job status and influences promotion and other rewards.

There are indications, however, that Japanese wives would forge more integrated marriages if they had sufficient power. Although the great majority of wives polled in public opinion surveys in the mid-1970s indicated satisfaction with their marital relationships, specific points of dissatisfaction toward husbands centered around their absence from home, their inadequacy as conversation partners, and their lack of empathy.[17] Television commercials occasionally promote various household products on their ability to attract husbands home. In one prime time ad for a food flavoring, a young wife looks up from her simmering stew pot with a broad smile when the doorbell rings and exclaims, "He came straight home today, too!" As in the United States, commercials may not say much

[16] Fujin Chōsakai 1974:12, 329, 378.
[17] Fujin Chōsakai 1974:102-04.

about their products, but they offer a glimpse of what people crave in their lives. Of the 22 wives in the intensive interview series, half indicated a desire to have more leisure activities with their husbands, and seven of these women also stated that they would appreciate more household or child care help from their husbands as well. Slightly over a fourth of the questionnaire survey participants also indicated that they would like more household help from their husbands.

If, in Japan's future, women derive more rewards from their public, non-familial roles as men realize fewer, the stage will be fully set for a qualitative change in family life. Although I must leave the serious prediction of educational trends and female occupational structure in Japan to educators and labor economists, there are some fairly visible facts which suggest that an upgrading of women's occupations is not at hand. First, the de facto two-track educational system provides few female students with specialized skills suitable for building careers. Second, female labor currently performs an important function for Japanese capital by absorbing economic setbacks through firing and layoffs, much as migrant labor does in Western Europe.

The various socioeconomic factors I have identified have very subtle and indirect effects on that most intimate of human problems, the separation of sexual expression from fertility. By process of elimination, however, there are no other institutions in Japanese society besides marriage itself that could plausibly become agents of change for a different set of fertility control methods. It is highly unlikely that modern contraceptive methods will diffuse through Japanese society merely by virtue of "modernization" or imitation of the West, because Japanese birth control is not outdated or held back by "cultural lag"; rather, as I have attempted to show, it is an adaptation to the political economics of health care and contraceptive marketing that meshes with the dominant themes in Japanese marital life-styles and sexuality.

Appendices

Selection and Characteristics of the Questionnaire and Interview Samples

The Questionnaire Study

The questionnaire form (presented in Appendix B) is the first in Japan to include questions on coital frequency and preferences for specific features of contraceptive methods. The sensitive nature of the questionnaire required that it be distributed in an atmosphere of purely professional interest and detachment; medical facilities were chosen as distribution points since they provide this kind of setting. This method of distribution greatly reduced the randomness of the sample, but was absolutely necessary to insure respondent participation.

The questionnaire forms were distributed voluntarily by doctors, family planning counselors, or paramedical personnel at eight facilities in the Tokyo-Yokohama conurbation. A pretest was conducted in late October of 1975 at a private Ob-Gyn hospital, and, after a few slight revisions, the form was distributed at the other seven locations. The form required between 15 and 20 minutes to complete. Respondents also received a separate stamped postcard for those who wished to be informed of survey results. Completed forms were received from the last distribution point in April 1976. The seven locations included two other private hospitals, two large Red Cross hospitals, and one other large voluntary hospital, a maternity hospital operated by a midwife, and the personnel welfare office of an electronics plant that provides family planning services. Forms were distributed to outpatients receiving their first examinations, primapara child care class participants, well-baby clinic mothers, and contraception clinic patients. Distributors were asked to avoid unmarried women and patients with infertility complaints. Questionnaire forms were completed by respondents on the premises, with two exceptions: participants at a well-baby clinic at one of the large voluntary hospitals were provided with pre-stamped return mail envelopes, and respondents at the midwife's maternity hospital were interviewed with the questionnaire as a closed-ended set of questions and responses in order to assure cooperation.

Once the completed forms for each distribution point were collected, the characteristics of the samples were compiled and presented to distributors for comparison with their patient populations. Cases of suspected subfecund couples and non-cohabiting individuals were also reviewed case-by-case with distributors. Of 1,020 forms distributed, 687 were returned; of these, 52 were excluded from further analysis because the respondents were over age 44, were not coresiding with a husband, were suspected of infertility problems, or did not designate their age on the form, in that order of frequency. The effective return rate was thus 62.3 percent.

Average age of wives in the survey is 29.5, and their average number of living children is 1.5. If we compare the sample with census figures, respondent ages are skewed downward by greater representation of women in their late 20's—about 40 percent of the sample, as opposed to 25 percent of the married female population under 45 in urban areas.

The questionnaire respondents are also better educated than all women their age in the Tokyo area; although the sample roughly matches the proportion of high-school graduates among the urban female population between the ages of 20 and 44, it considerably overrepresents women with higher levels of education (about 27 percent of the sample, as opposed to 9 percent of the population in the same categories as they appeared in 1970 census data). Average household income is nearly a third higher than per household incomes for Tokyo and Yokohama.[1]

As in other phases of the research, women with the least education and the heaviest work burdens were the most dif-

---

[1] Comparison is made with 1974 figures from Nihon Māketingu Kyōiku Sentā 1975:86, 90.

ficult to include. Distributors noted that a large proportion of respondents were well educated and had husbands with higher incomes than their total patient populations. Working women were also underrepresented, according to distributors, especially family employees. One of the hospital distributors with a large family enterprise patient population also reported that working women over the age of 40 were more likely to decline to participate in the study.

A Note on Statistical Techniques

Statistical test results were judged significant when they attained the .05 level of probability or less. In regressions involving a dummy dependent variable, ordinary least squares analysis was applied, since distribution of the dependent variable values approximated a 70-30 split or better.

Interviews

The content of the interviews overlaps with many discussions held with informants in the course of research, but the interviews differ from other data-gathering techniques in several important respects. First, the interviews were an attempt to get comprehensive information on both conjugal life-style and family planning from each couple involved. Data from discussions with other informants are much more fragmented. Second, both marriage partners were interviewed, allowing comparison of responses from separate interview sessions. (Unfortunately, however, we were not afforded the chance subsequently to cross-check conflicting answers with interviewees because we had promised that spouses would not be informed of one another's responses.)

The interviews were designed to progress in content from less to more sensitive topics. Age, ages of other family members, region of origin, and education were used as opening questions. Both spouses were asked open-ended questions about their housing and sleeping arrangements, relations with relatives, and domestic division of labor, with special attention to child-care help. Wives were asked if they were satisfied with the extent of their husbands' participation in these various areas of family life, and husbands were asked if they thought their wives were satisfied. Husbands and working wives were asked brief questions about the nature of their work and their feelings about workplace society and recreation.

The interview then progressed to the more personal area of marital affect, with the questions of how the spouses met, most- and least-liked qualities then and now, and shared leisure activities, followed again by questions about the wife's satisfaction. Then desired number of children for both spouses at marriage and at present was taken up, along with the issue of ideal birth interval and the forms of assistance given the wife after childbirth. This in turn opened the way for discussion of the wantedness of each child and other conceptions that the couple may have experienced, including experience of induced abortion. History of contraceptive use was then discussed, including the way in which methods were decided on, sources of information, liked and disliked features, and reasons for discontinuing use. Both partners were also asked if they had an interest in other forms of contraception, and husbands with completed families were asked their opinions of vasectomy. In the last topic area, conjugal sexuality, interviewees were asked about coital frequency, relative strengths of both partners' sexual desire, and opinions on differences between male and female sexual desire in general. The first ten couples were asked if and how childbearing had affected marital sexuality, a question that was subsequently omitted; in its place, couples were asked what point in their marriage provided the most enjoyable sexual relations. If time and circumstances permitted, questions about religious beliefs and personal hobbies were asked.

The interviews were conducted from late April to late November of 1976. Twenty-two couples (44 husbands and wives) were interviewed. Eighteen couples were living in the Tokyo-Yokohama conurbation, three couples lived in the Kansai area, and one in Nagoya. I conducted my own interviews with the husbands, and Sawanobori Nobuko, an independently operating researcher who had previously done interview research on women's attitudes toward menstruation and tampon use, conducted separate interviews with their wives.

We could not use tape recorders because of the sensitivity of the interview subject matter. Instead, we took notes in the course of each interview, and statements were reconstructed after the end of each session. Average time for the interviews was one hour and 40 minutes.

I used a network of personal and professional contacts to find volunteers for the interviews. Doctors, midwives, and social workers provided 12 of the 22 couples interviewed. All prospective subjects were informed of the subject matter of the interview. Interviewees were not offered any material incentives beforehand, but were given gifts at the end of the interviews and were offered reports of research results.

Interviews with wives were conducted at their homes. Only one couple had a joint interview, and the wife was re-interviewed afterward. Half the husbands were also interviewed at home, the rest at their workplaces or public places such as coffee shops or local parks.

Members of the interview sample were older than questionnaire survey participants; the average age for wives was slightly more than three years greater than the average for the questionnaire sample. Seventeen couples were living in nuclear households. Predictably, the interview couples' family stages were more advanced; only six couples planned on having more children. Of the remainder of couples, however, only four had children over five years of age. Couples participating in the interviews were also more highly educated; women with high-school educations or less were represented in about the same proportion as in the questionnaire sample, but there were six women with four-year college educations and only two with junior college level education. (Among Tokyo area women in the age group studied there are about two junior college graduates for every college graduate, a ratio found in the questionnaire sample also.) The interviewee sample was also slanted toward husbands in higher occupational strata: only two respondents could be called blue collar, and two more might be called semi-skilled. The rest of the husbands were in skilled occupations or had administrative positions. Twelve had college degrees, and none had not entered high school.

There were no indications that any of the couples interviewed had any unusual features in their personalities (such as exhibitionistic tendencies) or social backgrounds that would attract them to participate; rather, it appears that they were drawn to volunteer by virtue of the nature of the network link involving them. The sample is highly biased toward the better-educated, however, which probably reflects both greater personal contact with health care specialists and a greater willingness to discuss one's own family planning experiences with a foreign specialist.

Translated Questionnaire Form

(p. 1.)

I am from Columbia University and have come to Japan in order to conduct comparative research in family planning between Japan and the United States.

This survey contains questions on family planning that are somewhat personal, but please answer them as frankly as possible. The results of this survey will be made into *statistical figures* and will be used only for *purely academic goals*. Thus, you need not write your name; please fill out this form *anonymously*, place it in the envelope provided, and deposit it in the designated box.

For those who wish to have a compilation of the results, please place your request by filling out the *request postcard*. I shall send it to you subsequently.

Samuel Coleman
Columbia University

(p. 2.)

1. Your age ___   Your husband's age ___

2. Please place an "x" by the following individuals currently residing with you (excluding those living separately).
   ___ husband
   ___ father-in-law   ___ your father
   ___ mother-in-law   ___ your mother
   ___ husband's brothers   ___ brothers (#__)
   (#__)   ___ sisters (#__)
   ___ husband's sisters (#__)

How many children do you have? Please specify sex and
age.
___ male, ___ years old   ___ female, ___ years old
___ male, ___ years old   ___ female, ___ years old
___ male, ___ years old   ___ female, ___ years old
Please specify others (for example, cousins or adopted children).
In all, how many people? ___

3. Excluding bathroom, kitchen, and hallway (and including
   Western-style rooms), how many mats of living space do
   you have? [One mat equals about six feet by three feet.]
   ___ less than 5 mats   ___ 20 to less than 25 mats
   ___ 5 to less than 10 mats   ___ 25 to less than 30 mats
   ___ 10 to less than 15 mats   ___ 30 mats or more
   ___ 15 to less than 20 mats

3A. Who sleeps in your bedroom besides you and your hus-
    band?
    ___ only ourselves   ___ together with
    ___ together—with per-   child(ren)
         son(s) other than   ___ husband sleeps
         children   separately

4. Place an "x" by the school you last entered.
   ___ grade school   ___ junior college
   ___ junior high school   ___ college / old system
   ___ old system junior high   high school
        school / new system   ___ graduate school
        high school   ___ other
   ___ specialty school
        (excluding sewing,
        flower arranging, etc.)
        please write specifically: _____

4A. Place an "x" by the school your husband last entered.
____ grade school   ____ junior college
____ junior high school   ____ college / old system
____ old system junior high   high school
        school / new system   ____ graduate school
        high school   ____ other
____ specialty school
        please write specifically: _____

(p. 3.)

5. What is your husband's occupation?
____ self-employed / family   ____ factory worker /
        enterprise; please write   driver / construction
        (fish market, printing   worker, etc.
        etc.) ____   ____ craftsman (carpenter,
____ administrator for com-   box maker, toy maker,
        pany of 30 employees   etc.)
        or more / government /   ____ technical specialist
        association   (technician, teacher,
____ general company em-   etc.)
        ployee, civil service   ____ specialist, professional
        employee   (physician, engineer,
____ service (repairs, hotels,   lawyer, college
        etc.) / sales, store clerk   instructor)
____ agriculture   ____ unemployed

5A. Is your husband's work full-time?
____ full-time (includes   ____ part-time
        self-employed,   ____ day laborer, temporary
        agriculture)

5B. What is your husband's (net) monthly income?
____ less than ¥120,000   ____ ¥180,000 to less than
____ ¥120,000 to less than   ¥240,000
        ¥180,000   ____ ¥240,000 or more

6. What is your occupation?
   ___ administrator for company of 30 employees or more / government / association
   ___ general company employee, civil service employee
   ___ service (repairs, hotels, etc.) sales, store clerk
   ___ self-employed / family enterprise; please write (fish market, printing, etc.) ___. Excluding parents and siblings, how many employees are there? ___ 0
   ___ 1 ___ 2-3
   ___ 4-5 ___ 6 or more

   ___ factory worker / driver construction worker, etc.

   ___ piecework at home (toy-making, flower-making, sewing, etc.)
   ___ technical specialist (teacher, nurse, etc.)
   ___ specialist, professional (physician, engineer, lawyer, college instructor)
   ___ agriculture
   ___ unemployed

6A. Is your work full-time?
   ___ full-time (includes self-employed, agriculture)
   ___ day laborer, temporary

   ___ part-time / side job
   ___ work at home
   ___ family business employee

6B. How many hours do you work on each working day (including commuting time)? ___ hours
    How many days a week do you work? ___ days

6C. What is your monthly (net) income?
   ___ less than ¥30,000
   ___ ¥30,000 to less than ¥60,000
   ___ ¥60,000 to less than ¥100,000
   ___ no income

   ___ ¥100,000 to less than ¥150,000
   ___ ¥150,000 or more

(p. 4.)

7. Does your husband give you help in the areas listed below? Distinguish between weekdays and Sundays, placing an "x" in the appropriate place(s) below.

	Sundays only	Weekdays, twice or more
Taking out and putting away bedding	___	___
Shopping for everyday food-stuffs	___	___
Clothes washing	___	___
Changing the children's cloth-ing	___	___

7A. Would you like your husband to help more around the house?

___ yes ___ no

8. Excluding his work, how often in one month does your husband return home later than 10 p.m. from company and friendly social mixing?

___ 0 times ___ 2 times ___ 3-5 times
___ 6-9 times ___ 10 times or more

9. Would you prefer that your husband work harder?

___ yes ___ no, it's fine the way it is
___ if anything, he works too hard

10. How many hours of sleep a night do you usually get?
___ hours

11. On the next page there is a section for investigating "pregnancy history." Please record the following items.
    1. Place a circle around your present age.
    2. Place a ⊕ under the age when you were married. Then, place the results of each pregnancy under the age at which you were pregnant.
    3. For spontaneous abortions, still births, place a 死.

4. For induced abortions, place a ⊕ .
5. For births (deliveries), place a ⌢⊕⌣ .

For example, if one had an induced abortion at age 22, one writes: 21   22   23
                                                 ⊕

As a further example, Mrs. A is now 28 years old. At the age of 22 she had an induced abortion. She married at age 25, and in the same year a child was born. The following year a spontaneous abortion occurred. In this instance, Mrs. A's history is as follows. [See original form for sample and pregnancy history chart.]

(p. 5.)

12. How many children do you feel are an ideal number for you?

___ 0   ___ 1   ___ 2   ___ 3   ___ 4
___ 5 or more

13. Since marriage, how many contraceptive failures (including those resulting in birth) have you experienced?

___ 1   ___ 2   ___ 3   ___ 4
___ 5 or more   ___ have not experienced

14. If you were to choose a contraceptive method, what would be the most important quality? Place an "x" by one answer only.
___ Safety to my health
___ Safety to my husband's health
___ Complete (failure-free) contraception

15. When choosing a contraceptive method, which of the items below is important to you? Place an "x" by one answer only.
___ One I can use myself without having to rely on my husband
___ One I can leave to my husband's care rather than myself
___ It makes no difference to me

16. How often do you have sexual relations?
    ___ twice a month or less   ___ four times a week
    ___ once a week   ___ five times or more a
    ___ 2-3 times a week   week

(p. 6.)

17. If you were to choose a contraceptive method, which of the following would be important to you? Place an "x" by one answer only.
    ___ No interference with my sexual feelings
    ___ No interference with my husband's sexual feelings

18. Are you presently using a contraceptive method (including sterilization surgery)?
    ___ yes   ___ no
    Those who answered "yes," please answer the following questions.

18A. How often do you use a contraceptive method? (Recipients of contraceptive sterilizations need not answer.)
    ___ sometimes   ___ often
    ___ without exception

18B. Who informed you about your present method(s)? Place an "x" by as many as needed.
    ___ I investigated for myself (radio, magazine, etc.)
    ___ Husband
    ___ Family members / friends
    ___ Druggist / salesperson
    ___ Doctor / midwife / public health nurse / nurse

18C. What method are you presently using? (Combined method
users please place an "x" by two or more.)

___ rhythm (Ogino
Method)
___ Basal Body
Temperature
___ IUD
___ condom
___ jelly
___ douche
___ sponge/tampon

___ sterilization—self
___ sterilization—husband
___ diaphragm
___ pill
___ tablet
___ interruptus

19. There is currently a movement to revise present abortion
law by recognizing abortion in times of danger to the
mother's life but not allowing abortion in cases of economic hardship. What is your opinion?

___ agreement
___ opposition
___ I haven't thought about it / can't decide

Thank you very much for your cooperation.

Selected Nationwide Japanese Surveys on Family Planning and Related Areas

Title: Mainichi Newspapers National Family Planning Opinion Survey
(Series, Mainichi Shinbunsha Zenkoku Kazoku Keikaku Seron Chōsa).

Sponsoring Organization: Population Problems Research Council, Mainichi Newspapers.

Date: biennial since 1950, except for the third survey, conducted one year late (1955).

Survey Instrument: a self-administered questionnaire form distributed to and later collected from the respondents at their homes by survey personnel.

Population: married women under age 50 currently residing with their husbands; until the seventh survey in 1963, both husbands and wives were given questionnaires.

Sampling: random sampling within a sample of census districts stratified by cities, municipalities, and rural districts; sample size has been between 3,500 and 3,800 cases, and return rate has averaged 83 percent.

Reports: distribution of responses are reported in the *Mainichi Shinbun* newspaper within months after each survey; the Mainichi Newspapers also prints a limited number of reports in both English and Japanese. Two books in English (Population Problems Research Council 1970 and Japanese Organization for International Cooperation in Family Planning 1977) provide cross-tabulations of many responses with age, residential and education variables.

Comments: information on current use of specific contraceptive methods is unavailable because the questionnaire format merges current and previous use into one question. ("Which of these methods do/did you mainly use?") Male and female contraceptive sterilizations were not distinguished until the fourteenth survey in 1977.

Title: Japan World Fertility Survey
Sponsoring Organization: Statistics and Information Department, Ministry of Health and Welfare.
Date: September, 1974.
Survey Instruments: interviews conducted by public health nurses, using a questionnaire form similiar to the Core Questionnaire and Fertility Regulation Module designed by the World Fertility Survey, with a separate self-administered questionnaire having questions on induced abortion and contraceptive practice, distributed at the interview and returned by mail.
Population: ever-married women under age 50.
Sampling: cluster sample of 2,944 cases; successful contact and interview rate was 97.1 percent, and mail response rate was 84.0 percent.
Reports: a set of cross-tabulations was published in Japanese in late 1976 by the Statistics and Information Department (*Kōsei-shō* 1976). A very brief statement of findings prepared by the department was published in English in 1979 by the World Fertility Survey (see citation in English bibliography).
Comments: the mail-in portion of the survey was made separate from the interview to avoid possible accusations of government invasion of privacy; neither of the government reports attempt to cross-match the interviews and self-administered forms.

Title: Fertility Survey Report (Series, Shussanroyoku Chōsa Hōkoku).
Sponsoring Organization: Institute of Population Problems, Ministry of Health and Welfare.
Dates: 1940, 1952, and every five years since.
Survey Instrument: a self-administered questionnaire form distributed to and later collected from respondents at their homes by survey personnel as part of a larger survey, the

Health and Welfare Basic Administrative Survey (Kōsei Gyōsei Kiso Chōsa), conducted yearly.

Population: coresiding married couples (one questionnaire per couple).

Sampling: in recent surveys, the Institute of Population Problems randomly subsamples women under age 50 from the larger national survey; the 1972 and 1977 surveys had 9,182 and 10,368 cases, respectively, representing 98 percent and 93 percent of eligible respondents (respectively). (Only the 1952, 1972, and 1977 surveys are based on nationwide samples.)

Reports: the Institute of Population Problems publishes summaries in Japanese about a year after the studies are conducted.

Comments: the surveys do not ask about specific contraceptive methods used or induced abortion, although they do have questions regarding contraceptive practice experience, intentions, and "number of pregnancies aside from births." (The 1972 survey has a question on contraceptive failures, but the report does not analyze the responses.)

Title: Birth Control Opinion Survey (Sanji Seigen ni Kansuru Seron Chōsa).

Sponsoring Organization: Office of Information, Secretariat of the Prime Minister.

Date: November 1969.

Survey Instrument: interviews, with questions pertaining to birth control on a separate self-administered questionnaire form collected later.

Population: currently married women between age 20 and 49.

Sampling: two-stage stratified; 2,597 effective responses were received, a return rate of 86.6 percent.

Reports: the Office of Information published a summary in March 1970, in Japanese.

Comments: the survey report contains extensive sections on contraception and abortion; next to the Mainichi surveys, the most quoted survey in family planning literature of the mid-1970s.

Title: An Investigation of the Status of Eugenic Protection, with Special Emphasis on an Attitude Survey (Ishiki Chōsa o Chūshin to Shita Yūsei Hogo Jittai Chōsa).

Sponsoring Organizations: Ministry of Health and Welfare and the Japan Medical Association.

Date: December 1969.

Survey Instruments: three self-administered questionnaires, including an opinion questionnaire to Ob-Gyns and two to their patients: one on social background characteristics, one on opinions on various family planning issues and knowledge about the Eugenic Protection Law.

Populations: Ob-Gyns designated to perform legal abortions, and patients requesting abortions from them.

Sampling: all facilities having designated physicians; of 11,352 hospitals and clinics, 10,442 responded; all patients requesting abortions at these facilities during a 10-day period; 29,952 women completed the opinion questionnaire, and, of them, 29,880 completed the social characteristics questionnaire.

Reports: one summary was published in Japanese in 1971 by the Ministry of Health and Welfare and the Japan Medical Association.

Comments: the survey was designed largely to address politically sensitive issues surrounding abortion law; the careful stipulation that the patients were "applicants" and not necessarily recipients of abortions reflects the sensitivity of the survey.

References in English

Akamatsu Tadashi Hanami. 1969. "Women Workers and Retirement After Marriage." *Japan Labor Bulletin*, 8(5):6-8 (May).

Ando Hirofumi. 1976. "Japanese Family Planning: The Case of the Condom." In Social Science Research Institute, ed., *Asia Urbanizing: Population Growth and Concentration and the Problems Thereof.* Tokyo: Simul Press, pp. 118-26.

Aoki Hisao. n.d. "The New Life Movement Through Enterprises in Japan." *Reference Materials for Seminars in Population/Family Planning.* Tokyo: Japanese Organization for International Cooperation in Family Planning.

Asayama Shinichi. 1975. "Adolescent Sex Development and Adult Sex Behavior in Japan." *Journal of Sex Research*, 2(2):91-112 (May).

Azumi Koya. 1968. "The Mysterious Drop in Japan's Birth Rate." *Transaction*, 5(6):46-48 (May).

Balfour, Marshall C. 1962. "Panel Discussion on Comparative Acceptability of Different Methods of Contraception." In Clyde V. Kiser, ed., *Research in Family Planning.* Princeton: Princeton University Press, pp. 373-86.

Berelson, Bernard. 1979. "Romania's 1966 Anti-Abortion Decree: The Demographic Experience of the First Decade." *Population Studies*, 33(2):205-22 (July).

Blake, Judith. 1973. "Elective Abortion and Our Reluctant Citizenry: Research on Public Opinion in the United States." In Howard J. Osofsky and Joy D. Osofsky, eds., *The Abortion Experience: Psychological and Medical Impact.* Hagerstown, Md.: Harper and Row, pp. 447-67.

Bott, Elizabeth. 1957. *Family and Social Network: Roles, Norms, and External Relationships in Ordinary Urban Families.* London: Tavistock.

Callahan, Daniel. 1970. *Abortion: Law, Choice and Morality.* London: Collier-MacMillan.

Cartwright, Ann. 1976. *How Many Children?* London: Routledge and Kegan Paul.

————. 1978. *Recent Trends in Family Building and Contraception.* Office of Population Censuses and Surveys, Studies on Medical and Population Subjects No. 34. London: Her Majesty's Stationery Office.

Caudill, William, and David Plath. 1966. "Who Sleeps by Whom? Parent-Child Involvement in Urban Japanese Families." *Psychiatry*, 29(4):344-66 (Nov.).

Cliquet, R. L., E. van Hyfte, and F. Deven. 1978. "Evolution of the Knowledge About and Use of Contraceptive Methods among Married Women in the Dutch-speaking Community of Belgium, 1966-1976: Preliminary Results of NEGO III." In H. G. Moors, R. L. Cliquet, G. Dooghe, and D. J. van de Kaa, eds., *Population and Family in the Low Countries.* Leiden: Martinus Nijhoff, Vol. 2, pp. 69-79.

Coleman, Samuel, and Phyllis T. Piotrow. 1979. "Spermicides—Simplicity and Safety Are Major Assets." *Population Reports*, Series H (Barrier Methods), no. 5 (Sept.).

Davis, Kingsley. 1963. "The Theory of Change and Response in Modern Demographic History." *Population Index*, 29:345-66.

Dore, Ronald P. 1958. *City Life in Japan: A Study of a Tokyo Ward.* Berkeley: University of California Press.

Ford, Clellan S., and Frank Beach. 1951. *Patterns of Sexual Behavior.* New York: Harper.

Ford, Kathleen. 1978. "Contraceptive Use in the United States, 1973-1976." *Family Planning Perspectives*, 10(5):264-70 (Sept./Oct.).

Haas, Margi. 1975. *The First Birth Control Movement in Japan 1902-1937.* Master of Arts thesis, Harvard University.

Hall, Robert, ed. 1970. *Abortion in a Changing World.* Vol. 2. New York: Columbia University Press.

Harvey, Philip D. 1972. "Condoms—A New Look." *Family Planning Perspectives*, 4(4):27-30 (Oct.).

Hayasaka Yokichi, Toda Hideo, Anthony Zimmerman, Ueno Tasuke, and Ishizaki Mineko. 1973. "Japan's 22 Year Experience With a Liberal Abortion Law." *Marriage and Family Newsletter*, 4(5, 6) (May, June).

Huddle, Norie, Michael Reich, and Nahum Stiskin. 1975. *Island of Dreams: Environmental Crisis in Japan*. New York: Autumn Press.

International Labour Office [ILO]. 1975. *1975 Year Book of Labour Statistics*. 25th ed. Geneva.

Jaffe, Frederick S. 1964. "Family Planning and Poverty." *Journal of Marriage and the Family*, 26(4):467-70 (Nov.).

Jaffe, Frederick S., and Steven Polgar. 1968. "Family Planning and Public Policy: Is the 'Culture of Poverty' the New Copout?" *Journal of Marriage and the Family*, 30(2):228-35 (May).

Japan, Ministry of Health and Welfare. 1976. *Vital Statistics 1975*. Vol. 1. Tokyo: Health and Welfare Statistics and Information Department, Minister's Secretariat, Ministry of Health and Welfare.

Japan, Office of the Prime Minister. 1972. *1970 Population Census of Japan*. Vol. 2: *Whole Japan*. Tokyo: Office of the Prime Minister, Bureau of Statistics.

———. 1976. *Japan Statistical Yearbook 1976*, no. 26. Tokyo: Office of the Prime Minister, Bureau of Statistics.

———. 1977. *1975 Population Census of Japan*. Vol. 2: *Whole Japan*. Tokyo: Office of the Prime Minister, Bureau of Statistics.

Japanese Organization for International Cooperation in Family Planning, ed. (JOICFP). 1977. *Fertility and Family Planning in Japan*. Tokyo.

Jones, Elise, and Charles F. Westoff. 1973. "Changes in Attitude Toward Abortion: With Emphasis Upon the National Fertility Data." In Howard J. Osofsky and Joy D. Osofsky, eds., *The Abortion Experience: Psychological and Medical Impact*. Hagerstown, Md.: Harper and Row, pp. 468-81.

Kantner, John F., and Melvin Zelnik. 1972. "Sexual Experience of Young Unmarried Women in the United States." *Family Planning Perspectives*, 4(4):9-17 (Oct.).

Katagiri Tameyoshi. 1974. "Logistic Supplies for Family Planning Programmes: Japanese Experience in Distribution

Channel of Contraceptives." Basic Paper no. 3, International Labour Office Asian Regional Seminar on Management of Family Planning Programmes, Singapore, Nov. 5-9.

Kinsey, Alfred, Wardell Pomeroy, and Clyde Martin. 1948. *Sexual Behavior in the Human Male*. Philadelphia: Saunders.

Kinsey, Alfred, Wardell Pomeroy, Clyde Martin, and Paul Gebhard. 1953. *Sexual Behavior in the Human Female*. Philadelphia: Saunders.

Kon Yasuo. n.d. "Community-based Distribution of Contraceptives in Japan." Tokyo: Japan Family Planning Association.

―――. 1976. "Present Situation of Family Planning and Maternal and Child Health Programs." In Kunii Chojiro and Katagiri Tameyoshi, eds., *Basic Readings on Population and Family Planning in Japan*. Tokyo: Japanese Organization for International Cooperation in Family Planning.

Kunii Chojiro. 1979. "How the JFPA Began." *Japanese Organization for International Cooperation in Family Planning News*, Supp., no. 57 (Mar.).

Lader, Lawrence. 1966. *Abortion*. Boston: Beacon Press.

Lee, Luke. 1973. "International Status of Abortion Legalization." In Howard J. Osofsky and Joy D. Osofsky, eds., *The Abortion Experience: Psychological and Medical Impact*. Hagerstown, Md.: Harper and Row, pp. 338-64.

Leppo, Kimmo, Osmo Koskelainen, and Kai Sievers. 1974. "Contraceptive Practices in Finland in 1971." In *Yearbook of Population Research in Finland XIII 1973-1974*. Helsinki: Vaestontutkimuslaitos (The Population Research Institute).

Leridon, Henri. 1979. "Contraceptive Practice in France in 1978." *International Family Planning Perspectives*, 5(1):25-27 (Mar.).

―――. 1981. "Fertility and Contraception in 12 Developed Countries." *Family Planning Perspectives*, 13(2):93-102 (Mar./Apr.).

Liskin, Laurie S. 1981. "Periodic Abstinence: How Well Do

New Approaches Work?" *Population Reports*, Series I (Periodic Abstinence), no. 3 (Sept.).

Lorimer, Frank. 1954. *Culture and Human Fertility: A Study of the Relation of Cultural Conditions to Fertility in Nonindustrial and Transitional Societies*. Paris: United Nations Educational, Scientific and Cultural Organization.

Luker, Kristin. 1975. *Taking Chances: Abortion and the Decision Not to Contracept*. Berkeley: University of California Press.

Matsumoto, Y. Scott, Koizumi Akira, and Nohara Tadahiro. 1972. "Condom Use in Japan." *Studies in Family Planning*, 3(10):251-55 (Oct.).

Miyamoto Junhaku. 1973. "Background Considerations on Induced Abortion." *International Journal of Fertility*, 18:5-12.

Muramatsu Minoru. n.d. "Conventional Contraception in Japan." *Reference Materials for Seminars in Population/Family Planning*. Tokyo: Japanese Organization for International Cooperation in Family Planning.

———. 1966. "Japan." In Bernard Berelson et al., *Family Planning and Population Programs: A Review of World Developments*. Chicago: University of Chicago Press, pp. 7-19.

———. 1967. "Medical Aspects of the Practice of Fertility Regulation." In Muramatsu Minoru, ed., *Japan's Experience in Family Planning—Past and Present*. Tokyo: Family Planning Federation of Japan, pp. 57-82.

———. 1970. "An Analysis of Factors in Fertility Control in Japan." *Bulletin of the Institute of Public Health* (Tokyo), 19(2):97-107 (Feb.).

———. 1973. "Incidence of Abortion in Japan: Analysis and Results." In *International Population Conference Papers*, Liege: International Union for the Scientific Study of Population, Vol. 2, Sec. 5.6, pp. 319-31.

———. 1976. "Family Planning in Japan." In Kunii Chojiro and Katagiri Tameyoshi, eds., *Basic Readings on Population and Family Planning in Japan*. Tokyo: Japanese Organization for International Cooperation in Family Planning, pp. 1-24.

———. 1978. "Estimation of Induced Abortions, Japan, 1975." *Bulletin of the Institute of Public Health*, 27(2):93-97 (Feb.).

Muramatsu Minoru, and Jean van der Tak. 1978. "From Abortion to Contraception: The Japanese Experience." In Henry P. David, Herbert L. Friedman, Jean van der Tak, and Marylis J. Sevilla, eds., *Abortion in Psychosocial Perspective: Trends in Transnational Research*. New York: Springer, pp. 145-67.

Nagano Yoshiko. 1973. "Women Fight for Control: Abortion Struggle in Japan." *Ampo*, no. 17 (Summer).

Neubardt, Selig. 1972. "The Japanese Experience: A Personal Observation." In Selig Neubardt and Harold Schulman, *Techniques of Abortion*. Boston: Little, Brown, pp. 137-51.

New York Times. 1973. "Infanticide in Japan: Sign of the Times?" Dec. 8, p. 30.

NIDI (Netherlands Interuniversity Demographic Institute). 1978. "The Netherlands Survey on Fertility and Parenthood Motivation, 1975: A Summary of Findings." *World Fertility Survey*, no. 12 (Dec.).

Nohara Makoto. 1980. *Social Determinants of Reproductive Behavior in Japan*. Doctoral dissertation in Sociology, University of Michigan.

Norbeck, Edward M. 1970. *Religion and Society in Modern Japan: Continuity and Change*. Houston: Tourmaline.

Nortman, Dorothy. 1977. "Changing Contraceptive Patterns: A Global Perspective." *Population Bulletin*, 32(3) (Aug.).

Okazaki Yoichi. 1976. "Changes in Fertility Behavior in Postwar Japan." In Kunii Chojiro and Katagiri Tameyoshi, eds., *Basic Readings on Population and Family Planning*. Tokyo: Japanese Organization for International Cooperation in Family Planning, pp. 35-60.

———. 1977. "Knowledge, Attitudes and Practice of Family Planning." In Japanese Organization for International Cooperation in Family Planning, ed., *Fertility and Family Plan-*

ning in Japan. Tokyo: Japanese Organization for International Cooperation in Family Planning, pp. 119-55.

Osofsky, Howard J., and Joy D. Osofsky, eds. 1973. *The Abortion Experience: Psychological and Medical Impact.* Hagerstown, Md.: Harper and Row.

Osofsky, Joy D., Howard J. Osofsky, and Renga Rajan. 1973. "Psychological Effects of Abortion: With Emphasis Upon Immediate Reaction and Followup." In Howard J. Osofsky and Joy D. Osofsky, eds., *The Abortion Experience: Psychological and Medical Impact.* Hagerstown, Md.: Harper and Row, pp. 188-205.

Piotrow, Phyllis T., and Calvin M. Lee. 1974. "Oral Contraceptives: 50 Million Users." *Population Reports*, Series A, no. 1 (Apr.).

Pohlman, Edward H. 1969. *Psychology of Birth Planning.* Cambridge: Schenkman.

Polgar, Steven. 1968. "Cultural Aspects of Natality Regulation Techniques." *Proceedings of the VIIIth International Congress of Anthropological and Ethnological Sciences,* Tokyo, pp. 232-34.

————. 1977. "Birth Planning: Between Neglect and Coercion." In Moni Nag, ed., *Population and Social Organization.* The Hague: Mouton, pp. 177-202.

Population Problems Research Council (Mainichi Newspapers). 1970. *Family Planning in Japan: Opinion Survey by the Mainichi Newspapers.* Tokyo: Japanese Organization for International Cooperation in Family Planning.

Querido, Levie, and Paul Schnabel. 1979. "Evaluating the Clinical Effectiveness of the Patentex Oval." In Gerald I. Zatuchni, Aquiles J. Sobrero, J. Jospeh Speidel, and John J. Sciarra, eds., *Vaginal Contraception: New Developments.* Hagerstown, Md.: Harper and Row, pp. 146-53.

Rainwater, Lee. 1960. *And the Poor Get Children: Sex, Contraception, and Family Planning in the Working Class.* Chicago: Quadrangle.

————. 1965. *Family Design: Marital Sexuality, Family Size, and Contraception.* Chicago: Aldine.

Reed, James. 1978. *From Private Vice to Public Virtue: The*

Birth Control Movement and American Society Since 1830. New York: Basic Books.

Rindfuss, Ronald R., James A. Palmore, and Larry L. Bumpass. 1982. "Selectivity and the Analysis of Birth Intervals from Survey Data." *Asian and Pacific Census Forum,* 8(3):5, 6, 8-10, 15, 16 (Feb.).

Roht, Lewis H., and Aoyama Hideyasu. 1973. "Induced Abortion and Its Sequelae: Prevalence and Association with the Outcome of Pregnancy." *International Journal of Epidemiology,* 2(1):103-13 (Spring).

Scrimshaw, Susan C. M. 1976. "Women's Modesty: One Barrier to the Use of Family Planning Clinics in Ecuador." In John F. Marshall and Steven Polgar, eds., *Culture, Natality, and Family Planning.* Monograph 21. Chapel Hill: Carolina Population Center, The University of North Carolina at Chapel Hill, pp. 167-83.

Shinozaki Nobuo. 1980. *Population Problems in Japan: Historical and Cultural Approaches.* Tokyo: Ministry of Health and Welfare, Institute of Population Problems.

Sorensen, Robert. 1972. *Adolescent Sexuality in Contemporary America: Personal Values and Sexual Behavior Ages Thirteen to Nineteen.* New York: World Publishing.

Steinhoff, Patricia. 1973. "Background Characteristics of Abortion Patients." In Howard J. Osofsky and Joy D. Osofsky, eds., *The Abortion Experience: Psychological and Medical Impact.* Hagerstown, Md.: Harper and Row, pp. 206-31.

Stokes, Bruce. 1977. *Filling the Family Planning Gap.* Worldwatch Paper No. 12 (May). Washington, DC: Worldwatch Institute.

Taeuber, Irene. 1958. *The Population of Japan.* Princeton: Princeton University Press.

Taeuber, Irene, and Marshall Balfour. 1952. "The Control of Fertility in Japan." In Milbank Memorial Fund, ed., *Approaches to Problems of High Fertility in Agrarian Societies: Papers Presented at the 1951 Annual Conference of the Milbank Memorial Fund,* New York, pp. 102-28.

Takahashi Kosei. 1973. "A Myth of Medicine: A Warning to

the World on Internal Pollution." *Ampo*, 17:68-76 (Summer).

Tietze, Christopher. 1960. *The Condom as Contraceptive.* New York: National Committee on Maternal Health.

―――. 1978. "Safety and Health Hazards of Abortion." *Singapore Journal of Obstetrics and Gynecology*, 9(1):49-56 (Mar.).

―――. 1979. *Induced Abortion: 1979.* 3rd ed. New York: Population Council.

Tietze, Christopher, and Sarah Lewit. 1969. "Abortion." *Scientific American*, 220(1):3-9 (Jan.).

―――. 1979. "Life Risks Associated with Reversible Methods of Fertility Regulation." *International Journal of Gynaecology and Obstetrics*, 16(6):456-59 (May/June).

Udry, J. Richard. 1974. *The Social Context of Marriage.* 3rd ed. Philadelphia: Lippincott.

United Community Services of the Greater Vancouver Area. 1974. *Babies by Choice Not by Chance.* Excerpted in Ben Schlesinger, ed., *Family Planning in Canada: A Source Book.* Toronto: University of Toronto Press, pp.166-69.

United Nations. 1976. *Demographic Yearbook 1975.* (Special Topic: Natality Statistics.) 27th Issue. New York.

―――. 1979. *Demographic Yearbook 1978.* (Special Topic: General Tables.) 30th Issue. New York.

United States Bureau of the Census. 1973. *Census of Population: 1970.* Subject Reports, Educational Attainment, Final Report PC(2)-5B. Washington, DC: U.S. Government Printing Office.

―――. 1977. "Fertility of American Women: June 1976." *Current Population Reports*, Series P-20, No. 308. Washington, DC: U.S. Government Printing Office.

United States Center for Disease Control. 1978. *Abortion Surveillance 1976.* Atlanta: Department of Health, Education and Welfare, United States Public Health Service.

United States Department of Health, Education and Welfare. 1976. "Abortion Surveillance 1974. Issued April 1976." Atlanta: Center for Disease Control, Public Health Service.

Vogel, Ezra. 1963. *Japan's New Middle Class: The Salary*

Man and His Family in a Tokyo Suburb. Berkeley: University of California Press.

Wagatsuma Takashi. 1976. "Recent Techniques of Fertility Control in Japan." In Kunii Chojiro and Katagiri Tameyoshi, eds., *Basic Readings on Population and Family Planning in Japan*. Tokyo: Japanese Organization for International Cooperation in Family Planning.

Westoff, Charles. 1972. "The Modernization of U.S. Contraceptive Practice." *Family Planning Perspectives*, 4(3):9-12 (July).

———. 1974. "Coital Frequency and Contraception." *Family Planning Perspectives*, 6(3):136-41 (Summer).

Westoff, Charles, and Elise Jones. 1977. "Contraception and Sterilization in the United States, 1965-1975." *Family Planning Perspectives*, 9(4):153-57 (July-Aug.).

Westoff, Charles, and Norman Ryder. 1977. *The Contraceptive Revolution*. Princeton: Princeton University Press.

Wilson-Davis, Keith. 1975. "Some Results of an Irish Family Planning Survey." *Journal of Biosocial Science*, 7(4):435-44 (Oct.).

World Fertility Survey. 1979. *The 1974 Japan National Fertility Survey: A Summary of Findings*. No. 14 (June). London.

Wulf, Deirdre. 1980. "The Hungarian Fertility Survey, 1977." *Family Planning Perspectives*, 12(1):44-46 (Jan./Feb.).

Yamamura Kōzō, and Susan Hanley. 1975. "Ichi Hime, Ni Tarō: Educational Aspirations and the Decline in Fertility in Postwar Japan." *Journal of Japanese Studies*, 2(1):83-125.

References in Japanese

Akasu Fumio. 1973. "Jinkō Ninshin Chūzetsu to Hinin no Tokushū ni Yosete" (Preface to the Special Edition on Induced Abortion and Contraception). *Sanka to Fujinka*, 40(9):1 (Sept. 1).

Akiyama Yōko, Kuwabara Kazuyo, Yamada Mitsuko (trans.). 1974. *Onna no Karada* (Women's Bodies, translation of *Our Bodies, Ourselves*, Boston: Women's Health Book Collective). Tōkyō: Gōdō Shuppan.

Aoki Yayohi (ed.). 1976. *Dare no Tame ni Kodomo o Umu ka* (Childbearing for Whose Sake?). Tōkyō: Fūtōsha.

Asahi Shinbun. 1973. "Seiri Yōhin to Josei: Naisōshiki wa Benri Da ga Fuan" (Feminine Hygiene Products and Women: Internal Products Are Convenient But Cause Anxiety). March 19, p. 21.

———. 1976a. "Isha Koso Kusurizuki—Tsukaeba Tsukau Hodo Mōkaru Iryō" (It's *Doctors* That Like Drugs—the More Drugs You Use, the More Profits from Medical Care). June 21 (evening edition), p. 3.

———. 1976b. "Saikin no Fūfu Zō—Honsha no Ishiki Chōsa kara" (An Up-to-date Depiction of Couples—From Our Opinion Survey). Part 1, Feb. 2, p. 17.

———. 1976c. "Saikin no Fūfu Zō—Honsha no Ishiki Chōsa kara." Part 2, Feb. 3, p. 13.

Bishō. 1976. "Himitsu ni Chūzetsu Shitai!" (I Want an Abortion—Secretly!). 6(19):138-52 (Oct. 9).

Bosei Hogo I Hō. 1971. "Sanfujinka ni Okeru Dōisho • Shōdakusho no Hōteki Igi" (Legal Significance of Consents and Permits in Obstetrics). 258(11):1 (Nov. 1).

Fuji Masaharu. 1974. *Nihon no Jizō* (Japanese Jizo). Tōkyō: Mainichi Newspapers, Inc.

Fujin Chōsakai (abb. of Fujin ni Kansuru Shomondai Chōsa Kaigi). 1974. *Gendai Nihon Josei no Ishiki to Kōdō* (Attitudes and Behavior of Present-day Japanese Women). Tōkyō: Ōkura-shō Insatsukyoku.

Fuse Akiko. 1970. "Tomobataraki Katei no Ningen Kankei" (Human Relations in Families with Working Wives). In Yamamuro Shūhei, Himeoka Tsutomu, eds., *Gendai Kazoku no Shakaigaku: Seika to Kadai*, Ch. 5, 77-100. Tōkyō: Baifūkan.

Gendai Seikyōiku Kenkyū. 1973. "Gendai Nihon ni Okeru Sei Kaihō—Sono Kyozō to Jitsuzō" (Mirages and Realities in Present-day Japan's Sexual Liberation). 6:24-33 (Sept.).

Higashi Junko. 1976. "Mizuko no Yurai o Sakanobotte Mireba—Hi no Me o Mizu Haha no Kao o Mizu ni Kieta Ko" (Tracing the Origins of *Mizuko*—Children Snuffed Out Without Seeing the Light of Day or Their Mothers' Faces). *Kazoku Keikaku*, 270:7 (Sept. 1).

Hirai Nobuyoshi. 1976. "Kazoku no Naka de no Chichioya no Yakuwari" (The Father's Role in the Family). *Josanpu Zasshi*, 30(1):26-29 (Jan.).

Hirohata Tomio, Kuratsune Masanari, Inaba Yutaka. 1976. "Gairai Kanja Shinryōroku ni Motozuku Jinkō Ninshin Chūzetsu Nado no Tōkeiteki Kenkyū" (Statistical Research on Induced Abortion Based on Outpatient Examination Records). *Nihon Kōshū Eisei Zasshi*, 23(4):281-87 (Apr. 15).

Honda Tatsuo. 1959. "Senzen Sengo no Fūfu Shussanryoku ni Okeru Shussan Yokusei Kōka no Bunseki—Toku ni Chūzetsu to Hinin no Yokusei Kōka ni Tsuite" (An Analysis of the Birth Control Effect on Marital Fertility in Pre- and Postwar Japan, with Special Reference to the Effectiveness of Control by Induced Abortion and Contraceptive Practice). *Jinkō Mondai Kenkyū*, 78:1-19 (Dec.).

Hoshii Iwao. 1974. "Jinkō Chūzetsu no Mujun—Hataraku Fujin o Mushi" (The Contradictions of Induced Abortion—Working Women Are Ignored). Kon Yasuo, ed., *Shōwa 49-nen Boshi Eisei Kenkō Kazoku Keikaku Nenpō*. Tōkyō: Nihon Kazoku Keikaku Kyōkai, pp. 102-04.

Inamura Hiroshi. 1975. "Kogoroshi no Kenkyū" (Study on Infanticide). *Acta Criminologica Japonica*, 41(1):40-55 (Jan.).

Itō Masako. 1976. "Watashi no Hatsugen: Kodomo wa 'Tsukuru Mono' ka" (My Opinion: Are Children 'Products'?). *Mainichi Shinbun*, Aug. 1, p. 17.

Jinkō Mondai Shingikai (ed.). 1974. *Nihon Jinkō no Dōkō* (Trends in the Japanese Population). Tōkyō: Ōkura-shō Insatsu-kyoku.

Josanpu Zasshi. 1976. "Nihon Fujin no Kazoku Keikaku Ishi-ki—Sono Bunkateki Kōsai" (Japanese Women's Family Planning Consciousness—Cultural Considerations). 30(2):80-89. (Feb.).

Kamiko Takeji. 1965. "Kaji Kettei—Isshūnyū Kazoku to To-mobataraki Kazoku no Hikaku" (Determining Housekeep-ing: A Comparison of Single-Income Families and Families Where Both Spouses Work). *Soshiorojī*, 12(2):14-52. (Oct.).

Kashima Noboru. 1975. *Kenka Roppō—Bijinesu to Danjo Mondai de Arasou Hon* (Legal Handbook for Disputes—A Book for Struggles in Business and Between the Sexes). Tōkyō: Tokuma Shoten.

Kazoku Keikaku. 1976a. "Kōrumansan ga Mita Nihon no Kazoku Keikaku" (Mr. Coleman's View of Family Planning in Japan). 271:4-5 (Oct. 1).

———. 1976b. "Kujō Sattō!! Hinin Kigu Hōmon Hanbai" (A Flood of Complaints!! Door-to-Door Contraceptive Sales). 268:4-5 (Nov. 1).

———. 1976c. "F.P. Manpo" (Family Planning Rambles). 268:1 (July 1).

Keizaikikaku-chō (ed.). 1973a. *Seikatsu Jikan no Kokusai Hi-kaku Chōsa* (International Comparative Time Allocation Survey). Shiryōhen. Tōkyō.

———. 1973b. *Seikatsu Jikan ni Kansuru Chōsa—Kokusai Hikaku to Seikatsu no Shitsu* (Time Allocation Survey—International Comparisons and the Quality of Life). Tōkyō.

———. 1975. *Shotoku • Shisan Bunpai no Jittai to Mondaiten* (Present Status and Problem Points of Income and Capital Distribution). Tōkyō: Ōkura-shō Insatsu-kyoku.

———. 1976. *Shōwa 51-nen Ban Kokumin Seikatsu Haku-sho—Kurashi no Naka no Atarashii Teiryū* (1976 Edition, White Paper on Life in Japan: New Undercurrents in Liv-ing). Tōkyō: Ōkura-shō Insatsu-kyoku.

Kimura Eiji, Shichijō Mon. 1976. "Ore wa Sanka-i" (I'm a Gynecologist). *Manga Jō*, 1(4):163-82 (Feb. 19).

Kon Yasuo. 1971. "Chiiki Hoken Katsudō to shite no Kazoku Keikaku Fukyū no Jissai" (The State of Family Planning Dissemination as Community Public Health Activity). *Kazoku Keikaku Shidōsha Kenshū Tekisuto*. Tōkyō: Nihon Ishikai, 17-22.

———— (ed.). 1973. *Shōwa 49-nendo Boshi Hoken Kazoku Keikaku Nenpō* (1974 Year Book of Maternal Health and Family Planning). Tōkyō: Nihin Kazoku Keikaku Kyōkai.

Kōsei-shō (Kōsei Daijin Kanbō Tōkei Chōsa-bu). 1968. *Shōwa 41-nendo Jinkō Dōtai Shakai Keizaimen Chōsa Hōkoku: Kon'in* (1966 Vital Statistics, Social and Economic Aspects Survey Report: Marriage). Tōkyō.

Kōsei-shō (Daijin Kanbō Tōkei Jōhō-bu). 1972. *Shōwa 45-nendo Jinkō Dōtai Shakai Keizaimen Chōsa Hōkoku: Shusshō* (1970 Vital Statistics, Social and Economic Aspects Survey Report: Fertility). Tōkyō.

————. 1974. *Shōwa 48-nendo Jinkō Dōtai Shakai Keizaimen Chōsa Hōkoku: Kon'in* (1973 Vital Statistics, Social and Economic Aspects Survey Report: Marriage). Tōkyō.

————. 1976a. *Sekai Shussanryoku Chōsa Hōkoku* (World Fertility Survey Report). Tōkyō.

————. 1976b. *Shōwa 50-nen Kōsei Gyōsei Kiso Chōsa no Gaikyō* (Overview of the 1975 Health and Welfare Basic Administrative Survey). Tōkyō.

————. 1981. *Shōwa 55-nen Yūsei Hogo Tōkei Hōkoku* (1980 Eugenic Protection Statistics Report). Tōkyō.

———— (Jinkō Mondai Kenkyūjo). 1973. *Shōwa 47-nendo Jitchi Chōsa Dai 6-ji Shussanryoku Chōsa Hōkoku, Sono 1: Gaiyō oyobi Shuyō Kahyō* (1972 Field Survey, Sixth Fertility Survey Report, Part 1: Summary and Tables of Principal Results). Tōkyō.

————. 1978. *Shōwa 52-nendo Jitchi Chōsa Dai 7-ji Shussanryoku Chōsa Hōkoku—Gaihō oyobi Shuyō Kekka Hyō* (Seventh Fertility Survey of 1977—General Report and Tables of Major Results). Tōkyō.

Kōsei-shō/Nihon Ishikai. 1970. *Shōwa 44-nen Ishiki Chōsa*

o *Chūshin to Shita Yūsei Hogo Jittai Chōsa no Gaiyō* (Summary, Survey on the Status of Eugenic Protection, with Emphasis on the 1969 Opinion Survey). Tōkyō.

————. 1971. *Yūsei Hogohō Shitei Ishi Burokku-betsu Kenshūkai Shiryō—Shōwa 46-nendo* (Designated Physicians' In-service Training Session Data, by Block). Tōkyō.

Koyama Takashi (ed.). 1967. *Gendai Kazoku no Yakuwari Kōzō: Fūfu/Oyako no Kitai to Genjitsu* (The Structure of Roles in the Present-Day Family: Husband-Wife, Parent-Child Expectations and Reality). Tōkyō: Kaifūkan.

Kunii Chōjirō. 1974. "Kazoku Keikaku to Yūsei Hogohō" (Family Planning and the Eugenic Protection Law). In Aoyama Michio, Takeda Akira, Arichi Susumu, Emori Itsuo, and Matsubara Jirō, eds., *Kōza Kazoku*, Vol. VII, *Kazoku Mondai to Shakai Hoshō*, Ch. 3, "Gendai Kazoku Mondai," 208-23. Tōkyō: Kōbundō.

Kurahashi Yumiko. 1972. "Shussan to Onna de aru Koto no Kankei" (The Relationship Between Birth and Being a Woman). *Fujin Kōron*, 675:60-65 (Aug.).

Maehara Daisaku. 1970. "Jigyōjo ni Okeru Kinrō Fujin no Kenkō Kanri" (The Administration of Public Health for Working Women at the Workplace). *Kōshū Eisei*, 34(5): 17-20. (May).

Mainichi Shinbun. 1975a. "Tōron—Piru Kaikin no Zehi" (Debate: Pros and Cons of Lifting the Ban on the Pill). May 22 (5).

————. 1975b. " 'Kodomo ga Umenai' Shufu Tonegawa ni Nyūsui Jisatsu" ("I Can't Bear Children." Housewife Drowns Herself in the Tone River). Sept. 18.

Mainichi Shinbunsha. 1952-1979. *Zenkoku Kazoku Keikaku Seron Chōsa Hōkokusho* (National Opinion Survey on Family Planning Report Paper). Series. Tōkyō: Mainichi Shinbunsha Jinkō Mondai Chōsakai.

Majima Suemaro et al. 1973. "Tōkyō-to to New York-shi ni Okeru Jinkō Ninshin Chūzetsu no Jittai no Hikaku" (Comparison of Induced Abortion in Tokyo and New York). *Nihon Sanka Fujinka Zasshi*, 25(12):1334-42 (Dec.).

Maruyama Kazuo. 1975. "Danchi—Sanfujinka Nikki"

(Housing Project—Gynecologist's Diary). *Asahi Shinbun*, Sept. 17 (15).

Masuda Kōkichi. 1969. *Amerika no Kazoku/Nihon no Kazoku* (American Family/Japanese Family). Tōkyō: Nihon Hōsō Shuppan Kyōkai.

Matsuyama Kōkichi. 1976. "Jutai Chōsetsu Shidō no Pointo" (Points on Conception Control Counseling). *Josanpu Zasshi*, 30(2):93-95 (Feb.).

———. 1981. "Dataiyaku no Nagori 'Tsūkeizai' " ("Menstrual Inducers"—Vestige of Abortifacients). *Sekisharu Medishin*, 8(2):34-37 (Feb.).

Mizushima Kanae. 1975. *Shinshitsu Haibun ni Miru Oyako no Shinsosei* (Parent-Child Intimacy as Seen in Sleeping Arrangements). Ochanomizu Daigaku Kaseigaku-bu, Daigaku-in 75-nendo Shūshi Ronbun.

Monbu-shō. 1976. *Shōwa 50-nendo Wagakuni no Kyōiku Suijun* (1975 Editions: The Level of Education in Japan). Tōkyō: Ōkura-shō Insatsu-kyoku.

Mori Miyanobu. 1975. "Kokuritsu Byōin de mo Bai Ijō no Hiraki Aru Bunben-hi no Hyōka wa Tekisei ka" (Are Delivery Fees Reasonable When Their Range is Double or More Even Among National Hospitals?). *Nikkei Medical*, 1:109-11 (Jan.).

Morioka Kiyomi. 1973. *Kazoku Shūki Ron* (Family Cycle). Tōkyō: Baifūkan.

Moriyama Yutaka. 1973a. "Yūsei Hogohō no Kaisei Mondai" (Problems in the Revision of the Eugenic Protection Law). *Sanka to Fujinka*, 40(9):2-7 (Sept.).

———. 1973b. "Jinkō Ninshin Chūzetsu no Suii (Tokei)" (Statistical Trends in Induced Abortion). *Sanfujinka no Sekai*, 27(1):21-28 (Jan.).

Muramatsu Hiroo. 1974. "Sei no Hanran to Kazoku Mondai" (Sexual Anomie and Family Problems). Aoyama Michio et al., eds., *Kōza Kazoku*, Vol. VII, *Kazoku Mondai to Shakai Hoshō*, Ch. 3, "Gendai Kazoku Mondai," 225-34. Tōkyō: Kōbundō.

Murayama Ikuko. 1976. "Ninshin/Shussan ni Fusei wa Dō

Kakawarieruka" (How Can We Involve Fathers in Pregnancy and Birth?). *Josanpu Zasshi*, 30(1):15-21. (Jan.).

Naikaku Sōridaijin. 1970. *Sanji Seigen ni Kansuru Seron Chōsa: Shōwa 45-nen Sangatsu* (Opinion Survey on Birth Control: March, 1970). Seron Chōsa Hōkokusho, Shōwa 44-nen Jūichigatsu Chōsa. Tōkyō.

―――. 1978. *Seishōnen Hakusho* (Youth White Paper). Tōkyō: Ōkura-shō Insatsu-kyoku.

Nakagawa Eiichi, Honda Hiroshi. 1973. "Toshi no Boshi Hoken ni Kansuru Kenkyū, Dai 2 Hō: Jūkyo Oyobi Shokugyō Tsūkin no Eikyō ni Tsuite" (Research in Urban Maternal Health, Part 2: Effects of Housing and Commuting). *Boshi Eisei*, 13(4):72-81 (Mar.).

Nakahara Takeo. 1975. "Ninshin Chūzetsu to Hōritsu" (Induced Abortion and the Law). *Sanfujinka no Sekai*, 27(1):9-13 (Jan.).

Negishi Etsuko. 1976. "Shishunki no Bosei Hoken Shidō" (Maternal Health Guidance at Puberty). *Kazoku Keikaku*, 273:1 (Dec. 1).

Nihon Bosei Hogo I Kyōkai. 1966. *Shitei Ishi Hikkei* (Designated Physician's Handbook). Tōkyō.

Nihon Fujin Dantai Rengō-kai. 1975. *Fujin Hakusho—Kokusai Fujin-nen ni Atatte* (Women's White Paper—On the Occasion of International Women's Year). Tōkyō.

Nihon Kazoku Keikaku Kyōkai. 1976. *Shōwa 51-nen Ban Jigyō-bu Annai* (Business Operations Division Guide, 1976 Edition). Tōkyō.

Nihon Kazoku Keikaku Renmei. 1969. *Wagakuni ni Okeru Hinin Ringu ni Kansuru Chōsa Kenkyū* (Survey Research on the Contraceptive Ring in Japan). Tōkyō.

Nihon Keizai Shinbun. 1973. "Kigyōnai Seikyōiku" (Sex Education in the Corporation). Aug. 29 (27).

Nihon Māketingu Kyōiku Sentā. 1975. *50-nen Ban Shi-chō-son Zeimu Kenkyūkai Kanshū Shotoku Kakusa Nenpō* (1975 Edition, Wage Differential Year Book, Compiled Under Supervision of the City, Town and Village Taxation Research Group). Tōkyō.

Nihon Seikyōiku Kyōkai (ed.). 1975. *Seishōnen no Seikōdō:*

Wagakuni no Kōkōsei/Daigakusei ni Kansuru Chōsa Hō-koko (Youth Sexual Behavior: Report of a Survey of Japanese High School and College Students). Tōkyō: Shōgakkan.

Nishikawa Shunsaku, Ariake Tamiko. 1974. "Joshi Rōdō-ryokuritsu no Hendō Yōin" (Factors in Shifts in Female Labor Force Participation Rates). *Nihon Rōdō Kyōkai Zasshi*, 16(182):12-21 (May).

Ogino Hiroshi. 1971. "Sono Ta no Jutai Chōsetsu no Hōhō" (Other Conception Control Methods). *Kazoku Keikaku Shidōsha Kenshū Tekisuto.* Tōkyō: Nihon Ishikai.

———. 1976. "Shinkonsha no Hinin Jisshi Jōkyō" (The Use of Contraception Among Newlyweds). *Rinshōka no Tame no Sei Igaku*, 3(9):34-37 (Sept.).

Okuyama Michio. 1975. "Jinkō Ninshin Chūzetsu ni Kansuru Iji Funsō to Sono Mondaiten" (Complaints Against Doctors Involving Induced Abortion and Their Problem Points). *Sanfujinka no Sekai*, 27(1):35-43 (Jan.).

Ōmura Kiyoshi. 1972. *Jinkō Ninshin Chūzetsujutsu: Fu/Chitsushiki Teiō Sekkaijutsu* (Induced Abortion Surgery: Appendix: Vaginal Approach Caesarean Section). Tōkyō: Kanehara Shuppan.

Ōta Tenrei. 1967. *Datai Kinshi to Yūsei Hogohō* (Abortion Prohibition and the Eugenic Protection Law). Tōkyō: Keieisha Kagaku Kyōkai.

———. 1976. *Nihon Sanji Chōsetsu Hyakunen Shi* (A Hundred-Year History of Birth Control in Japan). Tōkyō: Shuppan Kagaku Sōgō Kenkyūjo.

Pureibōi. 1975. "Hatsutaiken-ha no Tame no Kanzen Hi-ninjutsu" (Complete Contraceptive Techniques for the First-timers). 16:148-52 (Apr. 22).

Rōdō-shō (Fujin Shōnen-kyoku, ed.). 1975. *Shōwa 50-nen Ban/Fujin Rōdō no Jitsujō* (Women's Labor, 1975 Edition). Tōkyō: Ōkura-shō Insatsu-kyoku.

———. 1976a. *Shōwa 51-nen Ban/Fujin Rōdō no Jitsujō.* (Women's Labor, 1976 Edition). Tōkyō: Ōkura-shō Insatsu-kyoku.

———. (Daijin Kanbō Tōkei Jōhō-bu, ed.). 1976b. "Saikin

no Chingin Kōzō no Dōkō (Latest Trends in Wage Structure). *Rōdō Tōkei Chōsa Geppō*, 28(3):3-14 (Mar.). Tōkyō.

Sakamoto Seiichi. 1975. "Jinkō Ninshin Chūzetsu no Kihon Mondai—Sanfujinka no Tachiba kara" (Fundamental Problems of Induced Abortion—From the Gynecologist's Standpoint). *Shōwa 50-nendo Kazoku Keikaku/Yūsei Hogohō Shidōsha Kōshūkai*. Tōkyō: Nihon Ishikai, pp. 8-9.

Sankei Ribingu. 1976a. "Nokku Shitara—Sērusuman! Akushitsu na Hōmon Hanbai" (If There's a Knock—Salesman! Obnoxious Door-to-door Sales). 240:15-16 (Nov.13).

———. 1976b. "Otoko wa Naze . . . Kitaku Jikan o Renraku Shinaika" (Why Do Men . . . Why Don't Men Say When They're Coming Home?). 238:8 (Oct. 30).

———. 1976c. "Otoko wa Naze . . . Teishu o Kusarasu Kinkushū" (Why Do Men . . . A Collection of Tabooed Words That Depress Husbands). 241:12 (Dec. 4).

Satō Fumi, Hachiya Takako, Ogawa Mitsue, Komori Akira. 1977. "Atarashii Jutai Chōsetsuhō ni Tsuite no Jittai Chōsa" (A Survey on the New Conception Control Methods). *Bosei Eisei*, 18(1):36-40 (June).

Satō Tsuneharu, Shigeshiro Toshikuni. 1976. "Wagakuni Sanfujinkai no Hininhō ni Taisuru Kangaekata" (Attitudes Toward Contraception Among Japanese Gynecologists). *Sanfujinka no Sekai*, 28(1):81-84 (Jan.).

Shūkan Josei. 1976. "35-nin no Mizuko ga Migite no Hashi ni Notte Iru . . ." (35 *Mizuko* Sit on the Chopsticks in My Right Hand). 20(32):26-30 (Aug. 24).

Soda Takemune, Kubo Hidebumi, Muramatsu Minoru, Kimura Masabumi, Ogino Hiroshi. 1960. "Jinkō Ninshin Chūzetsu Chōsa Kenkyū Hōkoku" (Research Report on Induced Abortion). *Kōshū Eisei-in Kenkyū Hōkoku*, 9 (4):204-13 (Dec.).

Sōri-fu (Seishōnen Taisaku Honbu). 1971. *Shōwa 46-nen Ban Seishōnen Hakusho: Seishōnen Mondai no Genjō to Taisaku* (1971 Edition Youth White Paper: Youth Problems and Policies). Tōkyō: Ōkura-shō Insatsu-kyoku.

———. 1973. *Sekai Seinen Ishiki Chōsa Hōkokusho. Soku-*

hōhen (World Youth Attitude Survey Report. Preliminary Edition). Tōkyō (July).

Sōri-fu (Tōkei-kyoku). 1970. Kokusei Chōsa Hōkoku (Census Survey Report), Vol. III, To-dō-fu-ken/Shi-ku-chō-son-hen, Sono 13: Tōkyō-to. Tōkyō.

———. 1975. Shōwa 50-nen Kokusei Chōsa (1975 National Census). To-dō-fu-ken/Shi-ku-chō-son-betsu. Sokuhō Shūkei Kekka. Dai 2 Bu: Kantō. Tōkyō.

Taiyō Kōbe Ginkō (Keiei Sōdanjo). 1976. Nyū Famirī (20-dai Fūfu) no Seikatsu Ishiki (New Family—Couples in Their Twenties—Opinions on Life-Style). (July).

Takemura Yukiko. 1973. "Konzen Shidō ni Okeru Funin Mondai no Toriatsukaikata" (How to Handle the Issue of Infertility in Premarital Counseling). Seikatsu Kyōiku, 17 (6):39-67 (July 15).

Taniguchi Seichō. 1975. Nani ga Taisetsu ka? (What's Important?). Tōkyō: Akarui Nihon o Tsukuru Shirīzu Kankōkai.

Tōkyō Shinbun. 1975. "Shitte Okitai 'Tanpon' no Chishiki" (Things We Should Know About Tampons) (Aug. 1).

Tōkyō-to Minsei-kyoku. 1974. Shōwa 49-nendo Tomin Fujin no Ishiki to Jittai Chōsa: Sābisugyō ni Jūji Suru Fujin no Ishiki to Jittai (1974 Survey on Urban Women's Attitudes and Behavior: Attitudes and Actual Conditions of Women in the Service Industry). Tōkyō.

Tsuboi Hideo. 1974. "Tōkyō-tonai Sanfujinka Shinryōjo Oyobi Byōin ni Okeru Nyūin (Shisetsu) Bunben no Genkyō to Shōrai" (Present Status and Future of Inpatient [Facility] Deliveries at Tokyo Gynecological Clinics and Hospitals). Tōkyō-to Ishikai Zasshi, 27(7):582-97 (Dec. 15).

———. 1975. "Ankēto kara Mita Tōkyō-tonai Sanfujinka no Genjō to Tenbō" (The Present State and Future of Obstetrics and Gynecology in Tokyo as Seen in a Questionnaire Study). Sanfujinka no Jissai, 24(4):323-30 (Apr. 1).

Wagatsuma Takashi. 1974. "Kōdō Keikaku no Tenbō (Perspectives on Behavior Planning). Dai 1-kai Nihon Jinkō Kaigi Gijiroku. Tōkyō: Nihon Jinkō Kaigi Jimu-kyoku, 161-65.

Yamaori Tetsuo. 1973. "Jinkō Chūzetsu to Bukkyō Rinri—Seihi Kimerarenai" (Induced Abortion and Buddhist Ethics—Right or Wrong Undeterminable). *Yomiuri Shinbun*, May 5.

Yamashita Akira. 1970. "Kinrō Fujin no Kenkō Shōgai to Mondaiten" (Women Laborers' Health Hazards and Problem Areas). *Kōshū Eisei*, 34(5):264-69 (May).

———. 1974. *Hataraku Josei no Ninshin/Bunben to Ikuji* (Working Women's Pregnancy, Birth and Child-raising). Tōkyō: Nihon Bosei Eisei Joseikai.

Yoshida Tadao. 1976. *Jinkō Bakuhatsu no Kiki wa Kuru ka* (Is the Population Explosion Crisis Coming?). Tōkyō: Haha to Taiji no Seimei o Mamoru Kai.

Yuzawa Yasuhiko. 1971. "Gendai Seinen no Kekkonkan/Kateikan" (Modern Youth's View of Marriage and Family). *Gekkan Ekonomisuto*, 3:50-55 (Mar.).

Index

Library of Congress Cataloging in Publication Data

Coleman, Samuel.
Family planning in Japanese society.
Bibliography: p.   Includes index.
1. Birth control—Japan.
2. Contraception—Japan.   I. Title.
HQ763.6.J3C64   1983   363.9'6'0952   83-42552
ISBN 0-691-03133-9